ROUTLEDGE LIBRARY EDITIONS:
ACCOUNTING HISTORY

Volume 19

THE EVOLUTION OF SELECTED ANNUAL CORPORATE FINANCIAL REPORTING PRACTICES IN CANADA 1900–1970

THE EVOLUTION OF SELECTED ANNUAL CORPORATE FINANCIAL REPORTING PRACTICES IN CANADA 1900–1970

Edited by
GEORGE J. MURPHY

Routledge
Taylor & Francis Group
LONDON AND NEW YORK

First published in 1988 by Garland Publishing, Inc.

This edition first published in 2021
by Routledge
2 Park Square, Milton Park, Abingdon, Oxon OX14 4RN

and by Routledge
52 Vanderbilt Avenue, New York, NY 10017

Routledge is an imprint of the Taylor & Francis Group, an informa business

British Library Cataloguing in Publication Data
A catalogue record for this book is available from the British Library

ISBN: 978-0-367-33564-9 (Set)
ISBN: 978-1-00-304636-3 (Set) (ebk)
ISBN: 978-0-367-53216-1 (Volume 19) (hbk)
ISBN: 978-0-367-53218-5 (Volume 19) (pbk)
ISBN: 978-1-00-308096-1 (Volume 19) (ebk)

The Evolution of Selected Annual Corporate Financial Reporting Practices in Canada 1900-1970

GEORGE J. MURPHY

GARLAND PUBLISHING, INC.

NEW YORK & LONDON 1988

For a list of Garland's publications in accounting, see the final pages of this volume.

Library of Congress Cataloging-in-Publication Data

Murphy, George J. (George Joseph)
The evolution of Canadian corporate reporting practices, 1900-1970 / George J. Murphy.
p. cm.—(Foundations of accounting)
Originally presented as the author's thesis (Ph. D. —Michigan State University, 1970) under the title: The evolution of selected annual corporate financial reporting practices in Canada, 1900-1970.
Bbliography: p.
ISBN0-8240-6119-5 (alk. paper)
1. Financial statements—Canada—History. 2. Corporations—Canada—Accounting—History. 3. Auditors'report—Cananda—History. I. Title. II. Series
HF5681.B2M83 1988
657'.3'0971—dc19 86-24427

Design by Renata Gomes

The volumes in this series are printed on acid-free, 250-year-life paper.

Printed in the United States of America

To Angela . . . .

FOREWORD TO 1988 PUBLICATION

The original work represents a doctoral dissertation completed almost two decades ago in 1970 at Michigan State University. Changes in this edition have been limited largely to editing, stylistic, and bibliographic measures in order to clarify portions of the text and make it generally more readable. Some corrections to, and reinterpretations of, factual data are inserted; however, no substantive changes have been made to the original document.

A number of important events have developed since 1970 which deserve mention: the delegation of virtually unrestricted standard setting to the Accounting Standards Committee of the Canadian Institute of Chartered Accountants by federal and provincial statutes in the mid 1970s - a development unique to Canada and quite unlike that in England and America; the increasing pressure placed on the Accounting Standards Committee by the Ontario Securities Commission to provide standards and guidelines for issues that the Commission feels urgent (to date the Commission has not countermanded any of the Committee's standards); and lastly, the occurrence of a number of corporate financial scandals in the 1980s that have brought into question a concern for accounting principles and auditor's responsibilities.[1]

Whether the thesis foreshadows some of these events is left to the interpretation of the reader. To aid the thoughts of those who are generously disposed, the author notes that the thesis characterization of the significant and unique role of the Chartered Accountants throughout the whole period made delegation to their organization - if it was to take place at all - almost inevitable. Similarly, as a consequence of and complementary to this delegation, it should not be unexpected that the Securities Commissions would exact continuingly high and time-consuming performance of the Standards Committee. The author hopes that scandals are not systematic in their occurrence and therefore offers no excuses for their lack of prediction in the thesis. However, he now bravely forecasts that when the "dust settles" on the 1980s' scandals, the Institute's standard setting mandate is likely to be more carefully

---

[1]Comments on these developments can be observed in the author's "A Chronology of the Development of Corporate Financial Reporting in Canada: 1850 to 1983", The Accounting Historians Journal, Spring 1986, pp.31-62.

elaborated rather than diminished - a consequence which bears some resemblance to the original delegation of the mandate in the 1970s that followed the scandals of the mid-1960s.

The author appreciates the interest and encouragement, the criticism and editorial comment of Mr. Alister Mason, Toronto partner of Deloitte Haskins & Sells, Professors Robert Crandall of Queen's University and Wayne Hopkins of the University of Regina and Dean W. John Brennan, Mrs. Evadne Merz and Mrs. Barbara Wilson of the University of Saskatchewan.

January 1988
Saskatoon, Canada

ACKNOWLEDGEMENTS

I wish to express my appreciation to my thesis supervisor Professor Charles J. Gaa and to committee members, Professors Donald A. Taylor and Floyd W. Windal. I would also like to acknowledge the extraordinary generosity, throughout the whole of the doctoral program, of the Department of Accounting and Financial Administration, Michigan State University and of the members of that department. Acknowledgement must also be made to members of the College of Commerce, University of Saskatchewan, staff members of the Canadian Institute of Chartered Accountants, and members of various firms of Chartered Accountants. The library facilities and arrangements with the Alberta Institute of Chartered Accountants, with the Universities of Manitoba, of Saskatchewan, of Toronto and of Western Ontario, with the Toronto Public Library (Business Reference Section) and with Professor Georgia Goodspeed were most helpful and particularly appreciated. Lastly, I would like to thank my own employer, the College of Commerce, the University of Saskatchewan, for continual encouragement and assistance.

TABLE OF CONTENTS

LIST OF TABLES

LIST OF FIGURES

CHAPTER I
INTRODUCTION

Purpose of Study

The purpose of this study is to document the changes in selected annual corporate financial reporting practices in Canada from 1900 to 1970 and to enquire into the background and processes that have influenced such changes.

Corporate annual financial statements are a common means of business communication and are both used and useful in the allocation of resources within an economy. Knowledge of how corporate annual financial reporting practices evolved and what influenced their evolution should be helpful both in understanding our present practices and in influencing further change.

Specification of Selected Annual Corporate Financial Reporting Practices and the Time Period 1900 - 1970

The kinds of things that are envisaged in the phrase "the evolution of selected annual corporate financial reporting practices" are, to some extent, akin to what is included in the concept of disclosure of more and better financial information. The selected practices include: the evolution of the mandatory audit and the financial statements included thereunder; the evolution of the content of the auditors' standard certificate; the evolution of the balance sheet and profit and loss statements - including their content, classification, and general valuation base; the evolution of the earned surplus statement, footnotes to financial statements, secret reserves and extraordinary items-inasmuch as they bear upon the balance sheet and profit and loss statement; and finally, the evolution of corporate depreciation practices. The foregoing topics include most of the items that Littleton and Zimmerman suggest were cited by critics of American accounting practices up to the early 1930s:

1. Plant, equipment, patents, and goodwill often shown as one amount; similar combined treatment of depreciation and maintenance amounts.
2. Failure to report total sales or operating costs.
3. Bases of asset valuations not disclosed.
4. Publication of only the balance sheet.

5. Stock dividends not disclosed by issuer; shown as income by the recipient.
6. Upward asset revaluations justified on the basis of present and expected future profits.
7. Depreciation charges seemingly used to smooth annual income amounts.
8. Use of secret reserves.
9. Inadequate or unreported net worth accounting, particularly in allowing direct charges or credits to surplus; failure to separate earned and capital surplus. [Littleton and Zimmerman, 1962, p. 138.]

Similar to England, the incorporating statutes of Canada and of its constituent provinces have, over the years, made provisions for the presentation and content of corporate annual financial statements. This study is concerned, in the main, with the federal legislation (if companies intend to operate in several provinces they normally incorporate under the federal statute) and will attempt to deal with that broad group of industrial companies that the federal companies acts contemplate.[1] The enquiry commences at the turn of the twentieth century when corporate annual financial statements were beginning to be made public and terminates at 1970.

English and American Evolution

The evolution of some of the English corporate reporting practices has been outlined by Stacey [1954] and Rose [1965] and of some of the American practices by Hawkins [1963, pp. 135-168], May [1938], Littleton and Zimmerman [1962], Storey [1964] and Carey [1969]. Hawkins in commentary upon the evolution of financial reporting practices in America between 1900 and 1935 cites four principle factors:

> First, gradual recognition by some managers of their public responsibility. Second, increasing criticism of management accounting and reporting practices by a number of influential groups and individuals outside of the management class. Third, direct federal government regulation, such as the so-called Securities Acts of 1933-34. Fourth, the recognition by the American accounting profession and acceptance by the business community of some common accounting and reporting standards. [Hawkins, 1963, p. 136.]

---

[1]Such regulated entities as banks, insurance companies, railroads, utilities, and trust and loan companies are generally excluded from such legislation.

Hawkins [p. 136] goes on to state that "underlying and contributing to these forces for change have been a number of social, political and economic factors such as the emergence of a large number of small investors, the evolution of big business, and the increasing willingness of the public to seek government action to reform undesirable commercial practices".

Canadian Evolution

There exist no outlines of the evolution of annual corporate financial reporting practices in Canada (as at 1970). This study will attempt to remedy that deficiency. It is proposed that the evolution of Canadian reporting practices has been, over the years, an interesting interplay of English and American influence acting upon, and together with, the unique elements of the Canadian scene. The English influence is felt largely in the legal tradition of the Canadian Companies Acts that have set forth minimum disclosure requirements. The American influence is felt through large American investment and ownership and the proximity and articulateness of such strong professional organizations as the American Accounting Association and the American Institute of Certified Public Accountants. The uniquely Canadian influence is felt through the pronouncements of the Canadian Institute of Chartered Accountants, the various income tax acts and the business and financial critics responding to reporting practice inadequacies and business failures.

Methodology

The Historical Approach

The approach of the historian, in broad perspective, is not unlike that of the scientist. E. H. Carr suggests:

> The world of the historian, like the world of the scientist, is not a photographic copy of the real world, but rather a working model which enables him more or less effectively to understand it and to master it. The historian distills from the experience of the past, or from so much of the experience of the past as is accessible to him, that part which he recognizes as amenable to rational explanation and interpretation, and from it draws conclusions which may serve as guides to action. [Carr, 1967, p. 136.]

There is no attempt here to suggest that the close relationship between the observer and what is observed, and the manner of drawing and testing conclusions, do not constitute methodological differences between the approach of the historian and that of the natural scientist. However, the general concept in science of a simplified version - that is, a model - of the real world which explains and aids in prediction is consistent with the historical approach.[2]

Historical analysis has a relatively minor but quite distinguished tradition in accounting scholarship.[3] The general conviction of the usefulness of the historical approach is attested to by both economists and accountants.[4] Schumpeter [1954, p. 4] has stated that through history "we learn to understand why we are as far as we actually are and also why we are not further. And we learn what succeeds and how and why . . ." Littleton and Zimmerman [1962, p. 9] argue that "a perspective of the evolutionary development of the ideas behind known accounting actions can make current accounting theory more understandable and accounting criticisms more intelligently debatable," while Stans [1953, p. 583] suggests that "evolutionary steps always have a certain consistency and it is not to be expected that sudden turns will divert past movements into wholly new directions. The future is to a large extent, a projection of the significant events which have comprised the recent past."

This study attempts to trace the changes that have occurred in corporate annual financial reporting practices, to place those changes in their economic and social background and to find the threads of continuity which give meaning to their evolution.[5]

---

[2]For commentary upon the methodology of history and its limitations, see Carr (1967) and Walsh (1967).

[3]Notable contributions have been made by B. S. Yamey and N. A. H. Stacey in England and E. Peragallo, G. O. May, J. D. Edwards, J. L. Carey and A. C. Littleton in America. A bibliography of Accounting history has been written by R. H. Parker (1965).

[4]The Committee on Accounting History of the American Accounting Association has suggested that the Association should deliberately encourage the historical type of research [American Accounting Association, 1970, p. 55].

[5]W. H. Walsh refers to this process of locating events in their context as "colligation" [p. 25].

Chapter Outline

The study falls into five divisions: Chapter I includes purpose, background, scope and methods of enquiry. Chapter II includes the evolution of the mandatory audit and the content of the auditors' standard certificate; Chapters III to V include the evolution of the balance sheet and profit and loss statements, including their content, classification and general valuation base, and involving related commentary on the earned surplus statement, footnotes to financial statements, secret reserves and extraordinary items; Chapter VI includes the evolution of corporate depreciation practices; and Chapter VII includes the summary and conclusions. Within each chapter, the material is handled on a chronological basis.

Source Documents and Evidence

The chief source of evidence concerning changes in financial statement reporting practices is the annual publication, The Annual Financial Review - Canadian [1901-1940] for the years 1900 to 1939. This periodical, edited by the long-time Assistant Secretary of the Toronto Stock Exchange, W. R. Houston, invited all incorporated companies to send in copies of their annual statements and provides what is likely an unequalled and concise source of evidence for early Canadian annual financial statements. The style and format of the financial statement presentations are, in substance, consistent with a sample of actual corporate annual reports for the years 1901 to 1939.[6] The only alterations that the periodical makes to the corporate annual reports are:

1. In many instances, the periodical places the assets on the right hand side of the balance sheet and the equities on the left hand side. (In some instances, the annual corporate report itself displays the assets and liabilities in this "English" fashion.)
2. The profit and loss accounts are realigned into a "T" account

---

[6]The following corporate annual reports for the years indicated, were checked to the periodical: Cockshutt Plow Company Limited, 1920, 1930, 1939; Penmans Limited, 1925, 1934; Canadian Locomotive Company Limited, 1912, 1915, 1918, 1921, 1924, 1927, 1920; Canadian Canners Limited, 1923, 1925, 1926, 1931, 1932, 1934, 1936, 1938; Canadian Westinghouse Company Limited, 1904, 1908, 1916; Steel Company of Canada Limited, 1910, 1915, 1917.

form if not portrayed in this fashion in the corporate annual reports.

3. Authorized share description is sometimes given in an information section that precedes the financial statement rather than being incorporated in the body of the statement.
4. The auditors' report or certificate is not given, though auditors' names are often given.
5. The annual statement by the corporate president that is normally included in the corporate annual report is not repeated completely. However, extracts of the more important information-invariably involving corporate finances - are given.

While the "voluntary" nature of the inclusion of corporate annual reports in the periodical may subtract from the representativeness of the population, it is believed that, throughout the years, the periodical contained well over half of the stocks listed on the Toronto Stock Exchange. As an example, the number of stocks listed by the Exchange in 1934 was 445;[7] while the number of stocks included in the periodical for that year was approximately 250. It is believed however, that over the years, virtually all the largest Canadian public companies have been included in the periodical.

Subsequent to 1939, evidence of changes in corporate annual reporting practices is obtained from annual corporate reports themselves. Similarly, evidence of changes in the auditors' report or certificate is obtained directly from annual corporate reports for the total period involved.

Evidence of the background and processes that influenced changes in annual corporate financial reporting practices (as opposed to the changes themselves) are obtained from the various incorporating statutes, debates of the House of Commons and the Senate that relate to relevant changes in the incorporating legislation, committee reports (together with submissions and briefs by interested parties to these committees) recommending changes in incorporating legislation, financial press commentary, stock exchange requirements, accountancy textbooks, professional periodicals such as The Canadian Chartered Accountant and the

---

[7] The Financial Post, October 4, 1952, p. 22.

various provisions of income tax legislation.

The Canadian economic and social environment is influenced by England and America. Evidence of that influence is sought in the professional pronouncements and the professional and academic journals of those countries - notably The Accountant, The Journal of Accountancy and The Accounting Review - and in the commentary of some of their accounting historians - B. S. Yamey, N. A. Stacey, H. Rose, D. F. Hawkins, G. O. May, A. C. Littleton, H. R. Hatfield and W. A. Staub.

Samples of Annual Corporate Financial Statements and Auditors' Certificates

As indicated in the second section of this chapter, the type of company that is studied is that which is contemplated by federal companies act legislation. Such companies may be generally referred to as "industrials" and usually exclude such forms of regulated organizations as banks, insurance companies, railroads, utilities and trust and loan companies. To document the changes in annual corporate financial reporting practices that have occurred, a random selection of ten such companies (see Appendix B) is examined for each of the following periods: 1903 to 1919, 1920 to 1939, and 1940 to 1970. In addition, test readings of corporate reporting practices of thirty to forty companies are made approximately every ten years throughout the period (see Tables 1 and 2). It is believed that the foregoing samples, together with the descriptions and studies of similar evidence by academic and professional commentators of the time, provide sufficient evidence to obtain an awareness of the changes in annual corporate financial reporting practices that have taken place. The first period - that is, up to 1919 - includes World War I, the formation of the Dominion Association of Chartered Accountants, the initiation of the income tax laws, and the beginning of provincial and federal legislation that set forth minimum standards for audited annual financial statement disclosure. The second period - from 1920 to 1939- includes further significant federal legislation in 1934 and the difficult economic years of the "depression." The third period - from 1940 to 1970 - includes World War II, the initiation of the Research Bulletins of the Canadian Institute of Chartered Accountants and further significant federal legislation in 1965. From 1905 to 1939, the random selection is secured from the annual periodical, The Annual Financial

Review - Canadian and subsequent to that time is secured from the industrial firms listed in The Financial Post Survey of Industrials. The scrutiny of firms' financial statements for each consecutive year for the periods indicated, together with the test readings every ten years, provide the evidence that helps to make whatever changes that have taken place more discernible.

As previously mentioned, The Annual Financial Review - Canadian does not, unfortunately, include the auditors' report or certificate for the annual corporate financial statements that are presented. The auditors' certificates examined, therefore, for the period up to 1939 (coinciding with the first two periods of examination of the financial statements), are obtained from the files of annual corporate financial statements in the Business Reference Section of The Toronto Public Library. Since there were relatively few financial statement files that preceded 1930, requests were made of certain companies to forward copies of the company's auditor's certificate for the years prior to 1920. The requests were directed toward those companies whose auditors performed auditing services for three or more companies as indicated from a compilation of approximately ninety-five companies in the 1920 edition of The Annual Financial Review - Canadian:

Auditing Firm	Number of Companies Audited
Price Waterhouse & Co.	20
Geo. A. Touche & Co. and/or P. S. Ross & Sons	12
Marwick, Mitchell & Co.	8
Clarkson, Gordon, Dilworth & Co.	7
Riddell, Stead, Graham & Hutchison	7
C. S. Scott & Co.	5
Deloitte, Plender, Haskins & Sells and/or Deloitte, Plender, Griffiths & Co.	5
Edwards, Morgan & Co.	4
Creak, Cushing & Hodgson	3

The audit certificates of six to eight of the foregoing audit firms are examined for varying consecutive periods from as early as 1904 to 1939. Subsequent to 1939, the auditors' certificates that relate to the financial statements examined for the period 1940 to 1970 are scrutinized. Appendix A indicates the audit certificates examined, the companies to which these relate and the periods for which they are examined. As with the examination of financial statements, the review of actual audit certificates is supplemented by the descriptions and studies by academic and professional commentators of the time.

Perspective of the Study

A history can attempt to sketch in broad perspective the changes and influences that have taken place with regard to a general topic- that is, changes in annual corporate financial reporting practices. Alternatively, a history can concentrate on a particular aspect of the general topic in far greater detail - for example, the evolution of financial statement footnote practices. The broad-perspective approach can be used to aggregate and synthesize several already-existing detailed studies of particular aspects of the general topic or it can be used to sketch the main features of the general topic prior to those several features being studied in great detail. In the latter instance, besides contributing to the understanding of the general topic, the history can point to those aspects of the general topic that appear to be most fruitful for further and more detailed investigation. It is this latter approach to which this study is directed.

CHAPTER II

THE EVOLUTION OF THE AUDIT AND THE AUDITOR'S STANDARD REPORT

Purpose

The purpose of this chapter is to describe, for the period 1900 to 1970, the evolution of the legislation of mandatory balance sheet and profit and loss audits and of the content of the auditor's standard report. Changes in the auditor's report are documented by reference to specific audit reports. The examination of these selected audit areas helps to illustrate the influences that have shaped corporate reporting practices in Canada.

Legislation and Auditors' Reports Prior to 1910

Early English Legislation

The pattern of Canadian legislation with respect to audit provisions and the auditor's duties is derived directly from the English legislation. In England, the Joint Stock Companies Act of 1844 required that an auditor be appointed [Great Britain, 1844, C. 110]. In 1856, the mandatory aspect of this provision was abandoned; however Table B of this enactment sets forth the "articles" which were to apply to all companies that did not register their own articles:

> The auditors shall make a report to the shareholders upon the balance sheet and accounts, and in every such report they shall state whether in their opinion, the balance sheet is a full and fair balance sheet containing the particulars required by these regulations, and properly drawn up so as to exhibit a true and correct view of the state of the company's affairs and in case they have called for explanations or information from the directors, whether such explanations and information have been given by the directors and whether they have been satisfactory; . . . [Great Britain, 1856, C. 47].

The English Companies Act of 1862 provided for the Board of Trade to appoint inspectors to investigate a company's affairs provided that one-fifth of the shareholders made the request and conditional upon the Board being satisfied that the applicants are not "actuated by malicious motives" [Great Britain, 1862, C.89]. By 1900 the mandatory audit provisions were reinstated in the Companies Act of that year [Great Britain, 1900, C. 48, Sec. 21]. The duties of the auditor were an elaboration of the provisions of the 1856 Act but the "full and fair" phrasing was dropped and the "true and correct" wording, retained.

> Every auditor of a company shall have a right of access at all times to the books and accounts and vouchers of the company and shall be entitled to require from the directors and officers of the company such information and explanations as may be necessary for the performance of the duties of the auditors, and the auditors shall sign a certificate at the foot of the balance sheet stating whether or not all their requirements as auditors have been complied with, and shall make a report to the shareholders on the accounts examined by them, and on every balance sheet laid before the company in general meeting during their tenure of office; and in every report shall state whether, in their opinion, the balance sheet referred to in the report is properly drawn up so as to exhibit a true and correct view of the state of the company's affairs as shown by the books of the company; . . . [Great Britain, 1900, C. 48, Sec. 23].

No substantive changes arose in the relevant audit provisions in the Companies Act of 1908 [Great Britain, 1908, C. 69].

Early Canadian Legislation

The Province of Ontario reflected the English legislation more quickly than did the federal Canadian legislation. The Ontario Act of 1897 stipulated inspection clauses similar to those of the English enactment of 1862 [Ontario, Statutes, 1897, Sec. 77]. Additionally, the annual shareholders' audit, while not made mandatory, was contemplated if the letters patent or the by-laws of the company so directed. In the event that an audit did take place, the duties of the auditor were specified:

> The auditor shall make a report to the shareholders upon the balance sheet and accounts, and in every such report he shall state whether in his opinion, the balance sheet is a full and fair balance sheet and properly drawn up so as to exhibit a true and correct view of the state of the company's affairs, and in case he has called for explanation or information from the directors or officers of the company, whether such explanations or information has been given by the directors and whether it has been satisfactory. [Ontario, Statutes, 1897, C. 28, Sec. 77.]

The wording of this legislation is almost identical with that of the "model articles" of the English legislation of 1856.

The Ontario Companies Act of 1907 [Statutes, 1907, Sec. 123 and 130], following the pattern of the English enactment of 1900, made the shareholders' audit mandatory and the duties set forth in the enactment were identical with those of the English Act.

As late as 1900, there were no inspection or audit provisions in federal legislation. However, the Act of 1902 [Canada, Statutes, 1902, Sec. 79] in the manner of the English Companies Act of 1862 and the Ontario Companies Act of 1897, allowed shareholders (representing at least one-fourth in value of the issued capital) to petition a judge to appoint an inspector to investigate the affairs and management of the company. The requirement that the judge be assured that good cause be shown for such investigation and that the applicants "are not actuated by malicious motives in instituting" the action, marks the period as one of transition between the business freedom of the nineteenth century and the growing legislative concern and regulation that characterizes the twentieth century [Canada, Statutes, 1902, Sec. 79]. Legislative debate that preceded the passing of the Act was concerned with whether such inspection clauses would be used "to embarrass the company" [Canada, House . . ., Vol. 2, 1902, p. 5059]. The inspection clauses also included provision for the company, if it so wished, to appoint inspectors by resolution at the annual meeting.

By 1910 therefore, Ontario legislation, but not the federal Canadian legislation, had provisions for mandatory audits and outlined, in broad terms, the duties of the auditor with respect to his report on the financial affairs of the company. These provisions are seen to have almost identical wording with that of antecedent English legislation. Two underlying influences can also be detected at this early date. Firstly, one influence might be inferred from the comments of the Under Secretary of State (Canada) and former Assistant Provincial Secretary of the Province of Ontario, Mr. T. Mulvey. In his book, Dominion Company Law, he indicated that the legislative provisions for detailed disclosure of assets, liabilities and equities as required in the 1917 Companies Acts ". . . were first suggested by the Board of the Institute of Chartered Accountants of Ontario in the drafting of the Ontario Companies Act, 1907 . . ." [Mulvey, 1920, p. 54]. The inference is that the Institute of Chartered Accountants of Ontario would also be more than moderately interested in advocating the compulsory audit provisions of the Ontario Act of 1907. The second influence that attempts to explain why the mandatory audit requirements (and minimum balance sheet disclosure) of the Ontario Act of 1907 predated federal Canadian legislation by some ten years, relates to the fact that ". . . the commercial and financial history of Canada for the past dozen years reveals . . . that there has been but one collapse of a large corporation in that time and this was in connection with a business which, at the same period, suffered similar reverse in other countries . . ." [The Financial Post, Feb. 16, 1907, p. 1]. The combination of factors - the early influence of the Ontario Institute of Chartered Accountants on the Ontario legislation and the general lack of any company failures - may help to explain this lead-lag provincial-federal relationship. No evidence was located to indicate that federal Canadian legislators were content to have less strict regulation, which would have tended to increase, relative to Ontario, the numbers of companies that would incorporate under their jurisdiction.[1] In later years, this prospect was certainly a concern of the federal Canadian legislators when they began to lead the way in regulatory legislation.

Attitude Towards the Audit

The need for an audit - though not mandatory in England for general companies until 1900 and in Ontario until 1907 - was, nonetheless, beginning to be fairly well established by the turn of the century. J. D. Warde in his book, The Shareholders' and Directors' Manual, states that:

> The value of a thorough and systematic audit of the accounts and books of a company has not hitherto been adequately appreciated. The investing public are now, however, paying more attention to the importance of periodical audits and examinations by the professional accountant and auditor. The resulting advantages are increased freedom from fraud, greater security for shareholders and more confidence on the part of the public, in the management of companies through being furnished with evidence of their safety and prosperity from an independent source. [Warde, 1900, p. 104.]

Similarly, T. Mulvey, in his book Canadian Company Law, states in reference to existing federal legislation that:

---

[1]However some concern existed in Ontario in this regard. See under "Ontario and Canadian Federal Legislation" of Chapter III.

> Under this act . . . the appointment of an auditor and the making of an annual audit of the books of the company are not required. Proper business methods, however, demand periodic audits, not only for the information of the shareholders, but also for the benefit of the directors. [Mulvey, 1913, p. 102.]

Form and Content of Auditor's Report

The form and content of the auditor's report were quite varied prior to 1910. According to Col. H. D. Lockart Gordon [1961, p. 97] of the public auditing firm of Clarkson, Gordon and Dilworth, early auditors' reports were extremely brief either in the form of "audited and found correct" or "examined and found correct." Just such wording appears on the 1904 financial statements of Canadian Westinghouse Company Limited. By 1908, the auditor's report of that company took a form which it substantially held until 1917:

> I have audited the books of the Company for the twelve months ended 31st December, 1908 and have been furnished with vouchers for all expenditures, and certify to the accuracy of the above statement, which agrees with the company's books. [Canadian Westinghouse Company Limited Annual Report, 1908.]

In this instance the statements referred to were a "General Balance Sheet" and a "Profit and Loss Account." The latter statement was much more akin to our present-day retained earnings statement - adding together the opening balance and the current net earnings and deducting from this the dividends and a reserve for depreciation to arrive at the closing balance.

The auditor's report of The Dominion Textile Company Limited [1906] testifies to both the variety of reports as well as the fairly detailed enumeration of audit techniques. The latter feature continued well into the 1920s and 1930s for many companies. Additionally, though the auditor's opinion or certification is implied in some of the paragraphs, there is no explicit articulation of an opinion:

> We beg to report having completed our audit of the financial transactions of your Company for the year ended 31st March 1906.
>
> During the year our audit has been carried on monthly at which periods we have reported to your Directors.
>
> The financial transactions have been carefully and correctly incorporated in the Books of Account and the disbursements and purchases have been verified by vouchers.
>
> The monthly Cash Statements from the various Mills, duly supported by vouchers, have been correctly incorporated in the financial records.

The Cash on hand, Bank balances, and Loan Accounts have been checked from time to time and the latter verified by certificates from the Banks.

The Inventories of Raw Cotton, Merchandise on hand and in process of manufacture, supplies &c. at the various Mills, have been prepared in detail and the summaries signed and approved by your General Manager.

The annual Financial Statements setting forth the transactions both of the subsidiary Companies purchased and those under lease have been correctly drafted from the Books of Account and we have signed the same as being in order.

The clerical work during the year has been satisfactorily carried out and the manner in which the systems of Accounting have been adjusted to meet the requirements of the Company reflects much credit upon your Secretary and office staff. [Dominion Textile Company Limited Annual Report, 1906.]

The auditor's report of Ogilvie Flour Mills Company Limited in 1909 renders an opinion only on the balance sheet (in this instance the abbreviated Profit and Loss Account contains trading profits, and deductions for bond interest, dividends, and transfers to reserve accounts), and provides, additionally, some information concerning asset valuation:

We beg to report that we have audited the books of the Company in Montreal, Winnipeg and Fort William for the year ending 31st August, 1909, and that the Balance Sheet which we have signed is a correct statement of the Company's Assets and Liabilities on that date.

The provision made in respect of the Open Accounts and Customers' Notes covers, in our opinion, every possible contingency, and the Stocks on hand are valued on a perfectly safe and conservative basis.

The increase in Property and F ant accounts is for additions and extensions only, all ordinary Repairs, Alterations and Improvements being included in the Working Expenses of the year, and depreciation (if any) is in our opinion fully covered by the addition of $100,000 to Property Reserve. [Ogilvie Flour Mills Company Limited Annual Report, 1909.]

The auditor's report of The Steel Company of Canada Limited of 1910 is similarly concerned with asset valuation but bears more heavily the imprint of the influence of the English and Ontario legislation. Most of the wording of the last paragraph is taken directly from those sources.[2] It can be noted in this report that the opinion is expressed

---

[2]The English influence on early American auditor's reports is acknowledge in <u>The Independent Auditor's Reporting Standards in Three Nations</u>, a Report prepared by the Accountants International Study Group

twice - in both the first and last paragraphs - and that while the opinion is rendered on the profit and loss account as well as the balance sheet, the former account is in the abbreviated form mentioned previously; that is, it merely includes earnings, depreciation, dividends and the closing balance:

> We have examined the books and accounts of The Steel Company of Canada Limited and subsidiary Companies for the six months ending December 31, 1910 and certify that the balance sheet as at that date, and relative profit and loss account are correctly drawn up therefrom.
>
> The inventories of stock on hand as certified by responsible officials of the Company have been made on a basis of approximate cost.
>
> We certify that we have obtained all the information and explanations which we have required, and that in our opinion, the balance sheet is properly drawn up so as to exhibit a true and correct view of the state of the affairs of The Steel Company of Canada Limited and its subsidiary companies as at 31st December, 1910. [Steel Company of Canada Limited Annual Report, 1910.]

Legislation and Auditors' Reports, 1910 - 1920

General Outline

Littleton and Zimmerman [1962, p. 81] have outlined the contrast in the evolution of auditing between England and the United States. In the granting of the privilege of limited liability to corporations, English law has required that, in the public interest, there be disclosure of financial information and that such disclosure be attested to by auditors. As previously mentioned, this tradition in English law commencing in 1844, was temporarily abandoned in 1856 and subsequently restored in 1900. The continuing strength of the "laissez-faire" attitude in business and the lack of a sufficiently strong auditing profession probably accounts for the interruption of the mandatory audit provisions between 1856 and 1900. Littleton and Zimmerman postulate the assumptions of the English tradition:

> . . . that adequate accounts were a basic source of knowledge of enterprize financial affairs; that audited balance sheets, widely circulated, would be in the public interest because the data reported by the company directors could be searchingly scrutinized as to its dependability and that the directors of that day would benefit from a recommended arrangement of balance sheet data which could guide them to an adequate and understandable

[1969, para. 22]; and in Cochrane [1950, p. 448].

> accounting disclosure of company financial status. [Italics mine.] [Littleton and Zimmerman, 1962, p. 239.]

The American tradition for auditing did not evolve through legislation on behalf of the "public interest," but rather out of the need for an external independent commentary on credit-worthiness. As Littleton and Zimmerman suggest:

> . . . the strongest motivating factor [for audits] seems to have been the need of creditors, particularly banks, for dependable financial information as a basis for their extension of credit to businesses in the form of short-term promissory notes. [Littleton and Zimmerman, 1962, p. 109.]

Similarly, G. Wilkinson commented on the American evolution of the auditing function:

> The necessity to borrow capital with which to transact an extensive business, has brought very many corporations to the necessity of having their accounts audited and their balance sheet certified by independent accountants of known standing. The use by a business concern of an accountant's certificate in this connection is one of the highly valued developments of the last ten years. This is on the increase. Bankers are demanding it even among companies whose credit rating is of the best. [Wilkinson, 1914, p. 239.]

In Canada, a number of events led to the mandatory audit provisions of The Companies Act Amendment Act, 1917: banking failures and the subsequent banking legislation; an existing Canadian prototype in the Ontario legislation of 1907; a rash of corporate failures in 1914 and 1915; and, most importantly, the Tax Acts of 1916 and 1917. It is likely that when these events occurred and the question of mandatory audits was raised that the English tradition for legislative action was inevitable. There is, as well, some evidence to indicate that the American concern for credit-worthiness was also influential in supporting the acceptance of the audit function.

Banking Legislation

Certainly, one of the events that led to a concern for mandatory audits for all federal Canadian companies was the series of bank failures that precipitated The Bank Act of 1913. The ability of Canadian businesses in avoiding failures has been commented on previously; however, that ability did not extend to the banking industry:

> More Canadian banks have failed than are now in existence and some failures have been disastrous to the public, both depositors and noteholders, as well as shareholders. Within the last five years, seven banks have failed. ["Bank Audit . . ." 1911, p. 24.]

English legislation had prescribed mandatory audits for banks in 1879 and equivalent Canadian legislation followed some 34 years later in 1913 upon the occasion of these bank failures [Canada, Statutes, 1913, Sec. 56]. Similar legislation for the "near-banks" - the loan companies and the trust companies - followed in 1914 [Canada, Statutes, The Loan Companies Act, 1914, Secs. 59 and 60 and The Trust Companies Act, 1914, Secs. 47 and 48]. It should be noted that The Bank Act required auditors to render an opinion on both the balance sheet and the profit and loss. The Loan Companies Act, 1914 and The Trust Companies Act, 1914 are less clear with regard to the financial statements on which the auditor must provide an opinion.

An editorial in The Canadian Chartered Accountant acknowledged the influence of public opinion in the new legislation:

> The banks themselves, while not appreciating the necessity for any form of external inspection, accepted the principle of a shareholders' audit as a concession to public opinion, which it was realized had become aroused owing to the disclosures respecting the Ontario, Farmers and others of the then recently defunct banks. [Author's italics.] ["Bank Auditing," May 1923, pp. 450-455.]

Frequent editorials in The Journal of Accountancy expressed great interest in the mandatory audit provisions ["Canadian Bank Audits," 1913, pp. 309-12]:

> Ten years ago it would probably have occurred to no one to suggest the compulsory audit of banks, for the number of reputable accountants in Canada was very small. At present, however, the chartered accountants are well organized in most of the provinces and held in high esteem among business men. The plan that contemplates their employment for the audit of the Chartered Banks will not be opposed on the ground that Canadian accountants are incompetent, untrustworthy or insufficient in number. ["Bank Examinations . . ." 1913, pp. 41-42.]

The Companies Act Amendment Act, 1917

Legislation

The audit provisions of the English Companies Consolidation Act of 1908 with respect to the mandatory audit and the duties of the auditor relating to the financial statements were substantially the same as in the predecessor English Companies Act of 1900 and the Ontario Act of 1907. Canadian legislators in 1917 transplanted these provisions word for word in The Companies Act Amendment Act, 1917:

> Every company shall at each annual general meeting appoint an auditor or auditors to hold office until the next annual general meeting.
>
> Every auditor of a company shall have a right of access at all times to the books and accounts and vouchers of the company, and shall be entitled to require from the directors and officers of the company such information and explanation as may be necessary for the performance of the duties of the auditors.
>
> The auditors shall make a report to the shareholders on the accounts examined by them, and on every balance sheet laid before the company in general meeting during their tenure of office, and the report shall state;-
>
> (a) whether or not they have obtained all the information and explanations they have required; and,
>
> (b) whether, in their opinion, the balance sheet referred to in the report is properly drawn up so as to exhibit a true and correct view of the state of the company's affairs according to the best of their information and the explanations given to them, and as shown by the books of the company. [Canada, Statutes, The Companies Act Amendment Act, 1917, Sec. 11.]

It should be noted that the legislation requires the auditor to provide an opinion on the balance sheet but not on the profit and loss statement.

The Background

A sizeable increase in the number of commercial and industrial failures in 1914 and 1915 (see Appendix C) undoubtedly stimulated concern for a wider extension of mandatory audits. M. Goodman commented that:

> When the crisis through which we are now passing was first felt [the early war years of 1914 and 1915], hundreds of well known concerns were thrown to the wall, the stock markets were closed, and thousands of small and large investors lost their all. After a series of investigations by accountants, it was shown that a majority of these concerns failed because of insufficient accounting, over-optimism and lack of foresight.
>
> The bankers, the principal and largest sufferers again sought a cure and prevention with the result that today they are demanding statements . . . prepared and signed by Chartered Accountants. [Goodman, July, 1917, p. 44.]

Some concern for audit compulsion was also expressed by J. L. Apedaile:

> I am sure that if the auditor would . . . take a greater interest in the problems of the manufacturer, he would be able to assist the manufacturer to such an extent that we would require no legislation to make auditing compulsory, rather would we have the manufacturer consider it essential. [Apedaile, 1915, p. 146.]

Though the foregoing quotations indicate some general concern for industry-wide compulsory audits, no additional evidence of commercial or professional concern was located in a scanning of articles and editorials in The Canadian Chartered Accountant and The Financial Post up to 1917. A Bill introduced in the federal parliament was never acted upon [Mitchell, 1916, p. 1143]. Seeming lack of commercial and financial concern for the mandatory audit may be partially explained by the fact that a great number of public companies had already voluntarily accepted the idea of an independent audit.[3] Undoubtedly a concern for credit-worthiness motivated a voluntary audit. J. Parton indicates that:

> . . . it was some time in 1912 (as I recollect) that the banks began a general practice of requiring an independent audit of all businesses which asked for loans or bank accommodations. This caused resentment from the heads of such businesses, who complained about the cost; but the banks persisted in their idea, and it is gratifying to look back after all those years and remember how heads of businesses very soon changed their minds and realized the value of audits, not only so far as banks were concerned, but also for themselves. [Parton, 1961, p. 95.]

The speech that introduced the legislation to the House of Commons and the subsequent House debates provide little explicit reasoning for audit compulsion other than the fact that federal legislation lagged behind English and provincial legislation:

> The purpose of the bill is to amend the Companies Act so as to embody in it principles that of recent years have been embalmed in legislation in Great Britain in their Companies Act and for the most part have been accepted by our provinces. [Canada, House . . ., 1917, p. 5920.]

When attention was drawn to the fact that mandatory audit provisions and minimum corporate disclosure requirements - two of the main features of The Companies Act Amendment Act, 1917 - would be

---

[3]Of 147 companies listed as "Industrials" in the Annual Financial Review - Canadian, 1916, only 18 did not indicate who the auditors were. Of the 147 companies, only 11 indicated that they were incorporated under the laws of Ontario, where by this time, mandatory audits were compulsory.

burdensome to the smaller companies, the Minister of Finance dismissed this concern by indicating that this legislation had been operative in Ontario for ten years [Canada, House . . ., 1917, p. 5935].

The Taxation Acts of 1916 and 1917

The Business Profits War Tax Act, 1916 [Canada, Statutes, 1916, C. 11] and The Income War Tax Act, 1917 [Canada, Statutes, 1917, C. 28] undoubtedly influenced the enactment of the Companies Act Amendment Act, 1917. In 1916 the federal parliament found it necessary for war purposes to levy a tax on corporate profits in excess of a stipulated percentage return on capital. The tax was applied only to those companies whose capital was in excess of $50,000. Sir Thomas White, the Minister of Finance, in response to questions in the house, indicated on several occasions that his department would be hard pressed in terms of sufficient staff to administer the tax regulations if all businesses were taxable [Canada, House . . ., 1916, p. 2630]. Additionally, he acknowledged that "field auditors" would be needed.

Under these circumstances the desirability of the mandatory audit and minimum disclosure provisions of the 1917 Act is apparent. Firstly, corporate accounting would be made more uniform and comparable, thereby satisfying the tax need for "equity"; and secondly, corporate accounting as reflected in audited financial statements would be attested to by a respected professional, thereby decreasing the need for an expanded tax-audit department since there would be an independent and objective witnessing to the corporate financial statements.

The complementarity of the Companies Act Amendment Act, 1917 and the taxing legislation was reflected in remarks relating to corporate annual reports by Mr. Carvell:

> We have had a business profits tax for the first time in our history and now we have the income tax. It is these incorporated companies who are the very ones that will contribute under the new methods of taxation and I think it quite proper that the very fullest publicity should be given. [Canada, House . . ., 1917, p. 5937.]

Similarly, Parton reflects this complementarity relationship between taxation and corporate auditing:

> . . . it has been very gratifying to find the ready way in which the Minister of Finance and his assistants have accepted the statements signed by chartered accountants for the purpose of

their assessment. Encouragement has been given to clients to have their auditors interview the inspectors of taxation and generally, business men have been led to obtain a much higher realization of the services of the profession than ever before. [Parton, 1917, p. 99.]

United States Influence

The coincidence in time of the Business Profits War Tax Act, 1916, and the Income War Tax Act, 1917 with that of the Companies Act Amendment Act, 1917, has already been noted. The latter legislation undoubtedly muted the effect in Canada of another event that was of great significance in the United States. That event was the publication of the statement Uniform Accounting by the Federal Reserve Board of the United States [1917]. This statement was reprinted in The Canadian Chartered Accountant [Uniform Accounting, 1917, pp. 5-33] and its merit referred to the consideration of "leaders of accountancy in Canada . . . and to the young accountant" [p. 49]. The statement prescribed in fair detail and accepted auditing procedures for the "balance-sheet" audit and also provided a model auditor's report:

> I have audited the accounts of Blank & Co. for the period from ______________ to ______________ and I certify that the above balance sheet and statement of profit and loss have been made in accordance with the plan suggested and advised by the Federal Reserve Board and in my opinion set forth the financial condition of the firm at ________________ and the results of its operations for the period.

It seems likely that the audit provisions of the Companies Act Amendment Act, 1917 pre-empted the effect that Uniform Accounting might otherwise have had with regard to the duties of the auditor in respect to financial statements and the form and content of the auditor's report. Certainly the Canadian audit reports, subsequent to 1917, bear the heavy imprint of the wording of the Canadian legislation.

The Canadian concern for American events, as evidenced in the reprinting of Uniform Accounting, was in the established tradition of The Canadian Chartered Accountant.[4] Similarly, Thomas Mulvey [1918, p. 129],

---

[4]As a rough measure of that Canadian concern, it was found that of the 37 signed articles of three pages or more in volumes 7 and 8 of The Canadian Chartered Accountant, 12 of these were written by Americans, 6 by English and 19 by Canadians. The non-Canadian articles were invariably reprints from the American and English accounting journals.

the Undersecretary of State, acknowledged the awareness of Canadian legislators of the early statutes of New York State.

The Effect of the Companies Act Amendment Act, 1917

The variety in content of auditors' reports continued through the early part of the second decade of the twentieth century in Canada. Cockshutt Plow Company Limited's Report of 1911 was:

> I have made an audit of the books, accounts and records of Cockshutt Plow Company for the financial year ended June 30, 1911. I have examined the charges to capital accounts, have verified the cash and other current assets as of June 30th, 1911 and have also verified the profit and loss.
>
> I hereby certify that in my opinion the statements of assets and liabilities submitted herewith reflects the financial position of the Company at June 30, 1911 and that the accompanying statement of profits is correct. [Cockshutt Plow Annual Report, 1911.]

In this instance, some auditing techniques are delineated and the profit and loss statement is included in the opinion. The abbreviated profit and loss includes net profit after depreciation, interest, merchandise reserve, capital reserve, and contingent reserve.

Similarly, the report of Penmans Limited attests to both the balance sheet and the abbreviated profit and loss statements as well as drawing attention to the inventory valuation basis and the management certification of inventories:

> I have examined the books and vouchers of Penmans Limited for the year ended 31st December, 1913 and certify that the accompanying balance sheet and profit and loss account agrees therewith.
>
> I have been furnished with all the information required by me, and the inventories of stock on hand have been taken approximately at cost, as certified by responsible officials of the company.
>
> The statements appended hereto represent, in my opinion, a true and correct view of the Company's position as at the above date. [Penmans Limited Annual Report, 1913.]

The report of Ogilvie Flour Mills Company Limited provides a great deal of accounting and auditing information. In this instance, the report to the shareholders does not contain the auditor's opinion; rather, the latter is given in a small note at the bottom of the balance sheet and signed by the auditors. The report to the shareholders reads:

> We beg to report that we have audited the Books of the Company in Montreal, Winnipeg, Fort William and Medicine Hat, for

> the year ended 31st August, 1916, verifying the Cash and Bills Receivable on hand, the Bank Accounts, the Investments, and the Accounts Receivable, in respect of which ample provision has been made for all Contingencies.
>
> The Stocks on hand of Wheat, Flour and Supplies are certified as to quantities by the Superintendents of the various Mills, confirmed by the Mill Reports, and are valued on a safe and conservative basis, taking into consideration the unusually high price of wheat and the contingencies of the markets.
>
> No provision is made for general depreciation, but the cost for repairs and maintenance of the various Plants has been included in the Working Expenses of the year. [Ogilvie Flour Mills Company Limited Annual Report, 1916.]

The fulfilling by the auditor of the duties imposed by the English Companies Consolidation Act, 1908 and the Companies Act Amendment Act, 1917 in Canada provided a ready prototype for the form and content of his report. R. Kettle indicates that legal advice, secured by the Institute of Chartered Accountants of England and Wales in 1908, suggested that the auditor's report take the following form:

> We have audited the balance sheet of ABC Ltd., dated the 31st December, 1908 as above set forth.
>
> We have obtained all the information and explanations we have required.
>
> In our opinion, such balance sheet is properly drawn up so as to exhibit a true and correct view of the state of the Company's affairs according to the best of our information and the explanations given us and as shown by the books of the Company. [Kettle, 1928, p. 337.]

Companies such as Steel Company of Canada Limited, Canadian Locomotive Company Limited and Cockshutt Plow Company Limited incorporated most of this "legal" wording in their auditors' reports several years prior to the Canadian legislation of 1917. The audit report of Cockshutt Plow Company Limited of 1914 is a good example of strong adherence to the "legal" wording:

> We have examined the foregoing balance sheet as at June 30, 1914 and the accompanying profit and loss account for the year ended on that date, with the books of the company and the accounts from the company's branches and we have obtained all the information and explanations we have required. In our opinion, such balance sheet and profit and loss account are properly drawn up so as to show a true and correct view of the state of the company's affairs as at June 30, 1914 and the results of its operations for the year ended at that date, according to the information and explanations given to us and as shown by the books of the Company. [Cockshutt Plow Company Limited Annual Report, 1914.]

For other firms, such as Canadian Westinghouse Company Limited, Penmans Limited, Ogilvie Flour Mills Company Limited and Dominion Textile Company Limited, the changeover to a stronger acknowledgement of the "legal" wording occurred immediately subsequent to the 1917 legislation. J. C. Gray [1919, p. 199] suggests that sometimes a time-lag in observance of such wording existed since "it is still the practice of many accountants to issue their accounts with notations of 'audited and found correct,' 'certified correct,' 'audited' etc. attached." He goes on to state "needless to say, these offenders are seldom Chartered Accountants" [p. 199]. Nor, would it appear, are they the normal auditor's report that attached to large public company financial statements!

Cochrane has provided us with an example of the kind of wording which was used in the United States in this time period:

> We have audited the books and accounts of the ABC company for the year ended December 31, 1915, and we certify that in our opinion, the above balance sheet correctly sets forth its position as at the termination of that year, and that the accompanying profit and loss account is correct. [Cochrane, 1950, p. 450.]

It is fairly evident from a comparison of the foregoing example and the model report offered in Uniform Accounting by the Federal Reserve Board with the Canadian Company audit reports previously illustrated that the form and content of the Canadian auditor's report were styled after the Canadian and English legislation.

Report Wording Beyond the "Legal" Minimum

A good number of the audit reports inspected provided additional information with respect to inventory valuation, fixed asset capitalization policy, non-existence of depreciation, inability to segregate goodwill from the other fixed assets, management certificates testifying to asset-recording propriety, and descriptions of audit techniques relating in particular to cash and securities. It is impossible to know whether these represented substantive qualifications in the minds of the auditor, whether they were simply additional information being passed along for the shareholders' benefit, or whether indeed it was felt that these kinds of things should form part of the auditor's standard report wording. Certainly they were very common features of the auditor's report during this period of time. Their widespread existence is likely a testimony to the uncertainty that attached at that time to the state of the art of accounting and auditing principles and practices. An additional source of uncertainty flowed from the necessity to comply with the minimum disclosure requirements of the 1917 Canadian legislation. An example of this latter situation is the 1917 audit report of Steel Company of Canada Limited which indicated that the company was unable to segregate goodwill from the property accounts as required by the new legislation. This auditor's report is fairly typical of the reports inspected following the 1917 legislation:

> We have examined the Books and Accounts of The Steel Company of Canada, Limited, for the year ending December 31st, 1917, and certify that the Balance Sheet as at that date, and relative Profit and Loss Account, are correctly drawn up therefrom.
>
> The Inventories of Stock on hand, as certified by responsible officials of the Company, have been valued on a conservative basis.
>
> We have checked the Cash on Hand, and certificates verifying the Bank balances have been produced to us. The Investments in which the Company is interested we have verified by actual inspection of the securities.
>
> No recent physical appraisal of the several Plants has been made, which would indicate to what extent Goodwill is included in the Cost of Properties, and the Balance Sheet therefore shows these Assets in the same manner as they have appeared in all previous statements.
>
> We certify that we have obtained all the information and explanations which we have required, and that, in our opinion, the Balance Sheet, as at 31st December, 1917, is properly drawn up so as to exhibit a true and correct view of the state of the Company's affairs according to the best of our information and the explanations given to us and as shewn by the Books of the Company. [The Steel Company of Canada Limited Annual Report, 1917.]

The legislation of 1917 required that an audit opinion be rendered only on the balance sheet. Seven of the eight auditors' reports inspected throughout this period, rendered an opinion on the profit and loss statement as well as the balance sheet prior to the 1917 legislation. Only two of these seven reports, which happened to be by the same auditor - Canadian Westinghouse Company Limited and Penmans Limited - did not have opinions rendered on the profit and loss statement in the years subsequent to 1917 and prior to 1920. Little evidence, at this point therefore, is adduced to support the contention that the general effect of legislation tends to decrease the standard of reporting practices.

The profit and loss statement at this point of time is typically abbreviated as previously described.

Legislation and Auditors' Reports, 1920 - 1940

Background

The first decade of the inter-war years of 1920 to 1940 were, for England, United States and Canada, the time of "normalcy" - for "business-as-usual." However, the stock market crashes and the depression altered the attitude of society towards the largely unregulated capitalist system prevalent in all three countries. Though England and Canada in slow, measured and evolutionary steps had, since 1850, led the way in respect to statutory, mandatory audits and the elaboration of auditors' duties relating to the financial statements, the American Securities Acts of 1933 and 1934 brought the United States quickly abreast.

In Canada, by the beginning of this period, many of the audit aspects we are concerned with had been settled. Still to be debated, however, remained the problems of the inclusion of the profit and loss statement in the auditor's opinion, the introduction of the wording "according to generally accepted accounting principles applied on a basis consistent with that of the preceding year," the use of "generally accepted auditing standards," and the elimination of wording beyond the "legal" minimum. Some progress was made on all four issues during this period - particularly with respect to the elimination of the extra wording that so characterized auditors' reports of the earlier era. The period 1930 to 1940 may well mark the transitional decade for Canada as it turned more towards the influence of the United States and largely away from that of England. The geographic proximity, the increasing investment of the United States in Canada and the articulateness of the American Institute of Accountants were all compelling reasons for this transition. World War II, commencing in 1939, interrupted the increasing concern of the Canadian accounting and auditing profession - a concern which was quickly rekindled in the immediate post-war years.

English and Canadian Legislation

Neither the English Companies Act, 1928 [Great Britain, 1928, C. 45] nor the Canadian Companies Act, 1934 [Canada, Statutes, C. 33] made any significant changes in the statutory audit provisions under examination. The changes in Canadian legislation dealt mostly with increasing the information content of the annual financial statement. Professor R. G. H. Smails [1934, p. 283], writing at the time, implied the influence of the English legal case - the Royal Mail Steam Packet Company - which arose in 1930, shortly after the English legislation. The case related to the Company's representation of profits and whether the augmenting of these profits through the use of secret reserves should be disclosed in the statement. Though the influence of the case was recognized, that influence did not extend to the requirement to have the auditor render an opinion on the profit and loss statement; rather the influence seemed to find expression in a desire for more disclosure in the profit and loss and earned surplus statements. Smails states:

> The hand of the auditor would seem to be greatly strengthened by the specification of the items that are to be shown separately in the general statement of income and expenditure and the statement of surplus respectively, to be laid before the company in general meeting. Certainly, these statutory requirements will relieve auditors of such grave responsibility as lay upon the auditor of the Royal Mail Steam Packet Company, full advantage having been taken by the authors of the new act of the costly experience gained from this case. [Smails, 1934, p. 283.]

The only new auditing provision relating to the form and content of the auditor's report that found its way into the new Companies Act, 1934 was in respect to treatment of subsidiaries not consolidated in the parent's financial statements:

> Where the assets and liabilities and income and expenditure of any one or more subsidiaries of the holding company are not so included in the balance sheet and the statement of income and expenditure and statement of surplus of the holding company, there shall be annexed to the balance sheet of the holding company a statement signed by the auditors of the holding company stating how the profits and losses of such subsidiary or, if more than one, the aggregate profits and losses of such subsidiaries, have, so far as they concern the holding company, been dealt with in, or for the purposes of, the accounts of the holding company, and in particular how, and to what extent,
>
> (a) provision has been made for the losses of a subsidiary, either in the accounts of the subsidiary or of the holding company or of both; and
>
> (b) losses of a subsidiary have been taken into account by the directors of the holding company in arriving at the profits and losses of the holding company as disclosed in its accounts;
>
> provided that it shall not be necessary to specify in any such statement the actual amount of the profits or losses of any

> subsidiary, or the actual amount of any part of any such profits or losses which has been dealt with in any particular manner. [Canada, Statutes, 1934, Sec. 114 (2).]

The foregoing provisions are identical with the provisions of the English Companies Consolidation Act, 1929 with the exception that in the latter Act, the statement must be signed by the directors rather than the auditors [Great Britain, 1929, Sec. 126]. The provisions are repeated here at length because from this time to the next federal legislation in 1965, frequent and repeated references to the treatment of profits and losses in non-consolidated subsidiaries are found in auditors' reports.

United States Legislation and
Stock Exchange Requirements

The American Securities Acts of 1933 and 1934 made the audit of both balance sheet and profit and loss statement mandatory. George O. May expressed some doubt about the concomitant features of this legislation:

> Whether the time was then ripe for making audits by independent accountants of statements filed under the Acts mandatory seemed to me to be doubtful. But if audits were to be required and a heavy liability placed upon the profession for the proper discharge of the duty thus imposed upon it, there could be no reason for striking at its professional character by taking the responsibility for accounting rules and principles out of its hands and placing it in those of a policy-making body that was not expert, especially as there was not even any provision for a hearing or right of appeal to the courts against rules so made. [May, 1943, p. 62.]

As is known, the SEC, over the years, has effectively handed back to the profession the task of determining accounting and auditing standards.

Some tradition for advocating mandatory audits had existed from earliest times in the United States. An editorial in the Journal of Accountancy in 1905 states that:

> The time is also ripe for an agitation in favour of private publicity - that is for the rendering by corporations of complete reports of their financial condition to their stockholders and the certification of such reports by independent public accountants. ["Public Accountant . . .", 1905, p. 137.]

Similarly, five years later in 1910, J. E. Sterrett [1910, p. 245], the president of the American Association of Public Accountants, proposed external examination of corporate affairs by competent accountants.

Predating the American Securities Acts somewhat, the New York Stock Exchange in January of 1933 required that corporate auditors furnish the Exchange with a statement indicating whether in their opinion the balance sheet and profit and loss statement are drawn up fairly, whether they are in conformity with "accepted accounting practices" and whether these practices have been used consistently [Cochrane, 1950, pp. 451-55]. These Exchange requirements (though not necessarily conceptually originating with the Exchange) gradually found their way into the auditor's report.

The Auditor's Duty Respecting the Profit and Loss Statement

The English Tradition

As indicated by the Amendment Committee in 1906, early English sentiment did not favour the requirement that the profit and loss statement be audited [Hein, 1963, p. 517]. However, though the English Companies Act, 1928 made no mention of this need, the Royal Mail Steam Packet case of the early 1930s awakened interest in this particular matter. As reported by H. Morgan [1933, p. 510], opinion of Counsel sought at the time indicated that the "auditors cannot dissociate themselves from all responsibility for the correctness of that account and there may be cases in which it would be incumbent upon them to draw the attention of the shareholders to any feature of that account which in their view involved anything of any improper or misleading character." Morgan himself goes on to advocate that:

> . . . the duties of the auditor regarding the profit and loss account should be defined as in the case of the balance sheet. Responsibility for the profit and loss account certainly exists, and to discharge it, the auditor should be required to report specifically on the profit and loss account as well as on a the balance sheet. The public is entitled to the valuable protection which would be afforded by enacting, in effect, that the auditor's report should relate to all accounts required to be submitted to shareholders. [Morgan, 1933, p. 518.]

According to Morgan [1933, pp. 512-513] the only accounting body in England at this time that advocated that the profit and loss statement be included in the auditor's report was the Society of Incorporated Accountants and Auditors. It should be noted that it was only in the English Companies Act, 1928 that a general statement of profit and loss was required to be submitted to shareholders - the details of which were left to the discretion of management. Similarly, it was not until the English Companies Act, 1947 that the profit and loss statement was required to be audited.

The American Tradition

The evidence with regard to American auditors' statements on the information contained in the profit and loss statement may be somewhat conflicting. George Cochrane [1950, p. 450] has indicated that audited reports up to 1929 usually included an opinion on the profit and loss statement. However he acknowledges that "the profit and loss statement . . . was usually one figure, shown on the balance sheet as the amount added to prior year's surplus, without any supporting statement" [Cochrane, 1950, p. 450]. George Benston [1969, p. 519], however, in a review of financial statements for the years 1926 to 1934, indicates that a majority of corporations provided such detailed profit and loss information as sales and cost of sales.

In 1929, the Federal Reserve Board in conjunction with the American Institute of Accountants issued their bulletin, The Verification of Financial Statements. This publication placed much more emphasis on the importance and verification of the profit and loss statement than did their earlier statement of 1917, Uniform Accounting. As previously mentioned, stock exchange listing rules of 1932 and the Securities Acts of 1933 and 1934 required that the auditor comment on the profit and loss statement.

The Canadian Tradition

Canadian concern for audited profit and loss statements, during this period of time, was quite active. Both the English and American traditions were carefully reported and scrutinized in The Canadian Chartered Accountant. As previously indicated, it was not uncommon in earlier times for auditors to render an opinion on the profit and loss. The latter statement was usually something more than what Cochrane has suggested existed in the United States. It was invariably a separate statement, and besides showing the opening and closing balances representing accumulated undistributed profits to date, it usually indicated depreciation, interest, net operating profits, transfers to reserves and dividends. Commencing in the early 1920s, and following the 1917 legislation that required the auditor to report only on the balance sheet, it became the exception rather than the rule for the auditor to comment on the profit and loss statement. This reduction in the opinion may well have been due to a certain unwarranted caution on the part of the Canadian auditor for it seems that there is evidence to indicate that, even from earliest times, sufficient audit work was being done to render that opinion.

In 1912, George Grant indicated that verification procedures must extend to the profit and loss statement:

> . . . since the balance sheet must incorporate in some form or other the balance of the profit and loss account, the audit must extend to that account also. Indeed, it is in this particular account that manipulation can be made and it is this account which has to be especially carefully scrutinized. [Grant, 1912, p. 111.]

Editorial commentary in The Canadian Chartered Accountant, relating to the "Balance Sheet Audit" that according to Montgomery was so common in the United States, indicated that the profit and loss statement must be searchingly scrutinized before the auditor can certify the balance sheet:

> But every balance sheet contains a balance of the profit and loss account, . . . and how can an auditor certify to that balance without laboriously going over the year's operations. ["Auditing Balance Sheets," 1912, p. 208.]

George O. May, in 1937, acknowledged a difference in the auditing procedures between the United States and Canada. In reference to the audit report's assertion that the balance sheet shows a "true" and "correct" view of the "state of the affairs" of the Company, he mentions:

> . . . the certificate was commonly used in America with even less justification, as I see it, for many years. I do not think that the amount of work that was done justified it to the extent to which it was justified here [Canada] and in Great Britain. I have always thought that we American accountants were overselling accountancy to the American public, as well as running considerable risks, in the use of that certificate. There was certainly no distinguishing between the English and American certificate, although the character of the work done was very different. [May, 1937, p. 299.]

Differences in opinion regarding the Canadian auditors' legal responsibility existed. In 1933, R. G. H. Smails, in his well-known textbook, <u>Auditing</u>, indicated that:

> . . . since the auditor has no statutory knowledge of the form or content of the profit and loss statement which directors propose to publish he cannot be saddled with this further responsibility. But, of course, if the profit or loss for the year is stated in the balance sheet and not merely the accumulated surplus, the auditor will admittedly be responsible for the correctness of the profit or loss so stated. [Smails, 1933, p. 232.]

A different interpretation was presented by H. D. Clapperton in commenting upon the Royal Mail Steam Packet (Kylsant) case as it affected English and Canadian practice:

> It is interesting to note that it used to be the English practice to regard not only secret reserves as permissible but to draw on these without what might be regarded as sufficient disclosure. This attitude arose from the fact that, mistakenly, the professional accountants who reported on the accounts of the companies felt that they had no responsibility for the details of the profit and loss account. This was an error as was shown by the Kylsant case. In any event, the degree of disclosure made in the financial statements has been greater since that court case. [Clapperton, 1941, p. 81.]

Apart from whatever legal responsibility may have existed, there was growing concern that legislation should explicitly require that the profit and loss statement be audited. Commentary at the annual meeting of the Canadian Institute of Chartered Accountants in 1941 indicated that:

> . . . there appeared also to be substantial agreement with his suggestion that for the present, while the requirements of good auditing practice are ill defined, particularly in the minds of those outside the profession, there would be a desirable strengthening of the auditor's position with his client if custom or statute required the addition of phrases to the effect that the profit and loss and surplus accounts were also covered by his certificate, and that the accounts were drawn on a basis consistent with accepted practice and with that used in the previous period. ["The Form of the Auditor's Report," 1941, p. 242.]

<u>Concern for Report Wording</u>

The period 1920 to 1940 evidenced an increasing concern in Canada for clarifying and making more uniform the auditor's report. <u>The Financial Times</u> in 1927 indicated a need for this concern:

> The very strength of the accountant's position has rather favoured the growth in his statements of a loose form of

> phraseology which is not free sometimes from ambiguity. It is very necessary that this should be corrected and that the wording of certificates and reports should be such that double meanings are impossible and no opportunity given for drawing deductions not intended. [As reported in The Canadian Chartered Accountant, November, 1927, p. 193.]

Professor C. A. Ashley, writing in The Financial Post in 1933, indicated that the general public and some members of the accounting profession were greatly disturbed about auditors' reports. Regarding report qualifications on depreciation, receivables, reserves and inventories, he states:

> . . . it is becoming fantastic. Soon we shall be reading without surprise "subject to the assets and liabilities being correctly stated." [Ashley, 1933, p. 9.]

Concern was also expressed both for auditor independence through governmental appointment ["Election of Auditors . . .", 1933, p. 11] and for auditing procedures and methods through an "audit clearing house" [Wegenast, 1934, p. 9]. Undoubtedly, as well, the Royal Mail and the International Laboratories legal cases affected the auditors' concern for the scope of his audit. The former case, which has already been discussed, affected the auditor's willingness to comment on the profit and loss statement. The latter case, arising in 1931 in Canada, supported the argument that a balance sheet audit called for only a series of tests, not a detailed audit ["Low Audit Fees . . .", 1933, p. 9]. Clamour for change, however, was not sufficient to alter the relevant auditing provisions in the 1934 legislation and any criticisms were likely diminished from 1934 on by the spirited activity of American institutions in elaborating stronger guidelines.

By 1929, in the United States, Verification of Financial Statements recommended a test audit based upon review of the internal control [Cochrane, 1950, p. 450]. In 1932, the Special Committee of the American Institute of Accountants on Cooperation With Stock Exchanges recommended inclusion of a note suggesting: that the accounting records had been tested but that no detailed audit was made; that the profit and loss statement be included in the audit; and that the statements should reflect accepted principles of accounting consistently maintained during the year under review [Staub, 1942, p. 74]. With regard to the use of this model auditor's report, the Committee indicated that "the certificate is appropriate only if the accounting for the year is consistent in basis with that of the preceding year" [Staub, 1942, p. 74]. The inclusion of verification procedures relating to cash and securities was also contemplated. This model report was later included in the American Institute of Accountants' booklet Audits of Corporate Accounts in 1934 [American Institute, 1934, p. 47]. By 1939, the American Institute pamphlet Extensions of Auditing Procedures suggested that the concept of "consistency with that of the preceding year" be incorporated into the audit report itself [p. 12]. In 1941, following the report of the Securities and Exchange Commission inquiry into the McKesson and Robbins fraud, the American Institute [1941, p. 39], on the recommendation of the Commission, recommended that the wording be revised to acknowledge that the audit was performed "in accordance with generally accepted auditing standards."

The influence of American events is evidenced in an editorial in The Canadian Chartered Accountant in 1937 that discusses the merits of a model report recommended by the American Institute in 1934 - in particular, with regard to "a general review being made but not a detailed audit" and "in accordance with accepted principles of accounting consistently maintained" [Editorial, 1937, p. 178].[5] Similarly, the topics for discussion pertaining to the auditor's report at the Annual Meeting of the Canadian Institute in 1938 outline features which had already been agreed upon in the United States ["Auditor's Report . . .", 1938, pp. 63-65]. These topics related to a concern for testing transactions (rather than providing a detailed audit), certifying the profit and loss statement, replacing the "true and correct" wording, and acknowledging the consistency of application of accepted principles of accounting. Additional topics related to whether the Canadian Institute should defer action until the English Companies Act had been revised (an event which was not to happen for nine more years!) and whether the existing wording in the American Audit report should be adopted in its entirety in the Canadian legislation. Debate on these matters continued at the Institute annual meeting of 1941 ["Form of the Auditor's Report," 1941, p. 242]. Here there was additional acknowledgement that the report wording related

---

[5]See also Editorial, The Canadian Chartered Accountant, Vol. 32 (May, 1938), p. 325.

less to delimiting the auditor's legal duties or responsibilities and more to the general instruction of the reader.

The war had, by this time, intervened so completely in the affairs of the country that no Institute action was possible at that time. It was not until 1951 that the Institute was able to issue its own bulletin on the auditor's report.

Form and Content of the Auditor's Report

Relative to the earlier period, 1900 to 1920, the variety in audit report wording decreased during 1920 to 1940. However, relative to the situations in England and America, the variety that did persist was indeed strong and of increasing concern to the Canadian profession.

Decrease in Variety

By the mid-1920s, the wording in some of the audit reports inspected had centered simply around the wording in the legislation and was, to a great extent, devoid of a listing of audit techniques performed, commentaries on asset valuation and notations of management certificates. The 1925 report of Canadian Canners Limited illustrates this point:

> We have examined the books and accounts of Canadian Canners, Limited, for the year ended December 31st, 1925, and we certify that in our opinion the above balance sheet is drawn up so as to exhibit a true and correct view of the state of the company's affairs according to the best of our knowledge and the explanations we have required. [Canadian Canners Limited Annual Report, 1925.]

Similarly, the reports of Canadian Locomotive Company Limited and Penmans Limited were equally simple.

On the other hand, listings of audit techniques, notations of asset valuation and management certificates did persist. The 1933 report of the Steel Company of Canada Limited includes:

> Inventories of stock-in-trade, certified by responsible officials of the Company, have been valued on a conservative basis.
>
> We have verified the cash on hand, bank balances and all securities. [Steel Company of Canada Annual Report, 1933.]

The qualifications in the Massey-Harris Company Limited report of 1932 were fairly extensive and with regard to inventories and accounts receivable were not atypical of corporate and auditor response to the uncertainty that existed in the depth of the depression. Part of that report reads:

> Net current assets including cash in foreign securities which have placed certain restrictions on the export of funds, aggregate approximately $4,500,000. Subject to the foregoing and to the adequacy of the reserves against receivables, inventories and fixed assets, we report that . . . [Massey-Harris Annual Report, 1932.]

By the late 1930s all auditors' reports inspected were relatively unencumbered with listings of audit techniques and asset valuation commentaries. The wording of each report was fairly similar and tended to center about the legal wording. None of the reports as yet used the accepted American wording, "according to accepted principles of accounting consistently applied." As in the case of Massey-Harris Company Limited and Howard Smith Paper Mills Limited, some attention was being implicitly given to internal control and the need to test rather than to perform a detailed audit. The report of the latter company in 1936 was:

> We have made an examination of the Consolidated Balance Sheet of Howard Smith Paper Mills Limited and its subsidiary companies as at 31st December, 1936. In connection therewith we examined or tested the accounting records and other supporting evidence of the Howard Smith Paper Mills Limited and one of its subsidiaries and have received all the information and explanations required by us; we have been furnished with certified statements as at the same date of the other subsidiary companies not examined by us.
>
> As required by the Dominion Companies' Act, Section 114, we report that the profits of two small subsidiary companies are not included in the attached statements.
>
> In our opinion, based upon the examination and certified statements referred to above, the attached Consolidated Balance Sheet as at 31st December, 1936, of Howard Smith Paper Mills Limited and its subsidiary companies is properly drawn up so as to exhibit a true and correct view of the state of their combined affairs as at that date, according to the best of our information, the explanations given to us and as shown by the books of the companies examined by us and the statements furnished to us. [Howard Smith Paper Mills Limited Annual Report, 1936.]

On the other hand, no company audit report examined came close to Russell Industries Limited in its simplicity, brevity and its ignoring of the legal wording:

> We have audited the books of Russell Industries Limited for the year ending December 31, 1939 and we certify that our requirements as auditors have been complied with.
>
> We also certify that the foregoing balance sheet is in accord with the books and, in our opinion, correctly states the position

> of the company on that date. [Russell Industries Limited Annual Report, 1939.]

It has been previously mentioned that both prior to the 1917 legislation and immediately thereafter, auditors usually rendered their opinion on the profit and loss statement as well as on the balance sheet. During the period 1920 to 1940, however, the practice of including the profit and loss statement in the report ended. None of the eight audit reports examined represents an exception to this statement. Similarly, in a report on the variety in wording that did persist during this period, The Canadian Chartered Accountant, in 1938, enumerated twelve auditors' reports, of which only two rendered an opinion on the profit and loss [Vol, 33, pp. 135-139]. It would seem therefore that the legislation of 1917 and 1934 did eventually have the effect of reducing the scope of the auditor's report opinion.

Increasing Concern for Variety

Despite the decrease in the absolute amount of variety that was taking place in Canada during this period, there was a realization that relative to England and America, the variety that did persist was of some significance. K. W. Dalglish commented on this and on the force of American influence:

> In England one form of certificate is very rarely deviated from . . . so that in the United States also one form is being generally accepted. . . . a large number of annual reports . . . indicate that we are rapidly departing from uniformity. We of course are in the position of being influenced to a great extent by American practice. Auditors in subsidiary companies in Canada of American companies are sometimes asked to use the American form of report, and they have wound in with that form certain additional phraseology so that it will comply with the Dominion Companies Act. There has also been a tendency to use it or some similar form for purely Canadian Companies. For these various reasons, in arranging for this annual meeting it seemed that it would be an appropriate time to have a discussion on this subject. [Dalglish, 1938, p. 454.]

In 1937, Professor R. G. H. Smails, in commenting on the phrase "drawn up in accordance with accepted principles of accounting consistently maintained during the period," evidenced his concern for greater uniformity:

> The auditors of a few Canadian companies (presumably those with a large number of shareholders in the United States or with

> extensive connections of other kinds in that country) have incorporated a similar clause in their reports. There would seem to be much to commend this practice but the extent to which it is voluntarily adopted during the next few years might be taken as an index to the desirability of having it made obligatory by statute. [Smails, 1937, p. 165.]

The twelve auditors' reports that were presented in The Canadian Chartered Accountant in 1938 in an attempt to illustrate the problem of variety indicated a persistence in the listing of audit techniques, commentaries on asset valuations and management certificates [Vol. 33, pp. 135-139]. In three instances there was either reference to or implication of the fact that "no detailed audit" was carried out and in only one instance was there mention made that "accepted principles of accounting" had been "consistently" used.

The concern for greater uniformity was undoubtedly stimulated by the unfavorable comparison with England and America and the desire to indicate to the public, in particular the readers of financial statements, the kind of work that auditors perform. This concern was able to take some expression because, relative to prior periods, the late 1930 period saw some decrease in the alternative accounting and auditing practices that were acceptable. By this time, bases of asset valuations and management certificates were invariably found in the balance sheet proper and accepted auditing standards left little doubt about the verification of cash, banks, securities, accounts receivables, and inventories. Confirmation of accounts receivable and attendance at inventory taking had been made mandatory in the United States following the McKesson and Robbins fraud of 1939.

The Effect of the 1934 Legislation

The legislation had four main effects: firstly, since the legislation contemplated the issuance of consolidated statements, audit reports began to refer to acceptance of subsidiary financial statements not audited by them; secondly, in conformity with the requirements of the legislation, the audit report began to include commentary on the treatment of the profits and losses of subsidiaries that were not consolidated; thirdly, comments on asset valuations tended to disappear from the audit reports since this information was now required to be given in the financial statements; and fourthly, as previously mentioned, auditors continued not to render an opinion on the profit and loss statement. This last outcome began to change by the mid-1940 to 1950 period and by 1951 - even though federal legislation did not require it until 1965- virtually all audit reports included an opinion on the profit and loss statement.

Legislation and Auditors' Reports, 1940 - 1970

Background

World War II served to interrupt the deliberations of the Canadian profession in its pursuit of a standard auditor's report. It was not until 1951 that the Canadian Institute of Chartered Accountants was able to make recommendations in this regard. The Canadian auditor was, of course, not bereft of guidelines. He continued to do what he had started to do during the 1930s; that is, he used the wording of the legislative statutes and interwove into this, often in a somewhat unmethodical manner, the changes that had been and were being introduced in the United States.

During this period, the increasing strength and prestige of the Canadian accounting profession manifested itself in its research bulletins begun in 1946, and in the influence it demonstrated in altering the legislation affecting both auditing and accounting matters.

The Pronouncements of the American Profession

At the beginning of the period presently under review, the American Institute of Accountants recommended that the standard wording of the auditor's report take the following form:

> We have examined the balance sheet of the XYZ company as of February 28, 1941, and the statements of income and surplus for the fiscal year then ended, have reviewed the system of internal control and the accounting procedures of the company and, without making a detailed audit of the transactions, have examined or tested accounting records of the company and other supporting evidence, by methods and to the extent we deemed appropriate. Our examination was made in accordance with generally accepted auditing standards applicable in the circumstances and it included all procedures which we considered necessary.
>
> In our opinion, the accompanying balance sheet and related statements of income and surplus present fairly the position of the XYZ company at February 28, 1941, and the results of its operations for the fiscal year, in conformity with generally accepted accounting principles applied on a basis consistent with

> that of the preceding year. [American Institute of Accountants, 1941, pp. 40-41.]

In 1947 the American Institute issued Tentative Statement of Auditing Standards which described in detail what generally accepted auditing standards were. This allowed the Institute in 1948 to delete reference to both the reviewing of the system of internal control and the acknowledging that no detailed audit was performed. The recommended wording is repeated here because it has been basically unchanged since that time and because it represents, with one exception, the identical wording toward which the Canadian Institute carefully struggled from 1951 to 1968:

> We have examined the balance sheet of X Company as of December 31, 19__, and the related statements of income and surplus for the year then ended. Our examination was made in accordance with generally accepted auditing standards, and accordingly included such tests of the accounting records and such other auditing procedures as we considered necessary in the circumstances.
>
> In our opinion, the accompanying balance sheet and statements of income and surplus present fairly the financial position of X company at December 31, 19__, and the results of its operations for the year then ended, in conformity with generally accepted accounting principles applied on a basis consistent with that of the preceding year. [American Institute of Accountants, 1948, p. 164.]

By 1969, an American Institute committee has recommended that the auditor should express an opinion on the source and application of funds statement whenever it forms part of the corporate financial statements [Accountants International Study Group, 1969, para. 14].

English Legislation and Professional Pronouncements

The English Companies Act of 1947 [Great Britain, 1947, C. 47] provided the first changes since 1908 in the statutory requirements relating to the content and wording of the standard auditor's report. Where previously the auditor had been required to state whether or not he had received all the information and explanations he had required and to state whether the balance sheet was properly drawn up so as to exhibit a true and correct view of the state of the company's affairs according to the best of his information and the explanations given to him and as shown by the books of the company, he was now obliged to include in his report an opinion on the profit and loss statement as well as the balance sheet and to comply with the Ninth Schedule of the Act. The latter required an explicit statement by the auditors as to:

> Whether they have obtained all the information and explanations which to the best of their knowledge and belief were necessary for the purposes of their audit.
>
> Whether, in their opinion, proper books of account have been kept by the company, so far as appears from their examination of those books and proper returns adequate for the purposes of their audit have been received from branches not visited by them.
>
> Whether the company's balance sheet and . . . profit and loss account dealt with by the report are in agreement with the books of account and returns.
>
> Whether, in their opinion and to the best of their information and according to the explanations given them, the said accounts give the information required by the Act in the manner so required and give a true and fair view -
>
> a) in the case of the balance sheet, of the state of the company's affairs as at the end of its financial year; and
>
> b) in the case of the profit and loss account, of the profit or loss for its financial year; . . .
>
> [Great Britain, 1947, C. 47, Ninth Schedule.]

The foregoing clauses do not require an expression concerning conformity with "generally accepted accounting principles applied on a basis consistent with that of the preceding year." The latter wording was recommended by a noted accountant, F. R. M. de Paula, but was not introduced into the statutes [Hein, 1963, p. 517].

The rather lengthy wording required by the 1948 Act was drastically reduced in the provisions of the Companies Act, 1967. Here the auditor was simply required to state whether the balance sheet and profit and loss were "properly prepared in accordance with the provisions of the principal Act" [Great Britain, 1967, C. 81, Sec. 14]. The items contained in the Ninth Schedule of the 1947 Act are presumed to hold unless otherwise stated by the auditor. Hein [1963, p. 518] reports that recommendations to the Jenkins Committee that preceded the enactment included such abbreviated forms of auditors' reports as "audited in accordance with section X of the Companies Act, 196_." According to Hein, suggestions along similar lines were made by the Association of Certified and Corporate Accountants and The Institute of Chartered Accountants in England and Wales.

Under the requirements of the Companies Act, 1967, the Institute of Chartered Accountants in England and Wales recommended the following standard report:

> In our opinion, the accounts set out on pages ____ to ____ give a true and fair view of the state of the company's affairs at________________ and of its profit (or loss) for the year ended on that date and comply with the Companies Acts 1948 and 1967. [Accountants International Study Group, 1969, para. 100.]

No recommendations exist with regard to the presentation or the rendering of an opinion on the source and application of funds statement. Unlike Canada, that statement is largely unused in England [Accountants International Study Group, 1969, para. 13].

Canadian Legislation

The Corporations Act, 1953 [Ontario, Statutes, 1953, C. 19] of the province of Ontario represent the first modern corporate legislation in Canada relating to accounting and auditing matters. The audit requirements of that Act, together with an amendment in 1964 [Ontario, Statutes, 1964, C. 10, Sec. 2] requiring insertion in the report of the wording acknowledging adherence to "generally accepted accounting principles applied on a basis consistent with that of the preceding period" constitute the identical legislation enacted federally in 1964-1965 under the Canada Corporations Act. The Ontario Corporations Act, 1953 reads:

> The auditor shall make a report to the shareholders on the financial statement to be laid before the company at any annual meeting during his term of office and shall state in his report whether in his opinion the financial statement referred to therein presents fairly the financial position of the company and the results of its operations for the period under review.
>
> The auditor in his report shall make such statements as he considers necessary
>
> (a) if the company's financial statement is not in agreement with the accounting records;
> (b) if the company's financial statement is not in accordance with the requirements of this Act;
> (c) if he has not received all the information and explanations that he has required; or
> (d) if proper accounting records have not been kept so far as appears from his examination.
>
> [Ontario, Statutes, 1953, C. 19, Sec. 82(2) and (3).]

The Act also requires the auditor to make such statements as he considers necessary if adequate provision has not been made in the financial statements for losses of non-consolidated subsidiaries [Ontario, Statutes, 1953, Sec. 89 (2)(d)].

It should be noted that according to the Act, the financial statement includes the balance sheet, the profit and loss and surplus statements. In 1966 an additional amendment to the Act requires that the financial statement include a source and application of funds statement and that this statement be included in the auditor's opinion [Ontario, Statutes, 1966, C. 28, Sec. 6(2)]. The 1967 Interim Report of the Select Committee on Company Law commented:

> The research which the Committee carried out revealed that the financial disclosure provisions of the Ontario Act, as amended in 1966, are without a peer in the Companies Acts of any other jurisdiction which came to the Committee's attention. The credit for this high standard of financial disclosure for Ontario companies must be shared with the Institute of Chartered Accountants of Ontario, whose recommendations were incorporated into the Act when it was passed in 1953. [Ontario, Legislative Assembly . . . , 1967, p. 88.]

More particularly, with regard to the auditing provisions of the Act, they represent, with exception of subsection (b), the recommendations of the Institute of Chartered Accountants of Ontario in 1952 [Ontario, Legislature . . . , 1952, p. 2032] and the Institute of Chartered Accountants in 1953 [Canadian Institute, 1953, pp. 166-167].

The Canada Corporations Act, 1964 - 1965 is identical with the 1953 Ontario Companies Act as amended in 1964 [Canada, Statutes, 1964-65, C. 52, Sec. 124 (1), (2) and (3)]. The heavy influence of the Ontario legislation and the Canadian Institute was explicitly acknowledged by the Standing Committee on Banking and Commerce that was appointed to consider changes in corporate legislation [Canada, Senate Debates, 1964, pp. 515-518]. The Canadian federal legislation of 1964 - 1965 provided the first substantive federal changes in the auditing matters presently under review, since the audit was made mandatory in 1917. It should be emphasized that it was in this Act that the auditor was first obliged to render an opinion on the profit and loss statement. However, this half-century did not actually represent a stagnation in the auditing matters under consideration for at least three reasons: firstly, many corporations were required to report under the Ontario jurisdiction; secondly, the Canadian Institute of Chartered Accountants began issuing auditing recommendations in 1951; and thirdly - and possibly more significantly- the pronouncements of the American Institute acted as guidelines.

<u>Pronouncements of the Canadian Institute of Chartered Accountants</u>

In September of 1951, the Committee on Accounting and Auditing Research of the Canadian Institute issued its first recommendations on auditors' reports in Bulletin No. 6. The recommended wording was:

> I have examined the balance sheet of the __________ Company Limited as at ______________ 19__ and the statements of profit and loss and surplus for the year ended on that date and have obtained all the information and explanations I have required. My examination included a general review of the accounting procedures and such tests of accounting records and other supporting evidence as I considered necessary in the circumstances.
>
> In my opinion the accompanying balance sheet and statements of profit and loss and surplus are properly drawn up so as to exhibit a true and correct view of the state of the affairs of the company as at ______________ 19__ and the results of its operations for the year ended on that date, according to the best of my information and the explanations given to me and as shown by the books of the company. [Canadian Institute . . . , Accounting and Auditing Practices, 1951, Bulletin 6, p. 31.]

The second sentence of the scope paragraph represents a careful selection and paraphrasing of similar portions of the American Institute recommended wording of 1941 and 1948 with the exception of the phrase relating to "generally accepted auditing standards." The Committee gave a strong recommendation that the profit and loss statement be included in the auditor's opinion.

In 1959 a revised Committee recommendation, Bulletin No. 17, [p. 3] called for substitution of the phrase, "presents fairly" for "exhibits a true and correct view" and also for the inclusion of the phrase "in accordance with generally accepted accounting principles applied on a basis consistent with that of the preceding year." The Committee indicated that the recommendation of 1951 contemplated the implication of the phrase and that upon reconsideration it was felt that it should be more positively disclosed. In 1967 a revised Committee recommendation [Bulletin No. 25, p. 3] called for the rendering of an opinion on the statement of source and application of funds when this statement was included in the financial statements. The only remaining difference between the standard wording recommended by the Canadian and American Institute was the phrase "generally accepted auditing standards." In this regard, the Report of the Special Committee on Shareholders' Audits in 1968 recommended that when the Accounting and Auditing Research Committee completes its study of auditing standards, the standard "Canadian short form report could then be amended, if thought desirable" to include this phrase [Canadian Institute . . . , Special Committee on Shareholder Audits, 1968, pp. 350-351].

Form and Content of Audit Report

Variety in audit report wording, relative to the United States and England, persisted throughout the 1940s; however, the publications of the Accounting and Auditing Research Committees on auditors' reports commencing in 1951 strongly influenced the movement towards uniformity.

It has been noted that in the period 1920 to 1940, none of the audit reports examined rendered an opinion on the profit and loss statement. However, by 1943 five of the ten reports inspected did render an opinion and, with one exception, the remainder followed the Institute recommendation of 1951 at that time. The results of an analysis of 280 firms by the Canadian Institute in 1951 revealed that two-thirds of the auditors' reports included an opinion on the profit and loss statement [Auditor's Report, 1953, p. 35]. By 1956, only 19 of 300 firms analyzed in Financial Reporting in Canada did not do so [The Canadian Institute of Chartered Accountants, Financial Reporting . . . , 1957, p. 106]. One of the ten companies inspected, George Weston Limited, fell into this category. It was only in 1953 that the province of Ontario and in 1964-1965 that Canadian federal legislation required that the auditor give an opinion on this statement.

That portion of the "scope" paragraph that relates to the "review of accounting procedures and tests of the accounting records and other evidence" underwent a drastic and speedy change. In 1940 only two of the auditors' reports inspected provided some commentary on this matter. One of these companies was Distillers Corporation Seagrams Limited which was listed on the New York Stock Exchange at that time and which, since at least 1940, has observed the American wording of the auditor's report. By 1951 - 1952, all audit reports inspected, except Dominion Bridge Company Limited, used the recommended "scope" wording of the Institute.

By 1956, only 12 of 300 firms examined did not refer to the "extent of the examination" [The Canadian Institute of Chartered Accountants, Financial Reporting . . . , 1957, p. 106].

In 1959, Bulletin No. 17 of the Canadian Institute required the insertion of the phrase "prepared in accordance with generally accepted accounting principles applied on a basis consistent with that of the preceding year." Only one of the firms inspected had adopted this phrasing prior to 1959 and by 1962 only approximately twenty firms out of 300 had not [The Canadian Institute of Chartered Accountants, Financial Reporting . . . , 1963, p. 79].

In 1965, Bulletin No. 25 of the Canadian Institute recommended that the auditor render his opinion on the source and application of funds statement when it was presented in the financial statements. In 1963, only 4 percent of the firms presenting such statements supplied an auditor's opinion on them; in 1964, 43 percent; in 1965, 77 percent; in 1966, 90 percent; in 1968, 99 percent [The Canadian Institute of Chartered Accountants, Financial Reporting . . . , 1967 & 1969, pp. 132 & 133 respectively]. The influence of the Canadian Institute's pronouncements can be gauged by the fact that likely fewer than one-quarter of the 325 firms in the survey would be required under Ontario legislation in 1966 to provide such an opinion.

Wording beyond the standard audit report during this period related mostly to qualifications, reliance on other auditors and the treatment of profits and losses of non-consolidated subsidiaries. The 1964 - 1965 federal legislation required the auditor to make a statement only if adequate provision has not been made for losses of non-consolidated subsidiaries. This requirement led to a considerable reduction in auditors' comments on non-consolidated operations because prior to this time the auditor was obliged to explicitly state how such profits and losses were treated.

By 1968, as reported in Financial Reporting . . . , only 11 percent of the 325 firms analyzed did not conform to the Institute wording [The Canadian Institute of Chartered Accountants, Financial Reporting . . . , 1969, p. 130]. In most of these instances, and similar to the years 1965 through 1967, the reason for non-conformity was that the company inserted the American Institute wording in the scope paragraph that relates to "generally accepted auditing standards." Financial Reporting in Canada implies the strong American influence on this point:

> The number of occurrences of this type of departure is not surprising in view of the fact that Canadian companies associated with American companies or selling their securities in the United States are required to comply with the rules of financial reporting in that country. [The Canadian Institute of Chartered Accountants, Financial Reporting . . . , 1968, p. 131.]

Similarly, with regard to one of the auditors' reports inspected, the Canadian firm, British American Oil Company Limited [Annual Report, 1956], in the same year that it became associated with the American firm of Gulf Oil, incorporated into the audit report the American Institute phrasing relating to "generally accepted auditing standards" and to "generally accepted accounting principles applied on a basis consistent with that of the preceding year."

Since the kind of auditor's report that was typically used after 1951 normally took the form of the recommended wording of the Canadian Institute, there is no need to provide illustrative examples for the period 1950 to the present. Examples of the 1940 decade follow. In the first instance, the audit report of Burns and Co. Limited illustrates an unqualified report that closely follows the statutory wording:

> We have examined the accounts of Burns & Co. Limited for the year ended December 26, 1940, and in accordance with the provisions of The Companies Act (Dominion) we have to report that we have obtained all the information and explanations we have required and, in our opinion, the appended Balance Sheet as at December 26, 1940, is properly drawn up so as to exhibit a true and correct view of the state of the Company's affairs as at December 26, 1940, according to the best of our information and the explanations given to us and as shown by the books of the Company. [Burns & Co. Limited Annual Report, 1940.]

In the second instance, the 1949 report of Dominion Bridge Company Limited likely illustrates one of the last times that detailed audit procedures are listed and asset valuations given in the audit report.

> We have examined the books and accounts of Dominion Bridge Company, Limited and its entirely owned Subsidiary Companies for the year ended 31st October, 1949 and report thereon as follows:
>
> The Inventories of Stock on hand, as certified by responsible officials of the various companies, have been valued on a conservative basis.

> The Investments in which your Company is interested have been verified by actual inspection of the Securities or by certificates from the Depositaries in the cases where the Securities are deposited for safe custody or as security.
>
> In accordance with Section 114 of the Dominion Companies Act, we report that profits of partly owned subsidiaries are included in these accounts only to the extent of dividends declared by these subsidiaries.
>
> We report that we have obtained all the information and explanations we have required and, in our opinion, the accompanying Balance Sheet as at 31st October, 1949, is properly drawn up so as to exhibit a true and correct view of the state of the combined companies' affairs, according to the best of our information and the explanations given to us and as shown by the books of the Companies. [Dominion Bridge Company Limited Annual Report, 1949.]

The 1945 report of Canada and Dominion Sugar Company Limited is more typical of the period in its inclusion of the profit and loss statement and in its exclusion of any reference to the extent of the details of the examination made by the auditor:

> We have audited the accounts of Canada and Dominion Sugar Company Limited and its subsidiaries, Montreal Products Company Limited, Dominion Sugar Company Limited and The Canada Sugar Refining Company Limited for the year ending 31st December, 1945 and have received all the information and explanations we have required. We report that, in our opinion, the above consolidated balance sheet and the related statements of consolidated profit and loss and earned surplus have been properly drawn up so as to exhibit a true and correct view of the state of the combined companies' affairs at 31st December, 1945 and of the results of their operations for the year ending that date according to the best of our information, the explanations given us and as shown by the books of the companies. [Canada and Dominion Sugar Company Limited Annual Report, 1945.]

Summary

The provisions for the mandatory audit and the auditor's responsibilities in regard to financial statements as initially set out in the federal legislation of 1917 were heavily influenced by the English legislation of the preceding decade. No changes in legislation occurred, nor did Canadian Institute pronouncements begin, until the early 1950s. During the early part of that intervening period, audit report wording tended to follow closely the statutory wording. After the American Institute pronouncements had begun in the 1930s, there was an increasing tendency to be influenced from that source. All of the many American audit pronouncements during the formative 1930 to 1950 period were reprinted and commented on in the Canadian journal and the wording which the American Institute was beginning to formulate was gradually creeping into the Canadian audit reports. This influence has increased so that by 1970 the only remaining difference between the recommended standard wording of the American and Canadian Institutes is the reference to "generally accepted auditing standards."

The influence of the Institutes of Chartered Accountants in Canada has become of increasing importance in shaping the auditor's report, particularly since their first recommendation in 1951. Committees appointed to enquire into changes in the Companies Acts have, since 1950, carefully requested the views of the Institutes. The current legislation illustrates this influence since there is no minimum prescribed form which the report must take. Items with which all Canadian Companies Acts have concerned themselves since 1907 - whether the financial statements agree with the records and with the requirements of the Act, whether proper accounting records have been kept and whether the auditor has received all the information and explanations he has required - now need auditor commentary only if they are not being observed. The recommended Institute report wording is now uncomplicated by statutory wording.

It is noteworthy that, at two of the most fateful junctures in Canadian auditing history - the introduction of the mandatory audit on the balance sheet in 1907 and on the profit and loss statement in 1953- the influence of the Ontario Institute on the Ontario legislation has been acknowledged to be of the greatest importance. In each instance the provincial legislation predated the federal legislation by at least ten years. It is also interesting to note that with regard to the audit of the profit and loss statement, practices initially led legislation, later fell to the lower legislative level, and eventually reverted to a leadership role.

It has been noted that the recommended report wording of the Institute of Chartered Accountants in England and Wales is extremely brief and simple, containing no reference to the extent of examination of corporate procedures, nor to the consistent application of generally accepted accounting principles. Similar brief wording has been advocated in Canada by Ken LeM. Carter in 1943 [pp. 7-8] and by L. M. Nelson [1967, pp. 40-41]. Similarly, some American tendency toward a briefer report is evidenced by Mautz and Sharaf [1961, p. 203] and anticipated by Stettler [1961, p. 614] as that "millennium" when "further growth and development of the public accounting profession . . . results in almost universal meaning and application for generally accepted auditing standards and generally accepted accounting principles." However given the geographic proximity and industrial influence of the United States, the articulateness of the American Institute and the need for some Canadian audit reports to observe American Institute wording, it is unlikely that Canadian audit report wording would move independently toward the English position.

CHAPTER III

THE EVOLUTION OF FINANCIAL STATEMENTS, 1900 - 1920

Purpose

The purpose of Chapters III, IV and V is to describe the evolution of financial statements in Canada from 1900 to 1970 by reference to corporate legislation, financial press commentary, the professional and academic literature and a sample of corporate annual financial statements. Primary attention will be devoted to the evolution of the balance sheet and the profit and loss statement, including their content, classification and general valuation base; there will also be some attempt to comment on the evolution of the earned surplus statement, footnotes to financial statements, secret reserves and extraordinary items - inasmuch as they bear upon the balance sheet and the profit and loss statement. The examination of these selected areas helps to illustrate the influences that have shaped corporate reporting practices in Canada.

The understanding of the evolution of financial statements is aided by brief reference to the selected series of economic statistics provided in Appendix C. Between 1900 and 1966 the population, aided considerably by immigration, almost quadrupled; and the gross national product rose from approximately one billion to fifty-seven billions. During this period the relative proportions of investment in Canada by the United States and Great Britain almost reversed. By 1966, 80 percent of total non-resident investment of thirty-two billions had its source in the United States. The price indexes during this period reflect a significant rise during World War I and through to 1920 as well as the considerable drop during the depression years. Together with other major countries, stock prices rose markedly during the late 1920s and then plunged disastrously during the depression. Subsequent to World War II, stock prices began their long post-war ascent. The first years of World War I, 1914 and 1915, and the first three years of the 1920s witnessed a large relative increase in the number and value of commercial failures. Especially since 1940 the relative proportion of business transacted by larger firms has increased significantly. Firms having an output valued at less than one million dollars in 1965 accounted for 85 percent of the firms but only 12 percent of the total value of output.

English Legislation

Though the English Joint Stock Companies Act of 1856 [Great Britain, 1856, C. 47] abandoned the provisions for the mandatory audit and the preparation of the balance sheet for the annual meeting that the 1844 Act had imposed, it set forward a set of model articles that were to apply in the event that an incorporating company did not register its own particular articles [Edey and Panitpakdi, 1956, p. 362]. The model article provisions for profit and loss statements and balance sheets and the elaboration of their contents are remarkably modern and though these provisions were not mandatory, they undoubtedly served as guides in corporate reporting practices in England, Canada and the United States. Hatfield in 1911 acknowledged the significance of these model articles on American practices [Hatfield, 1966, p. 172; also Hawkins, 1963, p. 154]. Because some portions of the model articles relating to disclosure were in advance of legislative requirements one hundred years later in both Canada and England, they are reproduced here below and in Figure 1.

> 70. Once at the least in every Year the Directors shall lay before the Company in General Meeting a Statement of the Income and Expenditure for the past Year, made up to a Date not more than Three Months before such Meeting.
>
> 71. The Statement so made shall show, arranged under the most convenient Heads, the Amount of gross Income, distinguishing the Several Sources from which it has been derived, and the Amount of gross Expenditure, distinguishing the Expense of the Establishment, Salaries, and other like Matters: Every Item of Expenditure fairly chargeable against the Year's Income shall be brought into Account, so that a just Balance of Profit and Loss may be laid before the Meeting; and in Cases where any Item of Expenditure which may in Fairness be distributed over several Years has been incurred in any One Year the whole Amount of such Item shall be stated, with the addition of the Reasons why only a Portion of such Expenditure is charged against the Income of the Year.
>
> 72. A Balance Sheet shall be made out in every Year, and laid before the General Meeting of the Company, and such Balance Sheet shall contain a Summary of the Property and Liabilities of the Company arranged under the Heads appearing in the Form annexed to this Table, or as near thereto as Circumstances admit. [Great Britain, 1856, C. 47.]

TABLE B OF JOINT STOCK COMPANIES ACT, 1856

FORM of BALANCE SHEET referred to in TABLE B.

Dr.	BALANCE SHEET of the	£ s. d.	£ s. d.	Co. made up to 18		£ s. d.	£ s. d. Cr.
	CAPITAL AND LIABILITIES				PROPERTY AND ASSETS		
I. CAPITAL -	*Showing:* 1. *The total Amount received from the Shareholders; showing also:* (a) *The Number of Shares* - : (b) *The Amount paid per Share* : (c) *If any Arrears of Calls, the Nature of the Arrear, and the Names of the Defaulters* - - - - *Any Arrears due from any Director or Officer of the Company to be separately stated.* (d) *The Particulars of any forfeited Shares.*			III. PROPERTY held by the Company -	*Showing:* 4. *Immoveable Property, distinguishing* - (a) *Freehold Land* - - - - (b) " *Buildings* - - - - (c) *Leasehold* " - - - - 5. *Moveable Property, distinguishing* - - (d) *Stock in Trade* - - - - (e) *Plant* - - - - - - *The Cost to be stated with Deductions for Deterioration in Value as charged to the Reserve Fund or Profit and Loss.*		
II. DEBTS AND LIABILITIES of the Company	*Showing:* 2. *The Amount of Loans on Mortgage or Debenture Bonds.* 3. *The Amount of Debts owing by the Company, distinguishing—* (a) *Debts for which Acceptances have been given.* (b) *Debts to Tradesmen for Supplies of Stock in Trade or other Articles.* (c) *Debts for Law Expenses.* (d) *Debts for Interest on Debentures or other Loans.* (e) *Unclaimed Dividends.* (f) *Debts not enumerated above.*			IV. DEBTS owing to the Company -	*Showing:* 6. *Debts considered good for which the Company hold Bills or other Securities.* 7. *Debts considered good for which the Company hold no Security.* 8. *Debts considered doubtful and bad* - - *Any Debt due from a Director or other Officer of the Company to be separately stated.*		
VI. RESERVE FUND - -	*Showing:* *The Amount set aside from Profits to meet Contingencies.*			V. CASH AND INVESTMENTS	*Showing:* 9. *The Nature of Investment and Rate of Interest.* 10. *The Amount of Cash, where lodged, and if bearing Interest.*		
VII. PROFIT AND LOSS -	*Showing:* *The disposable Balance for Payment of Dividend, &c.*						
CONTINGENT LIABILITIES -	*Claims against the Company not acknowledged as Debts.* *Monies for which the Company is contingently liable.*						

Figure 1

The Companies Act, 1900 [Great Britain, 1900, C. 48] contained neither mandatory nor optional provisions for financial statement disclosure - although the requirement to provide a balance sheet at each annual meeting can be inferred from the mandatory audit provisions that pertained to the balance sheet. Edey and Panitpakdi [1956, p. 374] suggest that evidence given to the Committee that made recommendations for changes in the Companies Acts indicated that "the cost of assets and accumulated depreciation thereon should be disclosed; that goodwill should be valued separately; and that the main classes of assets and liabilities should be distinguished." The Committee itself, recommended that there be stated "the bases upon which assets were valued: whether at cost, by valuation or otherwise; the percentage or amount of depreciation which had been written off; and what other provision, if any, had been made for depreciation" [Edey and Panitpakdi, 1956, p. 374]. However the Act of 1900 incorporated none of these requirements.

The Companies (Consolidation) Act, 1908 differed in two ways from the 1900 Act with respect to financial statements. Firstly, the profit and loss statement was required to be prepared for the annual meeting-but only if the by-laws and regulations of the company so directed. Secondly, a balance sheet "giving such particulars as will disclose the general nature of those liabilities and assets, and how the values of those fixed assets have been arrived at" must be forwarded to the Registrar of Companies [Great Britain, C. 69, Sec. 26(3)].

By 1908 therefore, there were no mandatory provisions requiring that the profit and loss statement be prepared for the annual meeting; nor none outlining the detail to be contained in the audited balance sheet that was to be submitted to the annual meeting. The statement that was to be forwarded to the Registrar of Companies had merely to contain some notation on asset and liability valuation. No changes of consequence took place in England in this regard until the corporation legislation of 1928.

Canadian Legislation

As indicated in the preceding chapter, the early Canadian legislation concerning the mandatory audit and the auditor's duty respecting the financial statements corresponded directly with that of the English legislation. However, the early Canadian legislation with regard to balance sheet and profit and loss disclosure was in advance of the actual English legislation. The Canadian legislation may, on the other hand, have drawn on the optional disclosure requirements of the model articles of the English Act of 1856 and upon the rejected recommendations of and evidence submitted to the Committee that, immediately before 1900, enquired into changes that should be made in the English Companies Act.[1]

Ontario and Canadian Federal Legislation

The Ontario Companies Act of 1897 called for the preparation of a statement of income and expenditure which was to be laid before the annual or general meeting. Additionally, if the by-laws of the company so directed, the accounts to be presented at the annual meeting were required to include an audited balance sheet [Ontario, Statutes, 1897, C. 28, Sec. 75]. The Ontario Companies Act of 1907 mandated an audited balance sheet and elaborated certain disclosure requirements to which the balance sheet must adhere [Ontario, Statutes, 1907, C. 34, Sec. 36, SS 2 and 3]. These disclosure requirements are important for at least four reasons: Firstly, according to T. Mulvey [1920, p. 54], the Under Secretary of State (Canada) and former Assistant Provincial Secretary of the Province of Ontario, they constituted the model upon which the Canadian 1917 legislation was based; secondly, according to Mulvey again, and indicating the early influence of the accounting profession, these provisions were made upon the recommendations of the Institute of Chartered Accountants of Ontario; thirdly, these provisions represent the most advanced federal corporate regulation of the time as between Canada, England and the United States; and lastly, the passing of these provisions by the Ontario legislature gave rise to a concern that was later to be re-echoed in the Canadian parliament in 1934.

> In regard to other clauses of companies (Act) it was pointed out that the concurrent jurisdiction exercised by the Dominion makes such control impossible. These companies would simply get incorporation at Ottawa to do all they desired to do and the only effect of trying to impose conditions here would be that the

[1]See preceding comments.

Province [of Ontario] would be deprived of revenue.[2]

On the federal Canadian level, the first disclosure provision requiring that "the directors of every company shall lay before its shareholders a full and clear printed statement of the affairs and financial position of the company at or before each general meeting . . ." was enacted in 1877 [Canada, Statutes, C. 43, Sec. 87]. The more specific requirement that such statements be presented annually was incorporated in the 1902 Act [Canada, Statutes, C. 15, Sec. 88]. While it may be felt that some ambiguity attaches to the meaning of "a statement of the affairs and financial position," many companies between 1902 and 1917 - when the presentation of the profit and loss statement became mandatory - interpreted these provisions to apply only to the balance sheet.

The next federal change in disclosure occurred in the 1917 Act which is repeated here because it represents the first attempt, at the federal level in Canada, England or the United States to delineate the components of financial statements and because it represents with the exception of (3)(j) and 3(m) similar disclosure already in force under the Ontario legislation since 1907. Relevant parts of section 105 read:

> (2) At such [annual] meeting the directors shall lay before the company,-
> (a) a balance sheet made up to a date not more than four months before such annual meeting:
> Provided however that a company which carries on its undertaking out of Canada may, by resolution at a general meeting, extend this period to not more than six months;
> (b) a general statement of income and expenditures for the financial period ending upon the date of such balance sheet;
> (c) the report of the auditor or auditors;
> (d) such further information respecting the company's financial position as the special Act, letters patent or by-laws of the company require.
>
> (3) Every balance sheet shall be drawn up so as to distinguish severally at least the following classes or assets and liabilities, namely:-
> (a) cash;

---

[2]Abstracted from the February 6th, 1907 Ontario Scrap Hansard, in the Ontario Legislative Library in Toronto, and representing a chronological filing of newspaper clippings relating to the Debates of the Ontario Legislature. A formal record of the Debates was not maintained until the 1940s.

(b) debts owing to the company from its customers;
(c) debts owing to the company from its directors, officers and shareholders respectively;
(d) stock in trade;
(e) expenditures made on account of future business;
(f) lands, buildings, and plant;
(g) goodwill, franchises, patents and copyrights, trademarks, leases, contracts and licenses;
(h) debts owing by the company secured by mortgage or other lien upon the property of the company;
(i) debts owing by the company but not secured;
(j) amount of common shares, subscribed for and allotted and the amount paid thereon, showing the amount thereof allotted for services rendered, for commissions or for assets acquired since the last annual meeting;
(k) amount of preferred shares subscribed for and allotted and the amount paid thereon, showing the amount thereof allotted for services rendered, for commissions or for assets acquired since the last annual meeting;
(l) indirect and contingent liabilities;
(m) amount written off on account of depreciation of plant, machinery, good-will and similar items. [Canada, Statutes, The Companies Act Amendment Act, 1917, Sec. 105, SS 2 and 3.]

Background to the Canadian Legislation

Several factors were influential in the promulgation of the 1917 Act: the Taxation Acts of 1916 and 1917, the concern for mergers and the profit in corporate promotions, the bankruptcies at the beginning of World War I, the bank failures culminating in the bank legislation of 1913, and the existence of a pattern for legislation in the Ontario Companies Act of 1907. No evidence was uncovered from any source - the financial press, the debates of the House of Commons, economic and legal histories nor accounting literature existing in The Canadian Chartered Accountant - to indicate exactly why this legislation was passed at a time when the efforts of the whole economy were devoted towards the War. However, an analysis of the foregoing factors allows the legislation to be placed in its economic and social perspective.

The significance of the Taxation Acts of 1916 and 1917 have been commented on in the preceding chapter. The complementarity of the new requirements in the 1917 Act relating to profit and loss disclosure and to the segregation and delineation of assets, liabilities and equities in the balance sheet with the need for an equitable and successful tax collection system is fairly evident. The Taxation Acts were therefore likely the strongest and most immediate of the factors influencing the 1917 Companies Act legislation.

Earlier anti-combines legislation at the turn of the decade had reflected the willingness of the Canadian public to have the government regulate business. Andre Raynauld indicates that:

> In 1909 a wave of mergers swept through Canadian economy shortly after a similar movement in the United States: fifty-eight business firms and $361 million in capital were involved. Faced with an aroused public opinion, Parliament in 1910 passed an Act to provide for the Investigation of Combines, Monopolies, Trusts and Mergers. [Raynauld, 1967, pp. 149-150.]

The historian, O. D. Skelton, gives us some insight into the public concern for the merger movement not only in its monopoly aspects but also in its promotional aspects. This latter point is of some importance since changes in legislative requirements relating to balance sheet and profit and loss disclosure have often been accompanied by stricter legislative requirements relating to corporate stock promotion. In this regard, it is notable that prospectus legislation emulating the 1908 English Act was also enacted in the 1917 Act [Williamson, 1960, p. 14].

> More characteristic of the period [1896 - 1912] was the growth of out and out consolidation, following some 8 or 10 years after the main movement in the United States. The usual arguments were put forward as to the economies in operation which would result from combination, the specializing of product, the saving in executive and sales force, the elimination of cross-freights. The regulation of prices was usually an object, whether this involved an increase of prices already giving adequate profit, or merely an ending of cut-throat competition. There was however a new factor involved of greater potency: it was not so much the profit of operation as the profit of promotion that was sought. In increasing degree, the initiative in the formation of mergers came from financial promoters unconnected with the industry, and the motive lay in the possibility of selling the bonds and stocks of the greatly overcapitalized new companies formed, to a public as ready to rush to share in the hoped-for monopoly of a specific trust as to denounce trusts in the abstract. [Skelton, 1913, pp. 259-261.][3]

---

[3] O. Skelton goes on to list some well-known and extant corporations that found their strength if not their origins in these mergers: Dominion Steel Corporation Limited, Canada Cement Company Limited, Canadian Car and Foundry Company Limited, Steel Company of Canada Limited, Dominion Canners Limited, Penmans Limited, Canadian Consolidated Rubber Limited (Dominion Rubber), Dominion Textile Company Limited,

Similarly, the concern for control by both the public and the government was evidenced in 1910 by W. L. M. King, the subsequent long-time prime-minister of the country:

> The discussion which has been going on in the press in regard to these large combinations, that the largest industrial combinations of all in this country have escaped criticism all together, namely, the great railway concerns of Canada. I think that fact is of particular significance in connection with the legislation we are contemplating at the present time . . . what the public is looking to this government to do in connection with the large industrial concerns is something along the line of what we have already done in regard to these great railway interests. [Skeoch, 1966, p. 24.] (Author's note: by this time there was relatively close regulation concerning the railways, involving detailed reporting of financial statements and operations.)

The bank failures culminating in the Bank Act of 1913 have been commented on in the preceding chapter. Mention was also made of a rash of bankruptcies (see Appendix C), in 1914 and 1915. M. Goodman indicated the importance of and necessity for proper financial statements in these instances:

> These business houses [of finance] began to realize the inefficient business methods of their customers when failures took place . . . and that the majority of these customers had submitted false statements, made from improperly kept accounts and records, that accounts receivable were bad or fictitious, stock was overestimated, . . . haphazard methods of costing and selling existed; waste in manufacture and extravagance in expenditure was rampant. When the War hit us it brought down hundreds of these small and dozens of large concerns. It was therefore proven that the basis of commercial success . . . is good management, accurate accounting, accurate costing, strict methods of selling and truthful financial statements. [Goodman, 1917, pp. 123-124.]

The foregoing description of the decade preceding the 1917 Act indicates the kind of events that influenced the passage of this important legislation. Though the contribution of the Ontario Institute of Chartered Accountants with respect to the Ontario Act of 1907 was acknowledged by Mulvey, no indication of concern was located in The Canadian Chartered Accountant for the federal legislation in the years immediately preceding 1917. The president of the Institute, Mr. John Hyde [1918, pp. 93-103], at the Annual Meeting in 1918 drew attention to

---

Sherwin Williams of Canada Limited, and Maple Leaf Milling Company Limited.

the passage of the Act but made no further comment. It may well have been that the profession felt that the provisions which they had recommended for the Ontario legislation of 1907 represented a sufficient guide for the federal legislation. Mulvey indicated that Sec. 105 of the 1917 Act "was first suggested by the Board of the Institute of Chartered Accountants of Ontario in the drafting of the Ontario Companies Act of 1907 and was taken with a few verbal alterations from that Act" [Mulvey, 1920, p. 54]. Certainly the 1907 Ontario legislation relating to profit and loss and balance sheet disclosure was not only well ahead of other legislation but also well ahead of corporate reporting practices at the time. It is also evident that the concern for legislative regulation respecting corporate financial statement disclosure at the federal level is in the English tradition.

English and American Influence

While the influence of England and its traditions seem to predominate in Canada for most of the 1900 - 1920 period, the increasing American influence became quite noticeable towards the end of that era.

Several areas of English influence were important: firstly, the early part of this period represents the high point of the relative size of English investment - 85 percent of all foreign investment in Canada being English, but declining to 53 percent by 1920; secondly, the Chartered Accountancy profession itself was in its formation, influenced by English and Scottish accountants who immigrated to Canada [J. E. Smyth, 1953, p. 291];[4] and thirdly, as described in the preceding section the Canadian Companies Act legislation was largely in the English tradition.

Between 1900 and 1920 the relative proportion of American investment in Canada had increased from 14 percent to 44 percent. Though Thomas Mulvey [1918, p. 129], the under Secretary of State, acknowledged some inspiration from the legislation of New York State, the mandatory

---

[4]Good evidence on this point is incomplete. Certainly some of the foremost leaders of the Institute of Chartered Accountants of Ontario were born and trained in Canada (e.g. George Edwards, E. R. C. Clarkson). And it is not evident from any of the research undertaken by the author that, as happened in the United States, firms of British accountants set up shop in Canada.

audit provisions and detailed disclosure required in the financial statements of The Ontario Companies Act of 1907 were far in advance of the New York legislation existing at that time.[5] The American influence however, was felt in the publication of The Federal Reserve Board's Uniform Accounting and its subsequent reprinting in the July, 1917 edition of The Canadian Chartered Accountant. Magazine commentary in the same issue recommended the bulletin "as a guide to the young accountant" [July, 1917, p. 49] and E. J. Bennett [1922, p. 327] and J. C. Gray as well [1919, p. 194] acknowledged the influence of American reporting practices. It should also be noted that the general requirements of the English Companies Acts were of some influence in the American scene. The President of the American Association of Public Accountants, J. E. Sterrett, in 1910 indicated that:

> Everyone familiar with the subject has noted that a rapidly growing number of the best American corporations conduct their affairs according to standards that are in practical conformity with the requirements of the Companies Acts of England, thus demonstrating that the form of control embodied in the law which merely gives legal authority to good established business custom in that country would be equally applicable to American conditions. It is significant also that probably without exception, the corporations whose courses of conduct have been made the subject of severe criticism within the past few years have failed to follow a policy in accord with the principles just outlined. [Sterrett, 1910, p. 246.]

The influence of both England and America was felt in the accounting literature in Canada. Of thirty-seven signed articles of three pages or more in volumes 7 and 8, 1917 - 1919 of The Canadian Chartered Accountant, twelve of these were written by Americans, six by Englishmen and nineteen by Canadians. Similarly an advertisement by The Accountancy Book Publishing Company of Toronto in The Canadian Chartered Accountant in 1920 lists sixteen texts, all of which are American with the exception of the first and last four. They are reproduced here because they likely represent the most scholarly and frequently-used contributions of each country at the time:

Accountancy - Pixley
Accounting in Theory and Practice - Lisle

---

[5]Letter to the author from Ernest H. Bruer, State Law Librarian, The New York State Library, Albany, New York, April 22, 1970.

Advanced Accounting - Dicksee
Bookkeeping and Accounts - Spicer and Pegler
Accountancy of Investment - Sprague
Philosophy of Accounts - Sprague
Accounting Practice and Procedure - Dickinson
Accounting Problems - Greendlinger
Applied Theory of Accounts - Esquerre
Auditing Theory and Practice - Montgomery
Company Accounts - Coles
Principles of Depreciation - Saliers
Auditing, Accountancy and Banking - Dowlen
Companies and Company Law - Connell
Joint Stock Company Accounts - Hoskins
Manufacturing Accounts - Eddis and Tindall

[The Canadian Chartered Accountant, April, 1920, back cover.]

The Theory Relating to Corporate Reporting Practices

Littleton and Zimmerman have suggested the particular and more immediate reasons for the existence of corporate annual reports: "periodic reports were the consequence of the acceptance of the idea of enterprise continuity" [1962, p. 56] and again, "permanent capital, transferable shares, and the continuity of operations made periodic accounting reports a necessity" [p. 57]. On a more general level of reasoning, periodic corporate reports were a function of wider-spread ownership, dependence on financial markets and a slowly emerging acknowledgement of corporate social responsibility [p. 80].

Balance Sheet and Profit and Loss Emphasis

The evolution of the relative significance of the profit and loss statement as opposed to the balance sheet has been suggested by Prof. J. E. Smyth:

> When a country is developing rapidly as was true of both Canada and the United States in the early years of this century, investment is made for appreciation and not for a steady return of income. In this stage, the balance sheet has a significance it does not have in a more mature economy. After things settle down the measurement of income, rather than the appreciation of assets, becomes the criterion of success in business ventures. [Smyth, 1953, p. 204.]

Support for this conjecture is indicated by B. S. Yamey, one of the foremost English accounting historians, who draws attention to the importance of the profit and loss statement in the relatively well-industrialized England of the late nineteenth century and by C. Brown who indicates that the tendency to emphasize the profit and loss statement in America for external purposes occurred only in the early twentieth century. Yamey states that:

> The profit and loss account and the calculation of periodic profits acquired a new status in the course of the nineteenth century in company accounting. The calculation of profits, and particularly of the profit figure to appear . . . in the accounts presented to shareholders, came to dominate the accounting scene. In this metamorphosis, the valuation of assets, as they were to appear in the final accounts, was made subservient to the calculation of profits. This was so, even though the publication of profit and loss accounts was not made compulsory [by the Companies Act] until 1929. [Yamey, 1961, p. 757.]

While Brown indicates that:

> . . . there were essentially two shifts in emphasis from balance sheet data to income statement data. There was an internal or managerial shift and an external shift by stockholders, creditors and other parties outside the firm. The former shift . . . probably occurred with the advent of the corporate form of business organization characterized by the separation of owners and managers, between 1880 and 1925. On the other hand, the latter shift began in the 1920s, accelerated in the 1930s and was essentially completed by the early 1940s. [Brown, 1968, pp. 167-168.]

It is likely that in Canada the change in emphasis towards the profit and loss statement occurred only slightly earlier than the change-period indicated by Brown for the United States. It has been previously mentioned that the Ontario Act of 1897 required that a profit and loss statement be prepared annually for companies coming under its provincial jurisdiction and that the Companies Act Amendment Act put forth the same requirements in 1917 for the federal jurisdiction. Fleming's text of 1892 provides interesting commentary on the times and seems to give at least as much prominence to the profit and loss statement as it does to the balance sheet:

> There are a great many varieties of financial statements published, as to the form and arrangement. Usually, however, there are only three kinds, viz., Resource and Liability statement, Loss and Gain statements and statements [of] Receipts and Payments of Cash. Sometimes a company will publish all three kinds at once - <u>usually two</u>, sometimes only one. Where the company is a trading corporation, such as a Joint Stock Company, formed for the purpose of making profit for the shareholders, it would be expected that a Loss and Gain statement would be made to show the profits from various sources and the losses and expenses. This statement shows the progress of the business. The

> Resource and Liability statement is made to show the actual standing on a certain day. [Italics mine.] [Fleming, 1892, p. 164.]

Several other Canadian texts [Eddis, 1899; Eddis and Tindall, 1904; Hoskins, 1907; Shaw and McIntosh, 1903, Hoskins, 1901] of the times were reviewed but only J. D. Warde's Shareholders' and Directors' Manual in 1900 indicated that one statement was relatively more important than the other:

> The balance sheet is the most important statement laid before the shareholders, as, if properly drawn up, it shows the exact financial position of the company. [Warde, 1900, p. 113.]

These sentiments were echoed much later in 1919 by J. C. Gray, in a review of financial statement disclosure [1919, p. 194]. The form of the profit and loss statement advocated by Gray could hardly be much less than the statement legally required by the Companies Acts - specifying only depreciation, interest income and expense, and profit thereafter [p. 202]. On the other hand, Mulvey's [1920, pp. 54-65] Dominion Company Law incorporates a model set of financial statements prepared by the chairman of the committee of the Institute of Chartered Accountants of Ontario that made recommendations for changes in the Ontario Companies Act of 1907. This model set of statements places somewhat more emphasis on the profit and loss statement by indicating the greater detailed information that should be included therein. These statements are reproduced in Figures 2 and 3. It should be noted that the statement heading of Income and Expenditure is what we refer to as an income or profit and loss statement and that the Profit and Loss Account is what we presently refer to as a statement of retained earnings. A sanguine interpretation of The Companies Act profit and loss disclosure requirements is given by the committee chairman - an interpretation with which actual corporate reporting practices seemed to be at variance.

> The general statement of income and expenditure called for by . . . section 105 [of the Companies Act Amendment Act, 1917], if construed consistently with good business practice, contemplates something more than a statement of the amount of net earnings for the period and the disposition of such earnings. It is open fairly to the construction that a company should show the gross income received and the volume of transactions in respect of which such income has been earned, and the expenditure side of the account should disclose the various ways in which the gross income of the company for the period has been disposed of.

THE JOINT STOCK COMPANY OF CANADA, LIMITED

Balance Sheet, December 31st, 1917

ASSETS.

(a)	*Cash:*		
	In Bank	$ 14,250 00	
	In Offices	1,600 00	
			$ 15,850 00
(b)	*Accounts Receivable:*		
	Customers	142,500 00	
(c)	Directors	1,500 00	
	Officers	350 00	
	Shareholders	800 00	
			145,150 00
(d)	*Stock in Trade:*		
	Materials, at cost	210,500 00	
	Goods in Process, at cost	82,600 00	
	Finished Goods, at cost	105,250 00	
			398,350 00
(e)	*Deferred Expenses*		9,400 00
(f)	*Lands, Buildings and Plant:*		
	Fixed	778,800 00	
	Movable	14,600 00	
			793,400 00
(g)	*Good-will, Patents, etc.:*		
	Purchased	42,000 00	
	Valued	326,000 00	
			368,000 00
			$1,730,150 00

LIABILITIES.

(h)	*Accounts Payable, Secured:*		
	Bankers' Advances	$ 195,000 00	
	Mortgage Bonds and Interest	535,600 00	
	Taxes, estimated	12,200 00	
			$732,800 00
(i)	*Accounts Payable, Unsecured:*		
	Salaries and Wages	6,300 00	
	Trade and Current	38,600 00	
	Dividends, payable Jan. 15, 1918	21,700 00	
			66,600 00
(l)	*Contingent Account:*		
	Doubtful Debts	4,000 00	
	Discounts and Collections	2,800 00	
	Inventory Reserve	21,200 00	
			28,000 00
(m)	*Depreciation:*		
	Buildings and Plant	42,000 00	
	Good-will	92,300 00	
			134,300 00
(j)	*Capital Stock paid in*, Common	520,000 00	
	Allotted to Dec. 31, 1916 $600,000		
	Allotted during 1917 .. 150,000		
(k)	*Capital Stock paid in*, Preferred	130,000 00	
	Allotted to Dec. 31, 1916 $150,000		
	Allotted during 1917 .. nothing		
	Surplus	118,450 00	
			768,450 00
			$1,730,150 00
(l)	*Indirect Bills under discount* $65,200 00		

Figure 2

THE JOINT STOCK COMPANY OF CANADA, LIMITED

Income and Expenditure, 12 months ending December 31st, 1917

EXPENDITURE.		INCOME.		
Management, Selling and General Expenses	$ 194,000 00	Gross Profit on Sales		$ 375,000 00
Reserved for Depreciation and Contingencies	76,000 00	Sales	$ 1,260,000 00	
Balance, Net Earnings	105,000 00	Cost	885,000 00	
	$375,000 00			$375,000 00

PROFIT AND LOSS ACCOUNT

Dr.		Cr.	
Interest Account	$ 41,300 00	Balance of Profit brought forward from previous year	$ 110,350 00
Incomes Taxes, estimated	12,200 00	Net Earnings for 12 months ending Dec. 31, 1917	105,000 00
Dividends Nos. 6 and 7, Preferred Shares	9,100 00		
Dividends Nos. 2 and 3, Common Shares	34,300 00		
Balance, to Balance Sheet	118,450 00		
	$215,350 00		$215,350 00

Figure 3

> Conformably with this view, management and selling and general expenses and reserves for depreciation would be within the meaning of the section, as well as the other usual items in a Profit and Loss Account, namely, - interest, income tax and dividends. [Mulvey, 1920, pp. 64-65.]

In summary, it would seem that by 1920 in Canada, there was some notable emphasis being placed on the profit and loss statement - as indicated by both Companies Acts requirements and the accounting literature of the time. Recommended statement forms by Fleming in 1892 [pp. 166 and 168] and Eddis in 1899 [p. 160] are shown in Figures 4 and 5.

Establishment of the Cost Principle

George O. May has indicated that the cost principle was established earlier in England than in America:

> In America, the emphasis on [market] valuation was in earlier days far greater than in England, and it is only in very recent years that the propriety of recording appreciation on books of account has been questioned. [May, 1943, p. 90.]

The lack of uniformity in the acceptance of the cost principle in America in the early part of the twentieth century is attested to by Hatfield [1927, pp. 73-74] in a review of such authorities as Esquerre, Montgomery, Kester and the Journal of Accountancy. The evaluation of the lower of cost or market rule took much the same course with the rule being fairly well established in England by the turn of the century and in the United States somewhat later [Parker, pp. 158-165].

Early Canadian literature offers a medley of valuation schemes for inventories and various subdivisions of fixed assets. Fleming [1892] makes no explicit comment on valuation. Eddis and Tindall suggest that cost be used in relation to buildings:

> It is also quite possible that up to a certain point the building may increase in value, owing to increased costs in material and labor, and value of position, etc., but this question need not here be raised, except as an argument against unduly writing down, as no wise man of business would write up such assets and attempt to show a profit this way. [Eddis and Tindall, 1904, pp. 154-155.]

However, with regard to machinery they advocate that "probably the wisest course is to have all machinery revalued every five years, and readjust the reserves or the amount written off accordingly" [p. 156]. Similarly,

ONTARIO PEOPLE'S SALT MANUFACTURING COMPANY (Limited).

Statement of Profits and Losses for the Financial Year, Ending May 30, '92.

LOSSES		PROFITS	
Balance of loss from last year	$ 913.74	Profits on sales of Fine Salt	$ 7,640.20
Wages	1,657.91	" " Coarse Salt	3,896.36
Salary and Auditing	763.33	" " Land Salt	915.84
Directors' Fees	49.00		
Interest and Discount	154.11		
Barrels	1,239.79		
Bags	844.36		
Real Estate, written off	425.00		
Chattels and Office Furniture, written off	95.30		
Postage	30.76		
Telegraphing	11.95		
Petty and Legal expenses	27.85		
Printing Books and Stationery	22.25		
Rent, Insurance and Taxes	317.48		
Coal	1,358.00		
Coal - Freight	320.29		
Coal - unloading	260.32		
Coal - Duty and Harbor Dues	147.10		
Travelling Expenses	63.40		
Repairs	183.18		
Organization Expenses, 10% written off	369.60		
Dividend No. 1 at 5%	1,377.50		
Balance of profits carried forward to next year	1,320.18		
	$12,452.40		$12,452.40

Figure 4

ONTARIO PEOPLE'S SALT MANUFACTURING COMPANY (Limited).

Statement of Resources and Liabilities, taken May 30th, 1892.

RESOURCES.		LIABILITIES.	
Due from sundry persons	$ 792.18	Bills Payable	$ 750.00
Cash in bank and on hand	2,981.88	Interest on above not due	40.00
Real Estate - estimated value	18,800.00	Rent accrued not due	71.22
Salt in stock at works	2,909.58	Paid up capital	27,550.00
Barrels and materials for same	267.14	Balance of profits carried forward at credit of Loss and Gain a/c	1,320.18
Bags on hand	39.02		
Oil and other supplies in Expense a/c	13.95		
Coal on hand	10.00		
Chattels, tools, etc.	467.45		
Office furniture and fixtures	44.15		
Books, stationery, etc.	12.00		
Insurance - unearned premium	67.66		
Organization a/c	3,326.39		
	$29,731.40		$29,731.40

Figure 4 (continued)

BALANCE SHEET OF THE............MANUFACTURING CO.,

As on............1898.

Liabilities.		Assets.	
Nominal Capital....shares of $....each ..		Cash on hand	
Subscribed Capital....shares of $....each, $....per share called up ...		Cash in Bank	
Less calls in arrears		Trade Debtors -	
Creditors, trade -		Bills Receivable	
Bills Payable		Accounts Receivable	
Accounts Payable		Less provision for discount and bad debts	
Other Creditors, if any		Stock on Hand -	
Reserve Account, if any		Raw Material	
Profit and Loss Account:-		Manufactured, incomplete	
Balance available for dividend		" finished	
		Stores	
		Plant and Machinery -	
		At cost	
		Less depreciation at say 10% per annum ..	
		Office Furniture and Fittings -	
		Less depreciation at say 7% per annum ...	
		Freehold Land and Buildings	
		Leasehold Property less depreciation	
		Other assets	
		Preliminary expenses (if not written off) .	

Figure 5

Warde [1900, p. 113] suggests that "if it be possible to value the plant and machinery each year and charge the reduction to depreciation account, it is the best way." On the other hand, "an inventory of merchandise should be taken at its cost price and not at its market value, as there can be no profit until the goods are sold" [p. 111]. Unfortunately in none of the foregoing recommendations is there any indication of how "value" would be determined - though original undepreciated cost seems to represent an upper limit on valuation.

Roughly fifteen to twenty years later - by 1920 - the literature, aided by the income tax regulations, began to stress valuation at cost for fixed assets and valuation at the lower of cost or market for inventories. Parton [1917, p. 95], a subsequent President of The Canadian Institute of Chartered Accountants, indicated that "an annual appraisal of these [fixed assets] based on current market values, would probably produce such distortion in the profit and loss accounts as to make them utterly worthless and misleading, besides making the balance sheet unreliable, an appraisal being always the result of an individual opinion, while original cost is an undeniable fact." He then goes on to advocate the lower of cost or market valuation for inventories [p. 97]. Similarly, in 1917, the chairman of an Ontario Chartered Accountants' Committee that made recommendations for changes in the Ontario Companies Act of 1907 indicated that fixed assets should be carried at original cost, that depreciation be based on cost and that the inventory be valued at the lower of cost or market [Mulvey, 1920, pp. 55-61]. The strength of the lower of cost or market concept at this time was evidenced by editorial commentary in the July 1918 issue of <u>The Canadian Chartered Accountant</u>, which indicated that "the accountancy profession generally, has always accepted the principle that stocks of all kinds should be valued on the basis of cost price or market value, whichever is the lower" ["Stock Inventories," 1918, p. 50]. Theory was reinforced by the Taxation Act of 1917 which permitted inventories to be valued at the lower of cost or market [Breadner, 1918, p. 108] but also insisted that depreciation be related to the original cost [Breadner, 1918, p. 118].

An interesting though scarcely persuasive commentary on the establishment of the cost principle is the advertisement in the January 1912 edition of <u>The Canadian Chartered Accountant</u> by the Canadian

Appraisal Company:

> The correct determination of physical values is the foundation of a reliable audit . . . The common denominator of a client's plant account is the cost of replacement at a specified date.

The advertisement did not reappear after 1912.

Content and Classification in Financial Statements

The recommended balance sheet of 1917 in Figure 2 is a far more sophisticated presentation of financial position than that of the earlier statements in Figures 4 and 5. The 1898 statement of Figure 5 effectively categorizes various divisions of assets, liabilities and equities - though the determination of working capital is obviously not a criterion of presentation. The detail of fixed assets and inventories is given with depreciation deducted from the fixed assets and the receivables appropriately valued. The English presentation of assets on the right hand side is adhered to, but, unlike the English style, the vertical presentation is, apart from capital stock, in order of decreasing liquidity. Figure 2 of 1917 rearranges the assets, liabilities and equities into order we now see - though there is again no easy determination of the working capital position.[6] Inventories and accounts receivable are valued but valuation and accumulated depreciation accounts are collected and recorded under the liability side. The only footnote relates to contingent liabilities.

The 1917 financial statements are particularly interesting because they advocate - though not in a clear-cut fashion - the distinction that is presently made between profit and loss statements and retained earnings statements. Two differences are notable: firstly, as previously mentioned, the Profit and Loss Account is more akin to what is

---

[6]The editor's column of The Canadian Chartered Accountant reflects the confusion of the times in this regard. "The expression working capital has sprung into use within the past few years, from whence no one seems sure; meaning what, no one appears prepared to state definitely; and how to interpret, no one seems to agree with another. Its use in an agreement of some importance has given rise recently to considerable discussion and thought by some members of the legal and accounting professions, who are engaged in trying to decide what should be read into an argument based on so indeterminate an expression." [The Canadian Chartered Accountant, January, 1919, p. 132.]

presently known as the retained earnings statement; and secondly, this latter account includes interest and tax expense, items which are presently thought to be components of the income or profit and loss statement. The model statement is also notable because of the detail provided in the Income and Expenditure statement.

No uniquely Canadian commentary was located concerning the appropriate treatment of extraordinary items. Yamey [1961, p. 759], the English historian, provides some background to the current-operating concept when he indicates that in nineteenth-century England "the important role of the periodic profit figure . . . as an index of profitability, . . . [for] shareholders . . . suggests the tendency to leave the profit calculation largely unaffected by what was considered to be unusual, non-recurrent or irregular items of profit and loss." A. Lowes Dickinson [1909, pp. 11-12], whose background reflects both the English and American traditions, and whose text was to be later used in Canadian accounting courses, attempted to stipulate the only acceptable charges to the retained earnings account as: items not applicable to any particular year; expenditures on improvements and betterments representing the likely reduction in future operating expense rather than an increase in earnings; and discounts and premiums on bonds and stocks. H. C. Bentley [1912, p. 106], another American commentator somewhat later in 1912, comes closer to the current-operating concept arguing that "there is a growing tendency among accountants to show all surplus adjustments in the profit and loss statement [and] the writer believes that this practice tends to confuse and burden that statement with items which have no direct bearing upon current operations."

Attitude of the Times

We have seen that Canada was strongly influenced by the English company legislation of the nineteenth century. However in both the Ontario legislation of 1907 and the federal Canadian legislation of 1917, the regulation developed beyond its English counterpart. This English legal tradition, motivated by concern for the investor [Littleton and Zimmerman, 1962, p. 266], may have partly accounted for the relatively early Canadian concern for disclosure of corporate information. The Financial Post of 1907 speaks highly of the corporate disclosure of the time:

> In Canada nearly all the most important Companies have adopted a straight forward policy of publicity of earnings and condition, and the value of this is apparent on the day of panic or depression when the first idea is to throw over stocks because of a feeling that the bottom is bound to drop out of things. Then it is that a glance at a Company's profits and a few moments consideration fortifies the holder of stocks against insane selling. ["Stocks Disappearing," 1907, p. 1.]

In the United States at the turn of the century there were grave misgivings about the extent of corporate disclosure. Hawkins enumerates some of the background to the American scene:

> The principal reasons why corporate managers were so secretive with regard to their companies' financial affairs were four in number: there was no tradition of publicity . . . ; management believed the public had no right to information on these matters; managers feared that by revealing financial information they would unwittingly assist their competitors; and to many, the doctrine of _caveat emptor_ seemed as applicable to buyers of securities as to purchasers of horses. [Hawkins, 1963, p. 141.]

It is likely that only the third reason - fear of helping a competitor - motivated the Canadian manager. Expression of this is given in _The Financial Post_:

> Of course it was well known in the time of the Commercial Cable Company that the earnings of that Company were of very ample proportions and it was often suggested that it would be well not to encourage competition by holding up to the public eye, the percentage earned on the investment. ["Stocks Disappearing," 1907, p. 1.]

It may well be that the Canadian scene up to 1920 was generally conducive to more informative corporate annual reports than were being provided in the United States. On the other hand, Canadian firms participated in the secrecy that Hawkins has referred to as pervading the American scene. This secrecy was reflected in the attitude towards secret reserves. The Canadian pattern was undoubtedly influenced by the English litigation in Newton v. Birmingham Small Arms Co. Ltd.:

> The result will be to show the financial position of the company to be not so good as in fact it is. If the balance sheet be so worded as to show that there is an undisclosed asset, whose existence makes the financial position better than that shown, such a balance sheet will not in my judgement, be necessarily inconsistent with the Act of Parliament. Assets are often, by reason of prudence, estimated and stated to be estimated at less than their probably real value. The purpose of the balance sheet is primarily to show that the financial position of the company is at least as good as there stated, not to show that it is not

> or may not be better. The provision as to not disclosing the internal reserve fund in the balance sheet is not, I think, necessarily fatal to these special resolutions. [As reported in Dickerson, 1966, p. 20.]

The usual Canadian concern for the force of English legal precedence undoubtedly provided some ambivalence in the mind of the Canadian accountant and auditor with regard to secret reserves. Nonetheless, J. C. Parton, a sometime president of the Canadian Institute, had little difficulty in stating the theoretical accounting viewpoint:

> Sometimes excessive depreciation is charged so that the concern may be on the safe side. While this may be considered from that point of view laudable, it is nevertheless wrong, inasmuch as it creates a secret reserve and understates profits, thus making present shareholders suffer for the benefit of future ones. [Parton, 1911, p. 11.]

Similarly, J. Porter Joplin [1915, p. 198], an American C.P.A. writing in The Canadian Chartered Accountant of 1915, indicated that the investor has reasonable intelligence and neither needs nor wants corporate earnings smoothed by the use of secret reserves. However, Joplin [pp. 195-196] goes on to review English and American accounting authorities and to demonstrate a certain tolerance for wise and careful use of secret reserves. As will be indicated in the following section, there is evidence to indicate that Canadian corporate reporting practices reflected the "conservatism" of which secret reserves are a function.

Corporate Reporting Practices

To 1910

A tabulation of certain aspects of disclosure is given for certain companies from The Annual Financial Review - Canadian of 1911, 1920, 1931 and 1939 in Table 1. It can be seen that by 1911 there were relatively few companies providing the classification, segregation and valuation of balance sheet items that are now regarded as normal. It should again be noted that the phrase "profit and loss statement," when applied to financial statements of an era, earlier than 1930, is generally a statement separate from the balance sheet in which there are reflected not only the net result of operations but also adjustments of owners equity, together with the opening and closing balances - the latter when taken to the balance sheet reflects what is now referred to as "Retained Earnings" or "Earned Surplus." Roughly one-half of the financial statements examined provided some analyses of operations. In eleven of sixteen instances the analysis took the form of the just-described profit and loss statement. The Canadian General Electric Company Limited Statement (see Appendix D) is an example of this form; the Canadian Salt Company Limited statement is an example of the profit and loss analysis taking place in the balance sheet itself. In only nine of thirty-one instances was the net profit as described, after such charges as interest, depreciation, taxes, bad debts and before transfers to reserves. The format of the statements sometimes gave the impression that such charges as interest, depreciation and taxes were regarded as distributions of income. Table 1 indicates that confusion in what was to be a deduction <u>from</u> and a distribution <u>of</u> income persisted through until 1940.

TABLE 1

ANALYSIS OF FINANCIAL STATEMENT DISCLOSURE TO 1940

Year Financial Statements Examined	1911 31	1920 42	1931 42	1939 42
Classification and segregation of current assets, fixed assets and current liabilities	6	27	34	42
Fixed asset additions noted in balance sheet	1	7	3	2
Components given for - fixed assets	1	6	8	11
- inventories	4	7	1	6
Depreciation deducted from fixed assets	--	12	26	28
Intangible assets				
- set out separately	5	22	21	16
- grouped with tangibles	11	7	5	--
Footnotes - relating to contingent liabilities	8	13	22	16
- other	1	1	4	7
Valuation basis indicated for				
- accounts receivable	2	18	30	29
- inventories	2	15[a]	9[a]	42
- fixed assets	1	4	11	35

TABLE 1 (continued)

Year	1911	1920	1931	1939
Financial Statements Examined	31	42	42	42
Indication of fixed asset appraisal	--	3[a]	6	24
Profit and loss analysis:				
Analyzed in balance sheet	5	5	5	2
Commingled with retained earnings statement	11	26	26	16
Separate statements for each of retained earnings and profit and loss	--	3	2	22
Retained earnings analyzed in balance sheet, while profit and loss in separate statement	--	3	4	2
No analysis of retained earnings or profit and loss	15	5	5	--
Amount of depreciation recorded in profit and loss	9	27	27	39
Sales and cost of sales enumerated	1	6[a]	2[a]	5
Consolidated financial statements	1	5	19	20
Net profit figure before dividends and transfers to reserves identified[b]	9	18	15	21

[a]Includes information contained in extracts from Directors' Reports.

[b]Oftentimes net profit figure identified is before interest, depreciation, taxes, bad debts, and after transfers to reserves.

Source: The Annual Financial Review - Canadian (Toronto: Houston's Standard Publications). The financial statements examined represent the sequential alphabetical listing of the "industrials." For 1911 and 1920 the numbers of financial statements represent fully one-half of the industrial listing.

In addition to the analysis of financial statements necessary to prepare the information presented in Table 1, the statements of ten companies, as listed in Appendix B, were reviewed annually for the years 1901 to 1919. Selected company statements are reproduced in Appendix D. The statements examined were selected randomly from a list of those companies that presented financial statements for each of the twenty years. It was felt that the scrutiny of consecutive statements would allow the reviewer to become aware of both the continuity and change in the statements. It is possible that the strength and continuity implied by the fact that the ten companies prepared and supplied financial statements for a twenty-year period may mean that this group of companies is different from that group of companies in Table 1 which represent the first thirty-one companies in the "industrial" section of The Annual Financial Review - Canadian for 1911. The scrutiny of these ten companies revealed that a profit and loss analysis, taking place in either the balance sheet itself or in a separate statement or sometimes in the Directors' Report (Canadian Cycle and Motor Company Limited, 1902 - 1907) was presented in almost all analyses. These profit and loss analyses were usually very brief, containing little more than operating profit, transfers to reserve accounts, dividends, premiums on stocks and bonds, interest income and expense. The Montreal Cotton Company financial statement (see Appendix D) is particularly interesting because a fairly detailed Manufacturing Statement is also given. Almost all of the companies mentioned, prior to 1910, that depreciation had been deducted in arriving at operating profit. Similarly, most of the companies grouped not only fixed assets but also intangibles into one lump sum that often amounted to at least 80 percent of total assets.

Other features of this time period related to the use of reserve accounts, the acknowledgement of conservatism and the recording of appraisals. The word "reserve" at this time was indiscriminately applied to asset valuation accounts, liabilities and appropriations of retained earnings.[7] These accounts tended to be grouped under the liability side of the balance sheet - their more common names being general reserve, investment reserve, insurance reserve, contingent account, suspense, replacement reserve, rest account, depreciation reserve and inventory reserve. Oftentimes no year-to-year reconciling of what appears to be the reserve accounts that represented appropriations of retained earnings

---

[7]Also attested to by J. B. Sutherland, "Reserves and Sinking Funds," [1917, p. 102].

was possible.[8] Sometimes the balance in the profit and loss account (that is, after dividends and transfers) seemed to be almost nominal in comparison with the amounts arrayed in the reserve accounts.[9] It might be that there was an attempt to have the balance in this account reflect only that amount that was available for dividends. Several instances of the conservatism of the times and even of smoothing of income were noticed. The Directors' Report of Canadian General Electric Company Limited in 1905 indicated that ". . . advantages have been taken during past years of prosperity to write down assets to a most conservative basis." In the 1908 Directors' Report of Canada Cycle and Motor Company Limited there is mention that ". . . the valuation of all assets has been conservatively made, present prices which are lower in most cases than for some time, being used in the pricing of all our stock."

Acknowledgement of the significance of market when market was lower than cost was reflected by Ogilvie Flour Mills Company Limited in the pricing of their inventory in 1903; similarly, in 1908, Canadian General Electric Company Limited acknowledged that they priced their inventory at the lower of cost or market. It was, however, generally quite unusual, by 1910, to have inventory valuation indicated. Some indication of the recording of appraisals was evidenced by Canada Cycle and Motor Company Limited in 1908, Lake of the Woods Milling Company Limited in 1905 and Ogilvie Flour Mills Company Limited in 1904.

1910 to 1920

As indicated by Table 1, a definite increase in the classification, segregation and valuation had taken place by 1920. Most notable was the increasing instance in which the profit from operations together with such items as dividends and capital adjustments, were analyzed in a separate statement called the profit and loss account. In six of forty-two instances the profit and loss account included details of sales and cost of sales and in twenty-seven instances mention was made in the

---

[8]See Canadian Cycle land Motor Company Limited, 1905 - 1908; Canadian General Electric Company Limited, 1906; Carter Crume Company Limited, 1906; Dominion Iron and Steel Company Limited, 1909 - 1910; Ogilvie Flour Mills Company Limited, 1904.

[9]Examples of this are Canadian General Electric Company Limited and Carter Crume Company Limited.

profit and loss statement of the specific amount of depreciation.[10] Classification and segregation of current assets, fixed assets and current liabilities increased notably as did the setting forth of the valuation basis of accounts receivable (e.g. reserve for bad debts) and inventories.

Observations from the scrutiny of the ten sample financial statements for each of the years 1910 to 1919 continued the pattern set in the earlier decade. There continued to be acknowledgement of conservative valuation of assets and instances of inability to reconcile reserve accounts. Instances were noted wherein fixed tangible assets were recorded at higher values based on appraisal and the resulting increment was used to write off or write down the value of intangible assets such as goodwill, trademarks and franchises.[11,12] The directors or presidents report frequently provided information, not otherwise contained in the financial statements proper, relating to the bases of valuation of assets, fixed asset reappraisal, and sales and cost of sales detail. Indeed, the reports of the directors and presidents in many instances performed the same function of what is now expected from financial statement footnotes - that is, an elaboration of additional quantitative and qualitative information that will enable a more meaningful interpretation of the financial statement proper. Certainly at this time and throughout the 1920 - 1930 period footnotes to financial statements rarely went beyond an indication of the existence of such contingent liabilities as customer paper under discount and guarantees of affiliated company's indebtedness.

By 1920 none of the companies observed in either sample set, provided an amount of information equal to the recommended version provided in Figures 2 and 3. In actuality, some companies categorized

---

[10]Though no mention was made of depreciation in the profit and loss statement, some firms were obviously recording depreciation since accumulated depreciation was reflected in the balance sheet.

[11]Canadian General Electric Company Limited and Ogilvie Flour Mills Company Limited in 1914.

[12]J. C. Parton indicates instances of increases in land values sometimes being reflected in the accounts to the credit of profit and loss ["The Determination of . . ." , 1911, p. 8].

the accounts in such a manner that working capital determination was easier; but more generally only a small percentage of the firms valued all assets or provided any operating detail. Footnotes apart from indicating contingent liabilities were almost unknown. Most financial statements did not clearly set forth the net income after having deducted such items as depreciation, bad debts, long term interest and before making appropriations to reserve accounts.

The Tax Acts of 1916 and 1917 and the Companies Act Amendment Act of 1917 had only a very small impact on the reporting practices of the firms examined. The Companies Act required that intangibles and depreciation be severally distinguished and the taxation acts, though they permitted depreciation to be an appropriate deduction in determining taxable income, required that goodwill be excluded from the capital base upon which a normal return was to be calculated. These two sources of influence acting on these two aspects of reporting may well have served to provide the impetus for the increase in information concerning depreciation and intangibles that is evident in Table 1 and that was noted in the other ten sample firms. More generally however, the financial statements examined in 1910 (and in many instances before that time) provided as much disclosure as required by the Companies Act Amendment Act, 1917.

CHAPTER IV

THE EVOLUTION OF FINANCIAL STATEMENTS, 1920 - 1940

English and American Legislation

Following the periodic review of company legislation by the 1928 Greene Committee, the English Companies Act of 1928 [Great Britain, C. 45, Secs. 39-40] made mandatory the preparation of a profit and loss statement and such detail and categorization in the balance sheet as the distinguishing of current and fixed assets, preliminary and stock promotional expenses, goodwill and the treatment of subsidiary profits and losses. The prescription of the 1908 Act relating to the disclosure of the general nature of liabilities and assets and the valuation of the fixed assets, in the statement that was to be forwarded to the Registrar of Companies, was now made a feature of the financial statements that were to be annually prepared for the shareholders. No minimum disclosure requirements were given for the profit and loss statement; however, the balance sheet and profit and loss account were required to disclose "the amount if any which they propose to carry to the reserve fund, general reserve or reserve account." By comparison with the earlier Canadian Act of 1917[1] it can be noted that the English legislation has been far less particularized in its disclosure requirements. The English Act of 1928 was in advance of the Canadian Act of 1917 only with respect to the provisions relating to the valuation of fixed assets, the distinguishing of current and fixed assets, and the mild requirements relating to transfers of reserves.

Unlike the English legislation of 1928, the origination of the American Securities Acts of 1933 and 1934 was quite likely a function of the recognition of the real or imagined corporate malfeasance of the late 1920s and early 1930s. Some American commentators have disputed the widely held belief that annual financial statements were grossly inadequate prior to the securities regulations of 1933 and 1934. George O. May has stated that:

> . . . I feel that even prior to 1934, the reports made by corporations whose securities were widely distributed were, in

[1]See preceding chapter.

> general, certainly more complete and, in so far as I am in a position to judge, not less fair than those in any other commercial country. This is not to say that the standard was completely satisfactory; on the contrary, it should and I think will be improved, but it was not and is not a case of raising a standard deplorably low. [May, 1943, p. 16.]

Similarly, a most revealing inquiry indicated that of all the companies listed on the New York Stock Exchange in 1926, 100 percent segregated and disclosed the current assets and liabilities, 55 percent disclosed sales, 45 percent disclosed cost of goods sold and 71 percent disclosed depreciation [Benston, 1969, p. 519]. The extent to which sales and cost of sales were voluntarily disclosed in America would not have been surpassed in Canada for almost another forty years.

It is important to note that the American Securities Acts differed markedly from the English and Canadian Companies Acts in that the latters' only concern for accounting principles have related to disclosure requirements and secondly, no institutions were set up to review corporate annual reports. The Securities and Exchange Commission which administers the Securities Acts, issued regulations concerning the content and accounting principles of annual reports submitted to them and has set up procedures for their annual review so as to ensure conformity with these regulations. The detail of these regulations and the extent of disclosure required were far in excess of the requirements of the Companies Acts of either England or Canada. The extent and pervasiveness of their concern can be felt in SEC Accounting Series Release No. 7 [1938] which, in citing common deficiencies in annual reports submitted to them, elaborated such items as details of consolidation practices, appropriate segregation and classification of assets, liabilities and stockholders' equity, reconciliations of all surplus and reserve accounts, detail of profit and loss statement including sales, cost of sales, general, selling and administrative expenses. The SEC, however had control only over financial statements submitted to them, not those submitted to the stockholders and the author is unaware of the extent to which these two sets of financial statements may have differed.

Canadian Legislation

The federal Companies Act of 1934 [Canada, 1934, C. 33, Secs. 112-114] introduced several important and fundamental changes in mandatory financial statement disclosure. The profit and loss statement must disclose such items as directors' fees, depreciation, taxes, investment income, non-recurring profits and losses, amortization of any asset and interest on long-term debt. The transactions in the various surplus accounts must be disclosed and their year-to-year reconciliation demonstrated. The valuation basis of inventory, land, buildings and plant must be disclosed and, if the fixed-asset valuation is based on appraisal, the date of the appraisal and the name of the appraiser. The preparation of consolidated statements, though long since done in practice, was now officially permitted. Where consolidated financial statements were not prepared, the investment in the shares of and loans to the subsidiaries must be disclosed together with the treatment of their aggregate profits and losses. Several other less important aspects of financial statement disclosure were also elaborated by the Act.

Following a federal inquiry by the Commission on Price Spreads, the Companies Act was amended within the year [Canada, Statutes, 1935, C. 33, Secs. 17-19]. The major changes pertained to the prospectus legislation in the 1934 Act, however such financial statement reporting practices as this study contemplates were also altered. Increased disclosure relating to accounts receivable, inventory, investment and marketable securities valuation was required. The profit and loss statement was to disclose not only the directors' fees as required in the 1934 Act but the payments to legal advisers and executive officers of the reporting company as well. Additionally, a copy of the financial statements were to be filed with the Secretary of State.

Apart from the specification that current and fixed assets be categorized, the English Act of 1928 contained nothing that was not in the Canadian Acts of 1917, 1934 or 1935. On the other hand, the Canadian Acts specified the careful distinguishing of several balance sheet items not contemplated by the English Act. Of significance were the 1934 and 1935 requirements to specify certain items in the profit and loss, to demonstrate the reconciliation of the surplus accounts, to specify more clearly the valuation basis of inventories, accounts receivable and fixed assets and to permit the preparation of consolidated financial statements. Undoubtedly, the six-year interval between the 1928 English Act and the 1934-1935 Canadian Acts - containing as it did a stock market crash, a depression and the very important Royal Mail Steam Packet failure[2] gave rise to the closer Canadian regulation.

Background to the Canadian Legislation

Economic Events and Attitude of the Times

The concern for secretiveness in corporate reporting practices, and particularly with regard to the details of the profit and loss statement as displayed by management in the first two decades of the twentieth century, continued well into the third and fourth decades. Little public concern was vented in the 1920s when economic events were buoyant; however, with the fall in values relating to the stock market crash of 1929 and the depression of the 1930s, the Canadian public began to clamour for greater information in corporate annual reports. In 1931, R. G. H. Smails, the highly respected Queen's University professor, protested vigorously against the inadequacies of corporate financial statements, even though they were drawn up in accordance with the requirements of the existing Act. His statement reveals much of the attitude of the times:

> A study of the published balance sheets of one hundred Canadian companies selected at random has revealed that not one of them was free from remediable defects . . . In twelve cases, terminology employed was so ambiguous or highly technical as to be wholly unintelligible or intelligible only to a trained accountant; excessive grouping of assets and liabilities marred respectively forty-eight and sixty balance sheets; in seventy cases, the basis of valuation of assets was not revealed. These results indicate that little attempt is made to use the balance sheet as a means of informing shareholders and the public, and that the report is prepared perfunctorily merely to assist the requirements of the statute.
>
> The statement of profit and loss accompanying the balance sheet is rarely more than a summary of the surplus account showing the net profit from operations of all kinds, the amount of depreciation reserved, income tax incurred and interest and dividends paid on securities. Less exception can be taken to the paucity of information in this part of the report, for to disclose to shareholders details of trading income and expense would, in some cases, be to furnish rivals with valuable information - and perhaps to shake the consumers' faith in the intrinsic value of the product! But even here, secretiveness seems to be practised on occasion for its own sake without regard to any useful purpose served, and information that would be of great

---

[2]See under "Antecedents of the Canadian Legislation" of this chapter.

> interest to shareholders and no value to competitors is withheld at the dictates of ancient custom.
>
> The dawn of a new era of interesting and informative reports will not be ushered in by legislation; so much is admitted by all who have given the matter earnest thought. The statutes already require that a balance sheet be presented, that a certain minimum of detail be given in the balance sheet and that the accounts must be audited before presentation. They cannot usefully go further than this. [Smails, 1931, pp. 101-103.]

Professor Smails did not foresee that the legislative revisions of 1934 would usefully provide much closer corporate regulation and that financial statement disclosure, as set out in the incorporating statute, would strengthen the hand of the professional accountant and auditor in his bid to provide more informative annual reports. A study group of Queen's university professors in 1933 [Members of the Department . . . , 1933, pp. 274-277] were more hopeful of the fruitfulness of legislative changes when they suggested that the legislation should require greater elaboration of assets and liabilities, greater detail in the profit and loss statement, the distinguishing of capital from surplus, the filing of a copy of the corporate financial statements at a public office of record and the furnishing of either a consolidated balance sheet or the balance sheets of all controlled companies. The need to state the bases of asset valuations when current values differed significantly from historic cost values also became vividly apparent in the depression and was reflected in commentary in The Financial Post [unsigned article, January 21, 1933, p. 11]. The latter journal articulated on many occasions the list of shortcomings in financial statements [May 6, 1933, p. 11; June 24, 1933, p. 12; December 16, 1933, p. 11]. It is noteworthy that the 1934 Act remedied many of the foregoing deficiencies.

The public outcry raised against the inadequacies of annual reports was far less vigorous than that raised against abuses in corporate promotion and capitalization. The pattern established in the 1917 revisions to the Companies Act, wherein changes in financial statement disclosure accompany changes in requirements pertaining to prospectuses and to capitalization, is again exhibited in the 1934 and 1935 Acts. The aforementioned study group [Members . . . , 1933, pp. 264-281] listed such abuses as the uncontrolled allocation of the proceeds of no par value shares to distributable surplus, the transfers from capital surplus to distributable surplus permitted by federal legislation of 1930, the failure of prospectus provisions to cover security issues handled through an underwriter and the lack of information relating to the net value of the proceeds from the underwriter.[3]

Such abuses in corporate stock promotion and capitalization were likely a more immediate cause of the legislative revisions in the 1934 Act than the inadequacies of financial statement disclosure. Several commentators have ruminated on the legislative significance of abuses relating to stock promotion and capitalization. The economist, W. A. Macintosh indicated that:

> . . . we have had many instances in Canada in the field of investment banking and stock promotion where sound business and ethical standards were shattered or bent by the pressure of the speculation boom of 1928 - 1929. We have had a crop of illegitimate promotions involving flagrant stock watering, over capitalization, and misrepresentation, and the sane principles of public and private finance have been violated. The Prime Minister, Mr. Bennett, has already indicated that there are likely to be amendments to the Dominion Companies Act designed to curb some of the worst abuses which broke into the light of day during the speculative boom. [Macintosh, 1932, p. 407.]

Similarly, a member of the House of Commons and a subsequent cabinet minister, J. L. Ralston [1935, p. 87] suggested that "the Act was passed, as you know, not for the benefit of the Chartered Accountant, nor the lawyers, but it was passed to give additional protection to the public, especially through its prospectus provisions." Debates in the House of Commons [Canada, May 19, 1934, pp. 3454-3458] further emphasized the importance of the abuses of stock promotion and capitalization.

On a very broad level, the increasing recognition that corporations were creations of society and that they must serve and be responsive to the demands of society, became more apparent. L. G. Macpherson reflected these societal obligations:

> There is a growing feeling and acknowledgement that the information conveyed by the balance sheets of public companies is a public concern, and that such companies, having been granted certain rights and privileges, accordingly, have certain obligations to the public. [Macpherson, 1934, p. 92.]

---

[3]Additional commentary is provided in <u>The Financial Post</u>, June 10, 1933, p. 11; June 17, 1933, p. 3; June 24, 1933, p. 12; and December 16, 1933, p. 11.

In fact, consistent with other countries, the public was beginning to doubt whether private enterprise could adequately handle the difficulties of the times. In Canada, business became suspect [Smyth, November, 1953, p. 206]. Government inquiries such as the Special Committee on Price Spreads and Mass Buying[4] and the Macmillan Commission on Central Banking paved the way for tighter Companies Acts in 1934 and 1935 and the adoption of a central banking system in 1935. The corporate legislation changes in Canada coincided in time with new corporate legislation in France, Germany, India and the United States.

The American Securities Acts of 1933 and 1934 overlapped in time the Canadian legislation of 1934 and 1935 and it is therefore somewhat difficult to assess the importance of this field of influence on the Canadian legislators. The perusal of House of Commons Debates, The Canadian Chartered Accountant and The Financial Post offered only a couple of references to the setting up of a review board to approve annual corporate reports [Davison, 1933, p. 11; Canada, House . . ., May 29, 1934, p. 3458; "Call for Action," 1943, p. 361]; and the only legislative action taken in this regard was the requirements to annually file a copy of the corporate annual report with the Secretary of State-a requirement that had existed in English legislation for many years. Certainly the detail of the regulations and pronouncements that emanated from the Securities and Exchange Commission were far in excess of the 1934 - 1935 Canadian corporate requirements. Canadian financial and professional accounting commentary was replete with the recounting of the abuses being uncovered in America; and in large measure the tale being told about stock promotion and capitalization abuses and financial statement inadequacies was much the same as it was in Canada. In America, government intervention may have come as a sudden jolt, but in Canada the vehicle of correction, the Companies Acts, had existed for many years and undoubtedly, by contrast, the legislation of 1934 and 1935 can be regarded as an evolution rather than a revolution. When one combines the precedent of the fairly recent corporate revision in England in 1928 and the state of the economic and financial affairs in Canada at the time, together with an awareness of the significance of the English

---

[4]This Committee examined in detail the financial affairs of a great number of Canadian companies for the years 1924 to 1934.

Royal Mail Steam Packet case and the pressure being exerted for new legislation by the Conference of Commissioners on Uniformity of Legislation in Canada, it is likely that the Canadian legislation of 1934 and 1935 can be explained without important reference to the influence of the United States.

Antecedents of the Canadian Legislation

As suggested in the preceding paragraph, it is likely that the timing and content of 1934 corporate revisions can be explained by circumstances in Canada and England. The influences from England were twofold. Firstly, the most notable aspect of the English Act of 1928 pertaining to valuation of assets was incorporated into the Canadian Act, and secondly, the importance of the English Royal Mail Steam Packet (RMSP) case gave rise to a greater concern for increasing the detail required in profit and loss statements and for reconciling the various surplus accounts - two other additional important changes in the Canadian legislation. The RMSP case of 1929 and 1930, in which the managing director Kylsant was found guilty, related to the undisclosed use of secret reserves to bolster current profits. The effect of this case was particularly shocking since it followed so shortly after the English corporate revisions of 1928. The investigation and inquiry indicated just how closely woven were such things as secret reserves, inadequate disclosure of non-operating detail in the profit and loss statement and the necessity for a mandatory audit of the profit and loss. The RMSP case was followed closely in the Canadian financial press and in The Canadian Chartered Accountant, and it became a constant and continual reference point for critics of financial statements in Canada. Professor R. G. H. Smails implies its legislative significance for Canada:

> The hand of the auditor would seem to be greatly strengthened by the specification of the items that are to be shown separately in the general statement of income and expenditure and the statement of surplus respectively, to be laid before the company in the general meeting. Certainly those statutory requirements will relieve auditors of such grave responsibility as lay upon the auditors of the Royal Mail Steam Packet Company, full advantage having been taken by the authors of the new Act of the costly experience gained from this case. [Italics mine.] [Smails, 1934, p. 283.]

English commentary before the RMSP case by the Liberal Industrial Inquiry in 1928 and after the case by the Council of the Society of Incorporated Accountants in 1932 [Smails, 1932, p. 362], urged the importance of greater disclosure in the profit and loss statement. The Council suggested that:

> a) the profit and loss account should show the true balance of profit or loss for the period covered by such account,
> b) in the profit and loss account any debits or credits which are abnormal in character or extraneous in their nature to the ordinary transactions of the company together with any reserves from a previous period no longer required, should be stated separately,
> c) free reserves should be disclosed on the face of the balance sheet . . . [Johnson, 1933, p. 498.]

The economic and financial situation of the late 1920s and early 1930s, as recounted in the preceding section, was such as to inevitably warrant the imposition of tighter regulation upon corporate behaviour. The immediate and somewhat unlikely vehicle for the transformation of corporate abuse into corporate restraint was the Conference of Commissioners of Uniformity of Legislation in Canada. Since 1918, this Annual Conference, largely through the enthusiasm of the Canadian Bar Association, has advocated a rationalization of laws between the federal and various provincial jurisdictions. At their behest, dominion-provincial meetings of the provincial Attorneys-General and the federal Secretary of State were convened to consider the need for uniformity of legislation and draft uniform company acts have been prepared and recommended by conferences on uniformity to dominion-provincial conferences. In relation to the 1934 Act, Senator Meighen, a former prime minister, acknowledged that "the bill was prepared at the instance of a provincial conference held about a year and a half ago . . ." [Canada, Senate, 1934, p. 452]. The successfulness of the conferences on uniformity of legislation in Canada with respect to the rationalization of companies acts has, however, from earliest times and consistently throughout the 1930s been severely retarded by the jurisdictional rivalries (relating to the incorporation fees accruing therefrom) of the various provinces and the federal government.[5] The economic circumstances were such in 1934 that the federal government was obliged to take the lead in Companies Act revisions despite the unwillingness of the provinces to make their laws uniform.

The Dominion Association of Chartered Accountants also played some part in the corporate legislative revisions of 1934. A Council report to the annual meeting of 1931 indicated a proposal for uniformity of legislation relating to books of account, annual financial statements and appointment and duties of auditors. This task was undertaken in cooperation with the Conference on Uniformity. Similarly, a submission was made to the federal government relating to proposed changes in the Companies Act in 1934.[6]

English and American Influence

The preceding section outlines the areas of influence on the Canadian legislation of 1934 and 1935 and suggests that the English influence was much greater than the American. While this English influence may have continued to be strong with regard to legislation, the general English influence became increasingly less significant. That change mirrored the relative English and American investment patterns in Canada. From 1920 to 1939, the English percentage of total non-resident investment in Canada declined from 53 percent to 36 percent, while the American percentage increased from 44 percent to 60 percent.

The American influence was reflected in the interest in, and deference given to, the pronouncements of the American accounting theorists and organizations and of the Securities and Exchange Commission. The publication of Uniform Accounting by the Federal Reserve Board and the American Institute in 1917 and the subsequent revision entitled Verification of Financial Statements in 1929 were reprinted and carefully reported on in The Canadian Chartered Accountant. C. A. Clapperton

---

[5]This point has been acknowledged by many commentators, among whom are Grant Dexter, [1932, p. 253]; P. H. Hensel, [1935, p. 407]; and L. Hansen, [Canada, House . . ., 1934, p. 3507].

[6]Neither report was located by the author. Copies of the Companies Act submission could not be located by the Department of Consumer and Corporate Affairs, The Canadian Institute of Chartered Accountants nor the provincial Institutes of Chartered Accountants of Manitoba or Ontario.

[1927, p. 10] expressed the Canadian envy for such guidelines. Professor Smails, a noted Canadian author and himself a member of the Institute of Chartered Accountants in England and Wales, dealt the significance of the English influence the cruellest blow by referring to the American texts as being theoretically superior:

> We think the student would still do well to imbibe his theory from such American writers as Hatfield, Paton or Rorem, whose works in our opinion contain a surer theoretical foundation than do any of the English texts with which we are conversant. [Smails, 1935, p. 367.]

Actual American corporate reporting practices also served as standards to which Canadian practice was directed. The Financial Times rhapsodized on the extent of disclosure in the annual reports of The United States Steel and The General Motors Corporation and drew a sharp contrast with the Canadian scene ["Lucidity and Success," 1926, pp. 185-186], while T. Keen, almost ten years later, in 1935, in commentary on the English scene indicated that it is "only on the rarest of occasions . . . do we get a profit and loss account" [Keen, 1935, p. 92].[7] Similarly, by the late 1930s the Securities and Exchange Commission regulations and periodic Accounting Releases were being duly reported in The Canadian Chartered Accountant. These reporting requirements were, as indicated in the previous section, much stricter than those in Canada. The formal American Institute of Accountants research bulletins on accounting matters commenced only in 1939 and these tended to supplant the influence of the Securities and Exchange Commission Releases. The American Institute had of course, by this time, already established a great deal of authority in the audit report wording which evolved in the 1930 decade and which was traced in Chapter II.

Two other areas of American influence can also be recognized at this time - although no evidence can be adduced to indicate the intensity of their influence. Firstly, a great number of Canadian corporations were subsidiaries of American parent corporations. Many of these

---

[7]Supported by commentary in The Accountant, stating that "the methods followed by American and Canadian companies are, so far as the accounts which come to our notice are concerned, much ahead of general practice in this country. . . We hasten to add that this sort of thing is done equally well over here. Unfortunately the companies which do it form a small minority," reprinted in A. J. J. Fanshaw, [1936, p. 353].

subsidiaries were organized as private companies in Canada and consequently did not need to publish annual financial statements; others, however did prepare such statements. Secondly, many of the larger Canadian public accounting firms were, or became during the period, affiliated with American public accounting firms. They bore the same name, did the audit of the same companies (parent and subsidiary) and certainly in some instances shared the same firm audit and accounting manuals. The opportunity for influence would seem to be very great in these two instances; however, no evidence was uncovered by the writer to indicate whether the American influence would have been less without these institutional arrangements or whether these arrangements increased or merely served to maintain the American influence.

The Theory Relating to Corporate Reporting Practices

As Canadians had borrowed and adapted the accounting theory of England and America in the first two decades of the century, so did they continue to do, in the second two decades. Whereas, however, that borrowing had tended to be from England rather than America in the earlier decades [Edwards, 1921, p. 157], it later tended to come increasingly from America. A listing of texts from the Queen's University course of instructions indicates that from 1923 to approximately 1936 there were relatively few Canadian texts used and that the majority were either English or American.[8] From 1936 to 1940, most of the books were either American or Canadian. As noted in a previous section, Professor Smails [1935, p. 367] had felt that the American texts were theoretically superior. Undoubtedly a great deal of that impetus for progressive accounting thought must have been spurred by the coming into existence of the Securities and Exchange Commission, an agency which had the authority both to set accounting principles and to review annual corporate reports. The Companies Acts of England and Canada contemplated neither power and consequently, as Professor Smyth [Dec., 1953, pp. 289-290] implies, the accounting profession (in Canada) lacked such a spur. Certainly, the outpourings of the American Institute of Accountants, following the formation of the Securities and exchange Commission, became quite

---

[8]Letter from Director of Accounting Courses, Queen's University, to the author, August 13, 1968.

prolific and, if one is to judge by the continual reference of Canadian literature to them, of great influence in Canada as well. The Canadian Institute, aware of the heavy reliance on non-Canadian accounting texts went on record as being prepared to sponsor publications by Canadian authors. By far, one of the better Canadian books of the times, Auditing by Professor R. G. H. Smails, bore the Institute imprimatur.[9] During this period, the contributors to the literature in The Canadian Chartered Accountant were predominantly Canadian. Whereas, for the period 1917 to 1918, only half of the signed articles of three pages or more were by Canadians, 80 percent of such articles, for the years 1933 to 1935 were Canadian; 13 percent were English, and 4 percent American.

Toward the end of the 1930s and the early part of the 1940s, the literature in The Canadian Chartered Accountant began to reflect an increasing dissatisfaction with the extent of disclosure in corporate annual reports and in the disclosure requirements of the Companies Act. The war years of 1939 to 1945 intervened however and diverted much of the attention that was necessary to make important changes. But the concern expressed in those pre-war and early war years helped to lay the foundation for the first accounting pronouncement on financial statement disclosure of the Canadian Institute in 1946. F. S. Capon reflects some of the frustrations of the period that arise from what he believes to be a gap between the disclosure standards proposed by the Companies Act and the standards that are necessary for more adequate disclosure. He did not foresee at this time that the improvement he was looking for was to come through the pronouncements of the profession itself, rather than the Companies Act:

> The authority and responsibility of the public accountant are governed by the provisions of the Companies Act which attempts to list in detail the items that must be segregated in official financial statements. It is obviously impossible to cover adequately all the items that should properly be segregated in any particular case, however, with the result that it is frequently possible to avoid making significant disclosures without

[9]More frequently-used Canadian accounting texts during the 1920-1940 period were: R. G. H. Smails, Auditing, 1933; W. S. Ferguson and F. R. Crocombe, Elements of Accounting, 1936; R. G. H. Smails and C. E. Walker, Accounting Principles and Practice. 1926; C. A. Ashley, An Introduction to Auditing for Canadians, 1931; and A. F. Sprott and F. G. Short, Canadian Modern Accounting, 1921.

> violating the letter of the law. In such cases auditors are accused of yielding to the insistence of management, stilling their conscience by stressing that the Act did not specifically require the item to be shown. Furthermore, the detailed accounting requirements of the Act have caused a rigid form of financial statement to be developed over a period of years, and most statements which conform with the minimum requirements are for the most part unintelligible to all but trained accountants. In order to improve the form of the financial statement which are the prime responsibility of the accountants, and also to strengthen the hands of the public accountants, it appears to be necessary to make widespread amendments to the [Companies] Act. [Capon, 1943, pp. 380-381.][10]

Capon reflects a theme that continues to appear throughout the literature from earliest times, and that is that the auditor, in commenting upon the fairness of presentation of financial statements, needs support from either the Companies Acts or the Institute pronouncements.

Balance Sheets, Profit and Loss and Earned Surplus Statements

The tendency to place increasing emphasis on the profit and loss statement, that began in the 1900 - 1920 period, continued at an increasing pace during the 1920 - 1940 period. The theoretical support usually offered for the propriety of emphasizing the profit and loss statement was that the value of a company was a function of what it could earn and therefore attention should be paid only secondarily to the balance sheet. Such theory was enhanced by the depression years in which balance sheet values placed on corporate assets seemed to vanish. The rapid and long-lived reduction in the price level seemed to enhance the importance of the profit and loss statement.

Despite such emphasis, little evidence was located which advocated greater disclosure in the components of that statement. In most instances prior to the 1934 legislation, the profit and loss statement contained little more than the opening and closing balances, net profit on operations, income tax, interest, depreciation and dividends, and it was only by such commentators as Smails and Ashley, prior to this time, that greater detail was advocated. That advocacy did not extend to

---

[10]Other representative articles reflecting the need for improvement in corporate reporting practices were: C. A. Ashley, "The Use of Accounts," 1941; and H. D. Clapperton, "What are Profits?", 1941.

disclosure of sales, cost of sales, general, selling and administrative expenses but more usually only to those items, the disclosure of which would prevent recurrences of the Royal Mail Steam Packet case. In 1931, Professor Smails suggested that:

> . . . it is more difficult to generalize upon the [recommended form] of the profit and loss statement . . . [Disclosure] of the total net profit or loss from trading operations is a figure to which the shareholders are most certainly entitled and disclosure of which cannot prejudice the business in competition. Details of the non-operating income including income from investments, non-recurring profits or losses, appropriations from reserves (secret or otherwise) should be distinguished at least in total and in most cases detail may reasonably be demanded. [Smails, 1931, pp. 104-105.]

Smails reflected the widely-held fear that disclosure of such information as sales, cost of sales, general, administration and selling expenses would prejudice the business in competition. As has been indicated, Benston [1969, p. 519] has suggested that by 1926 roughly half of the firms in the New York Stock Exchange were disclosing much of this information! By 1941 advocacy of disclosure of such items in Canada was becoming much greater [Ashley, 1941, p. 395].

By and large, in the period of the early 1930s, demands for more disclosure did not extend to the detail of the operating portion of the profit and loss, but rather to the treatment of non-operating, non-recurring or what can now be referred to as extraordinary items. This concern was intimately related to the existence, use and abuse of secret reserves, and reconciliations of surplus accounts. Generally it was felt that disclosure of operating detail would give the competition an advantage, but that disclosure of any aspect included in operating profit that was of an extraordinary nature would be most meaningful since it was the pure, recurring, net operating figure which investors wished to capitalize to determine share price. If the recurring profit from operations was to be disclosed, it would follow that at least the changes in secret reserves would be observable. This latter eventuality would be enhanced if the surplus accounts were reconciled.

Concern for the foregoing aspects of disclosure can therefore be traced to the increased emphasis on operating profit as a commentary on valuation and to the Royal Mail Steam Packet case; and it was these two root causes to which advocates of greater disclosure continually referred prior to the legislation of 1934. That legislation met most of the foregoing demands for additional disclosure. The particular requirements of the Act implied that the statements of earned surplus and profit and loss were to be separated, and if one judges by the description of the items that were to be recorded in each statement, there was a presumption toward the all-inclusive concept. As will be pointed out later, the Act did heavily influence the separation of the earned surplus statement from the profit and loss statement in the presentation of corporate annual reports. However, the hope that the Companies Act would be able to establish guidelines as to whether extraordinary items should appear in the profit and loss statement or the earned surplus statement was either inappropriate or overly optimistic. C. Wade [1941, p. 103] in a review of "several hundred companies whose statements were examined for a varying number of years" indicates little consistency in the statement treatment of many extraordinary items.

Valuation

Accounting concern for the asset valuation base, by both theoreticians and businessmen, has, quite understandably, been a function of those periods of time in which notable price changes have occurred. In the immediate post World War I period when prices rose dramatically, H. T. Jamieson evidenced great concern for asset valuation. He falls short of advocating LIFO and accelerated depreciation but he does propound the essential argument for their use within the historical cost concept:

> This inflation in the cost of all things has caused fictitious profits upon the pre-war inventories of industry. Such profits are not real and do not reflect the true earning power of the business. The proof that they do not will be seen in the decline in prices that will before long take place, gradually, I hope. These falling prices will spell losses to those manufacturers who have counted as profits inflation in valuations of their plant and inventories. [Jamieson, 1920, p. 240.]

In the later 1920 period the appraisal and writing up of fixed assets was not uncommon and in the 1930 period the appraisal and writing down of fixed assets was similarly not uncommon. Of the forty-two test companies examined in The Annual Financial Review, Canadian of 1939, sixteen companies indicated that their basis of valuation had been that of an appraisal in the 1920 to 1929 period (with additions at cost), while seven companies indicated that their basis of valuation had been that of an appraisal in the 1930 to 1939 period. E. V. C. Smith [1935, pp. 12-13] indicates that the reasons for the writing down of assets was threefold: to reflect replacement cost, to decrease the depreciation charge and thereby increase profits, and thirdly to allow for dividends. No evidence was located with regard to the (presumed) write-ups in the 1920 period to indicate whether they simply wished to increase balance sheet values or to charge more depreciation - if indeed they did![11] Towards the end of the 1930 period, as prices began to rise, some interest was being expressed in the LIFO method of inventory determination as expostulated by American advocates ["Inventory Valuation," 1938, p. 80].

Canadian accounting theorists in the 1920 - 1940 period, as they did in the earlier two decades, generally tended to argue against the merit of recording appraisals in the accounts [Clapperton, 1927, p. 4; Smails, Nov., 1936, pp. 362-367]. The rise and subsequent fall of prices in the 1930 to 1940 period lent heavy support to the merit of their claim that current valuations should be ignored - thereby indirectly reinforcing the valuation basis of historical cost. The occasional lapse did, however, appear:

> Nor . . . [are the reasons against recording appraisals] a denial of the desirability in times of a steadily rising or steadily falling price level, of a periodical revaluation of fixed assets designed to bring the fixed asset values into line with those employed by newer concerns in the industry and so to adjust depreciation charges that selling prices of the product may be fixed neither too high nor too low for competitive purposes. [Smails, 1933, p. 112.]

The Rise of the Canadian Accounting Profession

It was in the 1930 - 1940 period that the Canadian profession began to rouse itself into new areas of expected professional conduct. Professor Smails had complained in 1930 that there was no standing committee of the Institute appointed which could have made representations to the government committees concerned with recommending changes in the Companies Act Amendments in 1929 [Smails, 1930, pp. 311-312].

---

[11] Boer informs us that in the United States one factor around which asset valuation concern was reflected, related to the rate base for regulated companies. [1966, p. 92.]

Perusal of The Canadian Chartered Accountant indicates that subsequently, an Institute brief was presented on the Companies Act of 1934 [Companies Act, 1934, p. 74] and that the Institute was concerned with drafting uniform legislation amongst the federal and provincial governments on the accounting and auditing aspects of corporation law ["Uniformity . . . ," 1932, pp. 287-288]. Similarly, provincial committees became active with regard to corporate legislation and the Security Frauds Preventions Acts ["Provincial News," 1933, p. 60 and R. R. Grant, 1933, p. 532]. The numerous investigation teams appointed by the Royal Commission on Price Spreads and Mass Buying were conducted by such well-known accounting firms as Peat Marwick Mitchell & Co. and Clarkson Gordon & Co. In 1934 following the example of the American Institute, which in 1931 published Accounting Terminology, a Committee was organized to prepare a publication on uniformity in accounting terminology ["Accounting Terminology," 1934, p. 298]. Previous to this in 1931, the Institute, recognizing a shortage in Canadian accounting texts, expressed willingness to sponsor such texts by Canadian authors ["Annual Meeting," 1931, p. 120].

In 1939 the examination system across Canada was reorganized so that there was introduced by the Canadian Institute a national uniform set of examinations by which to judge admission into the Chartered Accountancy membership. In 1939 again, a standing committee on Research was appointed and undertakings were made with Queen's University to develop a series of research studies ["General Notes," 1939, p. 288]. The immediate output of this latter endeavour was cut short by the intervention of the war.

The foregoing concern for such things as education, representations to legislative bodies, research, and codification of terminology indicate an increasing awareness of the Canadian Institute of the obligation it had assumed as the chief spokesman for the accounting profession in Canada.

Corporate Reporting Practices

By reference to Table 1, it is evident that many of the trends that began in the 1900 - 1920 period with regard to content, classification and valuation in corporate financial statements were extended and oftentimes accelerated in the 1920 - 1940 period. By the end of the period all companies made some attempt to classify current assets, current liabilities and fixed assets, and to indicate the asset valuation basis used. During the period, there was an increasing tendency for accumulated depreciation to be regarded as a deduction from the relevant asset account rather than being classified with "Reserves" on the liability side of the balance sheet; for intangible assets to be separated from tangible fixed assets (and oftentimes reduced to nominal value); for the replacing of the formerly used profit and loss statement with an earned surplus statement and an income statement; and for consolidated statements to be used - even before legal permission to do so in 1934.[12]

Much of the change in reporting practices is attributed to the 1930 - 1939 period and is very likely a function of the additional disclosure requirements of the Companies Act of 1934.[13] It can also be noted from the last line of data in Table 1 that one-half of the forty-two firms examined identified as net profit some figure that was <u>before</u> interest, depreciation and taxes and <u>after</u> transfers to reserve accounts. In effect, in many instances, interest, depreciation and taxes were regarded as appropriations of income while charges for reserves regarded as reductions of income. By 1939 there was a slight increase in the use of footnotes to provide information other than which pertains to contingent liabilities. Such items as descriptions of valuation, bases of consolidation, elaboration of asset groupings and details of executive remuneration as required by the 1934 Companies Act, were beginning to appear in footnotes. More generally, however, footnotes to financial statements were in a very fledgling state. The impetus that the Securities and Exchange Commission gave to the proliferation of footnotes in America had, at this time, no real counterpart in Canada [Bell, 1949, p. 256]. Oftentimes the information that is now expected to be found in footnotes was contained in directors' annual reports. In some instances, especially with regard to informing the reader about various asset valuation bases, the vehicle of communication was, in order of

[12]At least as early as 1915, there was advocacy of the merits of consolidated statements. [Kerr, 1915.]

[13]This contention also supported by Smith, [<u>Depreciation Policies . . .</u>, 1935, p. 102].

likelihood, firstly the directors' report, secondly, the body of the financial statement itself and finally, the footnotes.

The Canadian accounting literature revealed little, if any, discussion on the treatment of extraordinary items prior to the 1930-1940 period. What existed in the literature of the early 1930s was simply a plea that such non-recurring items be segregated from operating profits. The Companies Act of 1934 made such disclosure mandatory and it is therefore only since this latter date that there has generally been a visible problem with regard to whether an extraordinary item should be placed in the profit and loss, or alternatively, in the earned surplus statement. The Companies Act can be interpreted to presume a preference for the all-inclusive concept since it indicates several non-recurring items as being appropriate entries in the profit and loss statement; while, apart from dividends, it suggests that the only entry in the earned surplus statement should be adjustments affecting prior years. Corporate annual reports paid little attention to the legislative directives in this regard and as C. B. Wade [1941, pp. 98-108] has indicated, following an examination of "several hundred companies for a varying number of years," there was little uniformity amongst companies in the treatment of many non-recurring items. Approximately 80 percent of such items as the reduction in book values of assets or the transfers from reserve accounts were treated as direct adjustments of earned surplus; on the other hand, there was little unanimity in the treatment of such items as loss or gain on sale of investments or fixed assets, and the discount or premium on the redemption of bonds. Wade also notes that many companies themselves were also inconsistent in the way they treated the same item in two different years. The practice of treating extraordinary items inconsistently over time and between companies at a point of time got an early start in Canada.

The review of the financial statements of ten companies (see Appendix B) for each of the years 1920 to 1940 revealed further informative aspects of this period. For all firms examined, excluding Steel Company of Canada Limited and Canadian Locomotive Company Limited, whose annual reports had already anticipated the 1934 Companies Act's requirements, there were dramatic effects on corporate reporting practices. Within two years of the 1934 - 1935 revisions in the Companies Act, such aspects as valuation bases, separation of the earned surplus from the profit and loss statement, and specification of extraordinary items were quickly introduced into the annual reports. Valuation bases had often been described in annual reports prior to that time but more usually in the directors' report, and frequently for some companies, only in those years when price declines occurred.[14] Valuation bases given were sometimes not very explicit. In 1922, Dominion Rubber Company Limited indicated that the inventory of finished goods was such as to produce satisfactory profits in the ensuing period, and Steel Company of Canada Limited all through the 1920 - 1930 period and as late as 1932 indicated that inventory valuation was simply "fair and proper." More generally, there seemed to be strong acceptance of the lower of cost or market valuation basis for inventories. Certainly after the 1934 - 1935 Companies Acts it was uncommon not to find the basis of valuation given in the balance sheet as the lower of cost or market.

The examination served to document the appropriateness of the concern in the literature for the treatment of extraordinary items and the handling of reserve accounts. There were numerous situations in which there were a host of ambiguously designated reserve accounts, in which changes in reserve accounts and even earned surplus accounts[15] could not be reconciled from one year to another and also in which reserve accounts were used to write down assets. The depression itself seemed to help the rationalizing of reserves by forcing companies to return reserves to the profit and loss account in order to maintain a credit balance in the latter. Steel Company of Canada Limited included the following list of reserves in its 1921 financial statement:

Employees' pension fund appropriation
Furnace relining and rebuilding reserves
Reserve for accidents to employees
Contingent reserve
Betterment and replacement reserve
Fire insurance reserve
Bond sinking fund reserve
Depreciation account

---

[14]For example, Belding Corticelli Limited, 1927.

[15]For example, Acadia Sugar Company Limited, 1931.

According to the directors' report in 1923, the cost of a blast furnace stack was charged against the contingent reserve and also against the furnace relining and rebuilding reserve. In 1928, the various reserves were categorized under three headings called operating reserves, plant reserves and appropriated surplus. The Directors' Report indicates that:

> . . . the reserve accounts are shown separately in accordance with purposes for which they are required. This has seemed desirable for the reason that although the figures have always been clearly set forth, the misreading of the balance sheet has not been prevented.

In 1932 the Directors' Report reveals that securities were written down to market out of the contingent reserve and the reserve for accidents to employees - reserves which according to the directors' report, were no longer needed.

Since 1920, Cockshutt Plow Company Limited made a point of disclosing such information as would allow a year-to-year reconciliation of reserve accounts; on the other hand, no such information was given by Dominion Rubber Company Limited for the changes in their contingent reserve for the years 1920 to 1932. In Penmans Limited's financial statement of 1923, goodwill and trademarks amounting to $2.2 millions were written off directly to a reserve account. Other examples of either the writing off of assets directly against reserve accounts or the coincident charging of earned surplus with assets and crediting of earned surplus with transfers from reserve accounts were Dominion Glass Company Limited in 1925 and 1927, National Breweries Limited in 1938 and Belding Corticelli Limited in 1925, 1926 and 1931.

No evidence of statements of source and application of funds were noted. As indicted in Table 1, the not-infrequent habit of detailing the changes in fixed assets in the balance sheet itself around 1920 was notably decreased by the end of the 1920 - 1940 period. On the other hand, at least two directors' reports, Tooke Bros. Limited in 1931 and Steel Company of Canada Limited in 1934, drew attention to changes in working capital. Particularly, but not exclusively during the depression years of the 1930s, depreciation was frequently omitted in those years when the company had either little profits or suffered a loss.

In summary, the information presented in corporate annual reports during the 1920 to 1940 period was much greater than that provided in the previous period. Most of that increase in information occurred during the 1930 to 1940 period and much of it is attributable to the Companies Acts requirements of 1934 and 1935. No evidence was located to indicate that the legislation tended to reduce the quantity of information being provided. Most corporate annual reports had to increase the information being provided in order to satisfy the legislation requirements. Few corporate reports were unaffected. It is also likely that the quantity of information being provided in corporate annual reports in Canada was less than that being provided in America. Where the possibility may have existed that in the 1900 to 1920 period Canadian reporting practices were better, it is likely that Canadian reporting practices fell behind the American during the 1920 - 1940 period if one judges firstly, by Benston's study relating to the amount of information being provided in the income statement and secondly, by the Securities and Exchange Commission regulations and releases.

CHAPTER V

THE EVOLUTION OF FINANCIAL STATEMENTS, 1940 - 1970

English and American Legislation

Following the periodic review of company legislation by the Cohen Committee,[1] the English Companies Act of 1947, influenced somewhat tardily by the Royal Mail Steam Packet case of 1930 [Edey, 1956, pp. 128-129], initiated some notable revisions in English corporate legislation [Great Britain, 1947, C. 47]. Consolidated statements were required and when not provided, the reasons for not doing so were to be given together with disclosure of current and accumulated profits or losses of subsidiaries and the amount taken into the parent's accounts. The profit and loss account required the delineation of depreciation, directors' remuneration, interest, taxes, and investment income. Reserves were required to be categorized and their changes reconciled. Additional disclosure of balance sheet data was also required together with the provision of corresponding figures for the immediately preceding year in all financial statements. If not otherwise shown, the footnotes were to include information on stock options, dividends in arrears, contingent liabilities, capital expenditure contracts, foreign exchange conversion bases and market values of current assets and quoted investments.

The Companies Act of 1967 [Great Britain, C. 81] adopted many of the recommendations of the Jenkins Report.[2] Greater profit and loss and balance sheet disclosure was required, including the valuation of non-subsidiary investments. Directors' reports were required to indicate the sales and profit or loss before tax of each class of business, the market value of land where the latter is substantially different from the book value, the aggregate wages paid to employees, and political and charitable contributions. The exemption granted to private (closely-held) companies, allowing them to avoid public disclosure of their financial statements, was withdrawn.

---

[1]Appointed in 1943 to consider and recommend desirable amendments in the Companies Acts.

[2]Appointed in 1959 to consider and recommend desirable amendments in the Companies Acts.

The provisions of the Companies Acts of 1947 and 1967 represented a very notable increase in the amount of data which was required of English corporations. Up to these points of time the English companies acts had required far less information than their counterpart legislation in Canada and the United States.

During this period of time the Securities and Exchange Commission continued to regulate American corporate practices. Up to 1945, the Commission, through its Accounting Series Releases, was very active in requiring greater disclosure and setting standards. From that time to 1965 the Commission tended to defer to the pronouncements of the American Institute of Certified Public Accountants [Pines, 1965, pp. 730-733]. Since 1965 the pace of the Commission interest has quickened most notably in its concern in narrowing the range of acceptable alternative accounting principles.

Canadian Legislation

The Ontario Corporations Act of 1953 [Ontario, Statutes, C. 19, Secs. 82-93] constituted the first significant Ontario revision of the requirements relating to financial statement disclosure since the Act of 1907. This long overdue revision - which gave rise to Professor Smails' [1943, p. 197] comment that prior to the 1953 Act, the Ontario legislation was a "blot on the Canadian escutcheon" - was as significant and pace-setting an event in 1953 as the earlier legislation had been in 1907. The financial statement provisions of the Act were virtually written by accountants [Glassco,[3] 1955, p. 212] and the federal legislation, more than a decade later, was almost a direct copy. The disclosure requirements related to the details of the profit and loss statement (but did not include a request for sales, cost of sales and operating expenses!), the distinction between contributed and earned surplus, details of the balance sheet, financial statement footnotes (thirteen, in all), disclosure of subsidiary profits and losses and the extent of their treatment in the parents' accounts for non-consolidated subsidiaries, the requirement to state the reason for not consolidating subsidiaries, and the restriction of the term "reserve" to appropriations of retained earnings. Because of their significance in the genealogy of Canadian

[3]Glassco was president of the Canadian Institute in 1955.

financial statement disclosure requirements they are reported in Appendix E of this treatise. The requirement to disclose sales or gross revenues and to include a statement of the source and application of funds was included in amendments to the Act in 1966 [Ontario, Statutes, 1966, C. 28, Secs. 7-8]. The Lawrence Report of 1967 [Ontario, Legislative Assembly, Interim Report . . . .] in its review of the corporations acts, indicated that "no present need has been demonstrated for amendments of major significance to the financial disclosure provisions of the Ontario Act" and a Business Corporations Bill (not passed as of 1970), emphasizes a delineation of shareholders' rights and directors' duties ["Ontario Moves . . .", 1969, p. 10].

Following the Kimber Report [Attorney General, 1965] in 1965, the Ontario Securities Act was drastically revised, giving the ongoing surveillance of the Toronto Stock Exchange over to the Ontario Securities Commission. Together with changes relating to take-over bids, proxies and insider trading, financial statement disclosure requirements were made identical with The Corporations Act as amended in 1966 [Ontario, Securities Act, 1966, Part XII]. Flexibility and external expertise were built into the Securities Act by provisions for the appointment of a Financial Disclosure Advisory Board, whose task is to "consult with and advise the Commission concerning the financial disclosure requirements of this Act and the regulations" [Sec. 143]. Following the financial difficulties of Revenue Properties Ltd. in 1969, the Ontario Securities Commission set forth accounting guidelines for the treatment of profits arising from land sales ["Recognition of Profits . . .", 1969; "Pertinent Questions," 1969, p. 3]. This ruling is particularly significant because it represents the first time that accounting practices have been established by governments or their agencies, for non-regulated companies, that have gone beyond what the accounting profession has recommended. The powers of the Ontario Securities Commission would seem to be as pervasive as the Securities and Exchange Commission in America:

> The Commission may, where it appears to it to be in the public interest, make any direction, order, determination or ruling, (a) with respect to the manner in which any stock exchange in Ontario carries on business; (b) with respect to any by-law, ruling, instruction or regulation of any such stock exchange; (c) with respect to trading on or through the facilities of any such stock exchange or with respect to any security listed and posted for trading on any such stock exchange; or

> (d) to ensure that companies whose securities are listed and posted for trading on any such stock exchange comply with this Act and the regulations. [Ontario, Statutes, Securities Act, 1966, Part XIV, Sec. 139.]

A period of thirty years intervened between the federal legislation of 1934 - 1935 and its updating in 1965 in the Canada Corporations Act [Canada, Statutes, 1964-65, C. 52]. It is, with the addition of the requirement to disclose sales or gross revenue, virtually identical with the Ontario legislation of 1953. Bill C-4 contemplates the provision of source and application of funds statements, comparative figures, the allocation of sales and profit by business class and the withdrawal of the exemption for private companies of public disclosure of financial statements [Canada, House . . . ,Bill C-4, 1969]. Only with regard to the allocation of sales and profit by business class and the private company exemption would the federal legislation exceed that of Ontario.[4]

Background to the Canadian Legislation

For purposes of providing perspective for the legislation, the 1940 - 1970 period can be conveniently bisected into the first twenty years, in which there existed a relatively quiet effort on the part of professional accountants, members of parliament, investment analysts and some legislators to increase and alter the information in corporate annual reports; and the last ten years, in which there arose certain financial scandals and an increasing willingness on the part of governments to regulate corporate practices. As with earlier major legislative revisions, changes relating to annual corporate reporting practices accompany changes relating to corporate promotion and administration.

1940 - 1960

Writers in the professional literature during this period soon began to cast doubt on the adequacy of the corporate reporting practices required by the 1934 - 1935 legislation and the accounting concepts of profit involved. Leonard expressed this concern:

> How many financial statements are there which do not tend to understate earnings in good years by the use of unstated inventory reserves? And is it not good business? And how can any

---

[4]Other small differences are pointed out as at 1966 in M. P. Carscallen [1966, p. 42].

accountant, in practice, know how large these are and when they are utilized in the leaner years? And does not the inequitable income tax law which measures taxes on a one-year basis make it necessary for some businesses to do this as well as to make a disproportionate amount of repairs in the good years? [Leonard, 1942, pp. 12-13.]

Similarly, Professor Ashley indicated that:

> Economic research and business judgement require that much more frequent and detailed information should be given by all businesses on such things as stocks of goods, sales, numbers employed and wages paid. The old argument that such information would be of great value to competitors is no longer valid and would, if true, be of minor importance . . . The charge of inaccuracy is unfortunately too true to require elaboration; it is partly the result . . . that understatements of values were always permissible and usually praiseworthy . . . Financial institutions, industrial and commercial companies, all publish accounts knowing them to be incorrect and often with the deliberate intention to deceive, frequently from the most honest motives. How is it possible for anyone to attempt to make a satisfactory study of the trade cycle when the basic data are incomplete and unreliable. [Ashley, 1941, p. 395.][5]

Non-academics were also displaying their intolerance of corporate secrecy and lack of disclosure. The Chairman of the Royal Commission on the Textile Industry indicated that:

> . . . parliament which provides the tariff has the right . . . to see to it that true facts are made known as often as is necessary and practicable, concerning, among other things, the profits made by those who operate under the protection of the tariff. It should be made sure that governments, when approached for tariff changes, will always have reliable figures presented to them; that consumers should know what is going on, and that shareholders should be furnished with annual statements sufficiently clear and detailed to enable them to form a fair opinion of the value of their shares. Even under the amendments made to the Companies Act, 1934, presumably with this end in view, some of the balance sheets shown me are still quite deficient. They are reduced to the smallest possible compass, and their reference to inventories and reserves are of practically no value. Reserves in themselves are not necessarily illegitimate; they may be of use and value, but they should not be kept secret from those entitled to know of them, for instance, shareholders and taxing officials. [Turgeon, 1938, p. 127.]

and again:

> . . . the whole question of company accounting, and of the necessity of providing against possible manipulation in such

[5]See also Ashley [1943, pp. 1-9].

> accounting, demands attention as a result of the evidence to which I have referred. [p. 127.]

The clash of the old and the new orders - between those who were demanding more information in financial statements and those who were reluctant to offer it - is nicely demonstrated in the questioning of one of Canada's foremost accountants by a House of Commons Committee on Banking and Commerce in 1944:

> Q. Perhaps I can ask you this . . . If I were a shareholder of the Bank of Commerce, . . . and read your report to the shareholders, would I be able to ascertain from that, the amount that the directors had set aside last year as a hidden reserve? - A. No.
> Q. Why do you not tell your shareholders what the directors are setting aside for possible losses? - A. Why should you?
> Q. Is there any other answer than that? If not I will pass on. - A. No.
> Q. There is no other answer. - A. Wait a minute; I do not see any reason why you should tell them the amount recovered on loans written off and the amount appropriated in the year for prospective loans any more than you should tell them any other expenses or recoveries.
> Q. Are there any other expenses you hide from them? - A. You are not hiding. I do not think you are hiding them because you see -
> Q. If we are not hiding at all tell us what they are, and I want to warn you that everybody so far, bankers and government, have refused to help us get the amount. I do not want to trap you. If you are not hiding them what are they? - A. Net profit for the year after deducting dominion government taxes, including tax on note circulation, and after appropriations to contingent reserve fund, out of which fund full provision for bad and doubtful debts has been made, so many dollars.
> Q. Do you suggest that "so many dollars" discloses to them the amount of the hidden reserves? - A. Now you are all mixed up, if I may say so, between a hidden reserve -
> Q. You may certainly say so.
> . . . .
> Q. Did you mean it when you said they do not disclose their gross earnings? - A. Any individual bank does not disclose its gross earnings; it is net profit for the year.
> Q. Why does it not disclose their gross earnings to the shareholders? - A. Well, this is the form of statement that has been issued by the banks for generations, something like this; it has always been satisfactory and has always been taken as such.
> . . . .
> Q. But do you suggest that you are, as a shareholders' auditor, truly reporting the affairs of the bank to your shareholders when you do not tell them what the true gross earnings for the year are? - A. Most certainly.
> Q. Most certainly. You do not tell the shareholders what the bank has earned in a given year? - A. The gross?

Q. Yes. - A. Gross does not mean net.
Q. No, of course it does not. - A. I do not think there is any necessity to tell them what the gross earnings of the bank are. If they want it, they can get it, if it is not against the interests of the banks' shareholders.

. . . .

Q. Will you tell me what the reason is that you as the shareholders' auditor do not disclose to the shareholders the gross earnings of your institution for a given year? - A. Because they are interested in the net earnings.
Q. I beg your pardon? - A. Because they are interested in the net earnings and the amount of money that is going to be available for distribution to them as dividends.
Q. And not in the expenses necessary for the operation of the bank? - A. You do not show them the expenses ordinarily.
Q. They are not interested in those? - A. I do not think so for they have appointed directors and a management. [Canada, Committee on Banking & Commerce, 1944-45, pp. 860-867.]

Commentary by the editor of The Financial Post and by a committee of the Montreal Board of Trade also indicated that the quality of corporate financial reporting was low and that public opinion would insist that business recognize its social obligations [McEachern, 1955, pp. 261-265; "Comment and Opinion," 1953, pp. 45-46].[6] The Canadian Institute, recognizing its professional obligations, outlined standards of disclosure in annual financial statements in Bulletins 1, 14 and 20 in years 1946, 1957 and 1964 and also in lengthy briefs to the government, relating to the Companies Acts, in 1946, 1953, 1962 and 1969.

Though, as outlined above, there was no shortage of critics of corporate reporting practices during this period, there were no particularly large financial scandals to ignite what might be considered as the smouldering embers of dissatisfaction. This was so much so that the most pace-setting piece of legislation relating to financial statement disclosure in modern times in Canada, the Ontario Companies Act of 1953, was inquired into and passed without the particular prompting of any part of the community.[7] A scrutiny of the financial press at that time gives no indication of the reasons for the legislation. The author's

[6]A committee of the Montreal Board of Trade examined fifty-five annual reports as evidence to support their opinion.

[7]"Pace-setting" because it represented the complete acceptance of the recommendations of the Ontario Institute of Chartered Accountants and because, with a few minor alterations, stands in 1970 as both the Ontario and federal law on financial statement disclosure.

conjecture that the legislative revision took place because the statutes had not been revised since 1907 and were behind the federal legislation and because the model for revised disclosure had already been framed in the Canadian Institute of Chartered Accountants' Bulletin #1, was confirmed by the then Secretary to the Select Committee on Company Law, S. Lavine.[8] Mr. Lavine also indicated that the inquiry and revision were made possible at that particular time because "the number of members of the House of the government party far exceeded the total number of members in the opposition parties and the use of the Select Committee gave Mr. Frost [the Premier of Ontario] an opportunity of keeping many of his backbenchers actively employed, especially between sessions when most of the work of the Select Committee was done." The request for a brief which the Select Committee made of the Ontario Institute caught that group by surprise, but not unprepared, since a Canadian Institute committee had just prepared a brief to the federal government on the very same matters.[9]

<u>1960 - 1970</u>

The period of 1940 - 1960, relative to the 1960 - 1970 period, was the calm before the storm. The storm was represented by a mixture of corporate difficulties and disasters combined with the willingness - even eagerness - of governments to appoint committees of inquiry and to revise legislation. The legislation itself was as much a part of the storm as the corporate failures because governments were not only eager to respond to the public outcry but willing, as well, to lead the way in those areas which were becoming of increasing national and political importance, e.g. disclosure of sales and profit by class of business and the abolition of exemption from public disclosure of financial statements for private companies.[10] The inquiries and legislation were to some extent self-

[8]In correspondence with the author, dated June 10, 1970.

[9]Actually, the Canadian committee was simply reconstituted as the Ontario Committee. See testimony of G. P. Keeping [Canada, Senate, <u>Committee on Banking & Commerce</u>, 1964, p. 53].

[10]This legislation is directed largely at American subsidiaries.

generating in that particular areas being inquired into would reveal the shortcomings of related legislation.[11]

The most significant corporate failure was that of Atlantic Acceptance Corporation in 1965, but prior and subsequent to that time such well-known companies as British Mortgage and Trust, Alliance Credit Corporation, Prudential Finance Corporation, Windfall Oils & Mines Limited, Revenue Properties Ltd., Corporation Foncier de Montreal and the Commonwealth group of companies in British Columbia all experienced either failure or major financial crises. By and large, the reasons were a mixture of inappropriate corporate promotion, diversity of accounting principles and poor management. As a result, much of the federal and provincial legislation both enacted and contemplated related not simply to increased financial statement disclosure but also to the rights of shareholders, the duties of directors and restrictions on proxy solicitation, takeover bids, and insider trading.

The major areas of inquiry and the related legislation will be briefly recounted here in so far as they bear on or help to provide a description of the climate for increased financial statement disclosure.[12]

The Royal Commission on Canada's Economic Prospects of 1957 chaired by Walter Gordon - a senior partner of Clarkson, Gordon & Co., one of the largest public accounting firms in Canada, and likely the largest firm not directly related to any American public accounting firm - made Canada aware of the increasing significance of foreign investment and the fact that, under the incorporating statutes that exempt private (closely-held) companies from public disclosure of their financial affairs, little was known about the financial activity of a significant portion of the economy. The Commission recommended that the financial activities of private non-resident corporations be disclosed [Governor-General in Council, 1957, p. 393]. This Royal Commission and the American Labor-Management Reporting and Disclosure (Landrum-Griffin) Act of 1959 provided the background for the Corporations and Labour Unions

---

[11]The author appreciates the insight of R. D. Thomas, Executive Director of The Canadian Institute of Chartered Accountants on this point.

[12]See also E. C. Harris [1967, pp. 476-506].

Returns Act of 1962 [Canada, Statutes, C. 26], which required all Canadian corporations and unions to make disclosure of the details of their ownership by non-residents and also of their annual financial affairs. The latter data, however, was confidential to the government.[13] The Watkins Report of 1968 on Foreign Ownership and the Structure of Canada Industry delineated the extent to which there was a lack of public disclosure of financial affairs of Canadian corporations by indicating that in 1964, of the 375 largest non-financial Canadian corporate complexes, 43 percent of these were private companies and, in turn, 75 percent of these were non-resident companies [p. 214]. Concern for the public disclosure of such a significant portion of the Canadian financial scene has undoubtedly led to the inclusion of this requirement in the federal Bill - C4, mentioned in the previous section.

Other inquiries of the time, though some primarily directed at matters not directly related to financial statement disclosure of industrial organizations, brought to the attention of the community the significance of improved corporate reporting practices. The Report of the Royal Commission on Banking and Finance in 1964 (the Porter Report) indicated that:

> We also believe that corporate disclosure standards in Canada are inadequate and that more stringent requirements should be enacted into law as part of a program designed to encourage the development of a better-informed Canadian investor community willing to purchase Canadian equities.
>
> . . . .
>
> We have argued that the public dealing with financial institutions and markets can never be guaranteed against loss, but that the best safeguard against this possibility is legislation which provides for adequate disclosure and sets high standards of self-regulation, backed up by strong government supervision and powers to enforce proper practices. [Governor General in Council, 1964, pp. 560-561.]

And in elaboration:

> In our view, companies should be required under these acts to provide annually prompt and comprehensive information containing sales figures, comparative data going back several years and information about long-term lease payments and contingent liabilities such as obligations to unfunded pension plans. [Governor General in Council, 1964, p. 350.]

---

[13]Its availability to other departments of government was circumscribed. [Privy Council Office, 1968, p. 180.]

The Report of the Attorney General's Committee on Securities Legislation in Ontario in 1965 (the Kimber Report) indicated that:

> Establishment of conditions and practices in the capital market which best serve the investing public will normally be consistent with the best interests of the whole economy. For example, disclosure of financial information which depicts adequately the operations and financial position of companies is vital to the investing public; such disclosure also provides the capital market with the information necessary to make a more satisfactory allocation of resources. [Attorney General, 1965, p. 7.]

Recommendations of the Kimber report relating to the disclosure of source and application of funds statements, comparative figures, sales or gross revenues, and semi-annual reporting were incorporated in both the Ontario Securities Act of 1966 and in amendments to the Ontario Corporations Act. The appointment of the Kimber Commission was likely not a function of any "particular grievance or scandal" - though "the discussion of the Canadian Oil Company takeover [by Shell Oil Co. in 1962], while not directly relevant did highlight the status of our law" - but was rather a concern that the law was in need of review.[14] The Securities Act legislation of 1966 implemented the recommendations of the Kimber Report and those of the Royal Commission Report on Windfall Oils and Mines Limited of 1965 [Ontario, Lieutenant Governor in Council].

The Canada Corporations Act of 1964-1965 represented legislation initiated by the Senate (Bill S-22) and both Senate and House of Commons Committees of Inquiry on Banking and Finance preceded the legislation. The Senate Committee, in particular, held extensive hearings and entertained the briefs and submissions of a great number of interested parties [Canada, Senate, Proceedings of the Standing Committee on Banking and Commerce, 1964]. It was acknowledged that with regard to corporate financial statement practices, the legislation of 1934 - 1935 was simply out of date and that the federal revision was copied from the existing Ontario legislation [Canada, Senate Debates, 1964, pp. 515-518]. In the same year, 1965, the Ontario Government appointed a Select Committee on Company Law, the Lawrence Committee [Ontario, Legislative Assembly . . . , 1967], to review the Corporations Act of Ontario.

---

[14]According to correspondence by J. R. Kimber, President of the Toronto Stock Exchange with the author, dated July 3, 1970.

Recommendations related to rights of shareholders, the duties and responsibilities of directors and the role of auditors. Much of their recommendations are contemplated in the Bills, in 1970, amending the Corporations Act of Ontario ["Ontario Moves . . . ," 1969, p. 10]-legislation which the Premier of Ontario, John Robarts, calls "a shareholders' bill of rights and a directors' code of ethics" ["A Law for Amateurs," 1968, p. 5].

It was in 1965, during the time of many of these committees of inquiry, that there ocurred in Canada a major financial failure - that of Atlantic Acceptance Corporation. Its failure brought into question, among other things, the appropriateness of loans to affiliated companies, income reporting practices of financial institutions, and parent auditor's responsibility with regard to the subsidiary auditor's work. The failure of Atlantic Acceptance Corporation together with Prudential Finance Corporation in the following year, involved losses of 75 millions of dollars. It occasioned the appointment of a Royal Commission of enquiry[15] by the Ontario government and precipitated the contemplation of changes in the Investment Companies Act even before the Commission report was handed down ["Finance Company . . . ," 1968, p. 3]. Financial press editorials indicated the pervasiveness of the influence of this corporate failure:

> The whole Atlantic debacle caused so much misery in so many places that it spurred reform at many levels in the past four years. The provinces and the federal government drafted new laws for corporations, for trust companies, and for finance companies. Investors insisted on higher standards of disclosure. Auditors set new codes for examination of company accounts. Directors re-examined their responsibilities . . . [The Financial Post, 1969, p. 9.]

Other Factors

Other factors were of varying importance in the evolution of annual financial statement practices during the period 1940 to 1970. By-

[15]Recommendations of the report handed down in late 1969 relate to the restriction and surveillance of investment policies, financial statement disclosure and responsibilities of auditors. [Ontario, Lieutenant Governor, 1969; "Here are Recommendations . . . ," 1969, p. 22.] Note Mr. Justice Hughes' impatience at the slowness of the accounting profession in resolving issues [pp. 1589-90].

law No. 63 of the Toronto Stock Exchange enacted in 1948, simply requires the submission of "an annual report containing a financial statement (including a balance sheet and profit and loss or revenue and expenditure account) in the customary form." Generally, "the Exchange has taken the position that direction regarding the form of financial statements should come from the Canadian Institute of Chartered Accountants."[16] A far more active role has been played by the financial press of Canada in its concern for improved corporate reporting practices - notably the Financial Times and The Financial Post. In addition, the latter has sponsored, since 1951, the Financial Post Awards for company reports and has given a great deal of detailed publicity to what has been regarded as good and poor practices by a panel of judges which include representatives from the Canadian Institute of Chartered Accountants and the Investment Dealer's Association of Canada.

Public concern for changes in corporate reporting practices has undergone a notable change during the 1960 - 1970 period. Prior to this time, much of the pressure for change placed emphasis on more complete disclosure of practices - of what was being done. Since mid-1960 there has been increasing concern for the narrowing of the range of acceptable practices. Complementary with this concern is the implication that the obligation for performing the task of narrowing the range of acceptable practices lies with the professional accountants. The implied threat that the profession had better undertake this task or have governmental agencies do it can be inferred from the financial, professional and academic literature:

> Most commentators feel that, while in some degree the exercise of professional judgement will always be required in order to provide the most meaningful presentation of financial data in any given set of circumstances, the scope for alternative presentation can and should be greatly reduced. Ideally, alternative presentation should be acceptable only where it is necessary to reflect significant differences in circumstances. Criticism of the lack of uniformity in accounting has intensified in the mid-1960s after the failure of certain Canadian financial institutions and the serious financial difficulties experienced by others, where there was no clear prior warning in the published financial statements of these institutions. [Harris, 1967, p. 491.]

---

[16] According to L. Lowe, Vice-president, Stock list of The Toronto Stock Exchange in correspondence dated May 11, 1970.

The Kimber Report indicated that:

> It is evident that optimum disclosure will not be attained until financial statements of business organizations are presented on a basis consistent with one another. At the present time two basically comparable companies may have their accounts presented using different accounting principles with the result that their financial position and operating results may appear to be quite different in their financial statements. It is necessary to work towards consistency in all financial statements and the Committee believes this consistency, together with clarity of presentation, can best be accomplished in Ontario by the Institute of Chartered Accountants of Ontario developing uniform accounting principles to be applied in a uniform manner to all companies engaged in similar types of business. [Attorney General of Ontario, 1965, p. 29.]

R. H. Jones, a senior official of the management firm operating Canada's two largest mutual funds, warns that:

> . . . if fallacy, error or unrealism have crept into financial reporting it will be you [the chartered accountants] that the public will turn against and the consequences will be unpleasant.
>
> Let us not delude ourselves that there will not be a day of reckoning. The longer it is postponed, the greater will be its severity.
>
> . . . .
>
> There will always be the need for some latitude in financial reporting . . . But they must recognize that the latitudes have become excessive and that they are contributing to a virtual jungle of financial reporting. [Jones, 1965, p. 13.]

The Financial Post on several occasions devoted up to two pages to a careful elaboration of the effect on corporate earnings of the use of acceptable but alternative accounting practices.[17] Both The Financial Post and The Financial Times have editorially urged the accounting profession to swifter action [The Financial Times, September 15, 1969, p. 6]. The Director of Research of the Canadian Institute acknowledged that one of the main areas of general criticism "involves the lack of codification of generally accepted accounting principles, and the continued acquiescence in the use of alternative and perhaps conflicting accounting practices in similar circumstances" [Mulcahy, 1966, p. 288].

This turning of attention from disclosure of practices to the narrowing of the range of practices has placed great pressure on the

---

[17]See The Financial Post, September 11, 1965, p. 48; November 20, 1965, p. 32; and July 16, 1966, pp. 15-16.

accounting profession. In a few instances legislators have demonstrated that they are unwilling to wait for Institute recommendations. The Ontario Securities Commission issued guidelines on the handling of profits for land development companies in 1969 [Ontario Securities Commission, 1969]. The federal Bill contemplating amendment of the Canada Corporations Act, requires that sales and profits by business class be disclosed in annual financial statements. At the time of writing the Canadian Institute was hurriedly preparing its own recommendations on these two important issues. In some instances, the pressure has been placed on the accounting profession by the willingness of governments or governmental agencies to defer to forthcoming recommendations ["New OSC Recommendations . . .", 1970, p. 6].

English and American Influence

The 1940 to 1970 period continued the pattern set in the earlier decades of decreasing English influence. The committees of inquiry and the professional briefs made a point of indicating that such relevant documents as the English Institute Recommendations #8 and #18 in 1944 and 1958 respectively, the Cohen Report and the Jenkins Report which preceded the 1947 and 1967 English legislation respectively, and the English legislation itself, were carefully perused. However, what decreasing influence there was would have been filtered by the professional Canadian accountants, since as mentioned in a previous section, the 1953 Ontario legislation and the 1965 Canadian legislation with regard to financial statement disclosure were almost direct copies of the professional recommendations.

One aspect of the English influence occurred during this period and its impact is still felt. The LIFO method of calculating inventory cost is seldom used in Canada and this is quite likely because the Privy Council in Great Britain (the case originated at a time when final legal appeals were still taken to England) rejected this method for the determination of taxable income [Byrd, 1966, p. 242]. On a larger field of influence, a scrutiny of the recommended texts in the professional accountants correspondence courses administered by Queen's University indicates that few if any English-authored texts were in use during this period. The author is unaware of any English accounting texts that have been in use in Canadian Universities during the 1960 to 1970 period. The

English influence that remains has been described by Professor W. B. Coutts [1959, p. 134] as a function of "our common background of common law and judicial precedent . . . [which] ensures that [English models] can never be entirely irrelevant."

The American influence has not only supplanted that of the English but is of such significant proportions that the uniqueness of Canadian professional accounting is sometimes questioned. R. M. Skinner a former Chairman of the Committee on Accounting and Auditing Research of the Canadian Institute has suggested, in relation to the Moonitz and Sprouse studies of the early 1960s that:

> . . . there is an important question whether Canadian thinking can afford to develop along lines different from the American. If not, we must either be prepared to accept whatever conclusions the American Institute arrives at in its present studies in this area, or else we should move to participate with the American Institute in these studies. [Skinner, 1961, p. 468.]

This concern is particularly apt, since some of the Canadian Institute Recommendations have differed very little from their American counterparts.

More generally, in the absence of a Canadian Institute pronouncement on any particular accounting matter, it was assumed that the American Institute Bulletin's and Opinions would be followed [Wilson, 1956, p. 35]. The enormous amount of professional and academic accounting literature that emanated from America during this period was faithfully and carefully reported on and reviewed in <u>The Canadian Chartered Accountant</u>. Apart from a mere handful of Canadian accounting texts, the author believes that the bulk of those used in Canadian universities were either American texts or Canadian revisions of American texts. Emulation of American reporting practices rather than English was recommended.[18]

A continuing and significant source of American influence in Canada related to the activities of the Securities and Exchange Commission. The Kimber Report, which so heavily influenced the Ontario Securities Act of 1966, bears witness to the influence of the Securities

---

[18]See the extremely favorable commentary on the Financial Statements of Duplan Corporation ["Form of Financial Statements," 1945, pp. 345-348]; and the largely uncomplimentary remarks relating to the confusing mixture of operating and capital items in the English profit and loss account by W. B. Coutts ["Accounting Research," 1959, pp. 135-136].

and Exchange Commission, by the numerous references to the activities and rules of that organization. The placing of the surveillance of the Ontario Stock Exchanges under the eye of the Ontario Securities Commission is similar to the relationship between the American Stock Exchanges and the Securities and Exchange Commission. The action of the Ontario Securities Commission in handing down accounting guidelines relating to the determination of profits on land development sales initiated the Canadian pattern of a familiar tradition long established by the Securities and Exchange Commission in America.

More direct sources of Securities and Exchange Commission influence related to those Canadian Corporations which are required to comply with Securities and Exchange Commission financial disclosure regulations because they either form part of a consolidated report which is being filed with the Securities and Exchange Commission or because the Company is selling securities in the United States or is listed on an American Exchange. Whether compliance with such Securities and Exchange Commission regulations has altered the reporting practices of such firms in Canada has, as of 1970 gone untested. One indication of positive influence was the disclosure to the Securities and Exchange Commission of the details of the substantial investment portfolio of Canadian Pacific Investments Limited. Only later in 1965, were these details disclosed in the Company's annual report [Dow, 1965, p. 8]. Another, and in Canadian eyes, far less appealing influence of the Securities and Exchange Commission, was the requirement that any foreign company that had securities that were held by three hundred or more American residents and which had one million or more of total assets, must comply with Securities and Exchange Commission financial disclosure regulations. The Canadian Government[19] protested the legality of such a ruling and succeeded in obtaining deferral of its imposition.

Professional Activity

During the early 1940 period, several writers commented on the

---

[19]As did the Canadian Institute of Chartered Accountants. See letter to the Minister of Finance from the Canadian Institute Committee on Federal Legislation, December 21, 1965.

growing dissatisfaction towards existing financial reporting practices.[20] An article in The Canadian Chartered Accountant in 1943 commented that:

> . . . it is unfortunate that the profession lacks that vigorous leadership which instead of awaiting developments, would formulate and energetically strive for action on constructive proposals to the end that shareholders receive adequate and uncamouflaged statements of the affairs and, no less important, the results of the operations of their companies. It is not improbable that routine representations have been made periodically to obtain amendment of the companies acts; the gravamen of the charge is that the leaders of the profession have not inaugurated a crusade to rectify a condition that must sooner or later bring the profession into disrepute among those whom it purports to serve. ["Call for Action," 1943, p. 361.]

It was largely out of a general realization that reporting practices were inadequate that the Canadian Institute in 1946, in the first of its recommendations, issued Bulletin #1, A Statement of Standards of Disclosure in Annual Financial Statements of Manufacturing and Mercantile Companies. This bulletin was largely prepared by the Ontario Institute Committee on Accounting and Auditing because, as J. R. M. Wilson, a former President of the Canadian Institute and Chairman of the Canadian Committee on Accounting and Auditing Research indicated:

> Several of us felt that the profession of chartered accountancy in Canada was headed towards a point where either it must speak out and say what its standards were or that the investing public would demand that the Government step in and fill the void by laying down a set of standards of what financial statements should disclose.[21]

Concern for the need of the profession to self-generate leadership was elaborated later in 1955 by J. G. Glassco, president of The Canadian Institute:

> There is, however, in our situation in Canada cause for some concern. We have a real difficulty in knowing how to maintain suitable progress in research without a prod or stimulus such as our American colleagues have in S.E.C. True, the British profession is also free of any compulsion in this matter but there the profession is very much larger, and also the incorporated accountants and the chartered accountants of Scotland and

---

[20] See for example, H. D. Clapperton [1941, pp. 75-83]; F. S. Capon [1943, pp. 380-385]; and R. G. H. Smails [June, 1943, pp. 454-455].

[21] From an address, "Standards of Disclosure," given by J. R. M. Wilson before the Dominion Association of Chartered Accountants at Montreal, September 11, 1946.

> England and Wales, respectively, form three top-notch professional bodies, each seriously concerned with this task and each thereby tending to stimulate the effort of the other two. In Canada we are on our own and in such circumstances, we ourselves must make a special effort. [Glassco, 1955, p. 212.]

Nor had there been in Canada, prior to the Atlantic Acceptance disaster, a financial crisis sufficiently significant that would make reform relatively easy.

The pattern for issuing such recommendations had, of course, already been set by the American Institute in 1939 and the English Institute in 1942. Revisions of the Canadian Bulletin #1 were issued in 1957 and 1964. Throughout the years since 1964, the Committee on Accounting and Auditing Research has put forward not only many recommendations on specific issues but also sponsored many research studies, including since 1953, a biannual compendium of Canadian corporate reporting practices, Financial Reporting in Canada. The general impact of the Institute's recommendations has been regarded by some professional accountants as having the force of mild pressure [Lyons, 1965, p. 22]. This may be an understatement of their influence since, as can be demonstrated by a review over time of Financial Reporting in Canada, there have been some notable changes in corporate reporting practices and secondly because the standards set by the recognized accounting body in Canada are very likely to constitute the standards which judges, juries and the public generally would expect to see maintained. As of 1969, "where departure from recommended accounting treatment and statement presentation and the effect thereof on the financial statements are not disclosed in notes to the financial statements, the auditors should make such disclosure in their report" [CICA Handbook, p. 604, 2500.18].[22]

Mirroring the Institute Bulletins were the submission of lengthy briefs and submissions to the government relating to increased financial statement disclosure - the more notable of these were in 1946, 1953, 1963

---

[22]This recommendation to be effective requires sanction by provincial institutes' rules of professional conduct.

and 1969.[23] It has been noted in preceding sections that much of the existing Ontario and Canadian legislation relating to annual financial statements is a direct copy of these briefs. It was quite evident that the various committees of inquiry were not only pleased to accept, but expected to receive, the briefs of the Canadian Institute. Some of these, for example the Kimber Committee and the Lawrence Committee have simply deferred to the Canadian Institute in matters of corporate reporting practices [Attorney General . . . , 1965, pp. 28-29; Ontario, Legislative Assembly, 1967, p. 88]. However, the privilege of being the recognized leader has also brought with it a concomitant obligation-that obligation being to anticipate areas of reporting practices in which there is likely to be some legislative concern and to respond quickly with recommendations when those areas of legislative concern have been discovered. It has already been mentioned that the Ontario Securities Commission created great pressure by by-passing the Institute in the promulgation of its guidelines for real estate transactions and by pointedly deferring to the Canadian Institute on as-yet unreleased recommendations on business combinations ["OSC Takes Hard Line . . . ," 1970, pp. 5-6]. Similarly the Minister of Consumer and Corporate Affairs in contemplation of new disclosure legislation for 1970, has deferred to the Institute with regard to the details relating to diversified reporting [Mulcahy, 1969, p. 287].[24] It is likely that an enormously increasing amount of time will have to be spent by the Canadian Institute on such matters if it is to satisfy this almost-voracious appetite of legislators.

The Theory Relating to Corporate Reporting Practices

Apart from articles in The Canadian Chartered Accountant, the main sources of authoritative Canadian literature during this period were the recommendations and research studies of the Canadian Institute. The writer believes that the basic accounting books used both in professional

[23]See the November and December 1946 issues and the April issue, 1953 of The Canadian Chartered Accountant. Copies of the other briefs were obtained from the Canadian Institute.

[24]It should be noted that the English Companies Act of 1967 required the reporting of profit by business class.

accounting courses and in Canadian universities were either American texts or the Canadianized editions of standard American texts,[25] or the several texts by Queen's University professors.[26] The most notably original theoretical work was Wealth, Income and Intangibles written by Professor J. E. Sands [1963] of the University of Toronto. It was not dissimilar to Edwards and Bell's The Theory and Measurement of Business Income and was written at about the same time.[27] Towards the end of the 1960s, Howard Ross [1966 and 1969] authored two strong statements outlining the shortcomings of corporate reports based on historical costs. It may be well to record here the contributions in the literature of three particular Canadian academics, Professors R. G. H. Smails, J. E. Smyth and C. A. Ashley, whose individual and joint output span almost five decades. The first two professors authored a monthly column in The Canadian Chartered Accountant from 1930 to 1960; all three were articulate and leading exponents in the battle for improved financial statements. All three made representations and presented briefs to committees inquiring into desirable changes in legislation. All worked on various Canadian Institute committees and, as well, contributed innumerable articles to the professional and academic literature. A listing of some of their published books displays their encyclopedic business interests: Accounting Principles and Practice by R. G H. Smails and C. E. Walker, Auditing by R. G. H. Smails, The Working of a Cost System by R. G. H. Smails, Canadian Crown Corporations by R. G. H. Smails and C. A. Ashley, An Introduction to Auditing for Canadians by C. A. Ashley, Corporation Finance in Canada by C. A. Ashley and J. E. Smyth, Introduction to Accounting for Students in Economics by C. A. Ashley, The Basis of Accounting by J. E. Smyth, and The Law and Business Administration in Canada by J. E. Smyth and D. Soberman.

[25]Notably the Canadian editions of Finney and Miller texts by L. C. Mitchell and K. F. Byrd; of Karrenbrock and Simons by W. J. McDougall; and of Meigs and Johnson by J. D. Blazouske.

[26]Various texts by Professors R. G. H. Smails, W. G. Leonard, D. Bonham and J. R. E. Parker.

[27]The book was reviewed by Maurice Moonitz [1964, pp. 829-830].

The Cost Principle

The convention of basing corporate reports on historical cost had of course largely been established in the first two decades of the century and no truly strong challenges were made to its continuing use during this period. Nonetheless, a couple of instances of either the divergence or the desire to diverge from its use are notable. It may be well to note, in preface to these comments, that the important writings advocating departures from historical cost have all been carefully reported on and reviewed over the years in The Canadian Chartered Accountant. Readers of this journal had the opportunity to become acquainted with the statements of Sweeney, MacNeal, Jones, the AICPA Accounting Research Study No. 6 on price levels, the works of Sprouse and Moonitz, the Jenkins Report, the 1966 AAA Statement, and the books of Edwards and Bell and Chambers. However, it must be said that much of the Canadian periodical literature in the 1940s did not adequately distinguish the differences between general and specific price changes and its meaning is therefore sometimes difficult to interpret.[28]

During the 1940s, and occasioned firstly by the war's uncertainty and then later by the marked rise in the general price level, there arose some concern that corporate reports based on historical cost were unrealistic. The response of corporations was to include such items as "inventory reserve for future possible decline in inventory values," "reserve for contingencies," and "reserve for depreciation relating to increased cost of replacement" as charges against income [Thompson, 1948, pp. 231-244]. Generally such charges against income were decried,[29] and the revised income tax law in 1949 which allowed generous depreciation for tax purposes served to scotch much of the dissent against historical cost that arose from inadequate depreciation charges [Ross, 1964,

[28]A notable exception is J. G. Chaston [1947, pp. 70-73]; on the other hand, witness such comments by the Director of Research of the Canadian Institute as: "If the monetary unit retained a stable value over the years, depreciation charges based upon cost would in the end equal the amount originally invested in the building or equipment . . ." [King, 1948, pp. 77-78].

[29]See The Use of the Term Reserve and Accounting for Reserves-Bulletin No. 9 (Toronto: The Canadian Institute of Chartered Accountants, 1953). This Bulletin was very similar to Accounting Research Bulletins, Nos, 29 and 31 issued by the American Institute of Accountants in 1947.

p. 276]. Commencing in the early 1950s and continuing throughout the 1960 period, a number of extremely authoritative academics and businessmen urged the accounting profession to consider departure from historical cost. Mr. V. W. Scully [1952, p. 181], a subsequent President of Steel Company of Canada Limited, in commentary on an English Institute recommendation of adherence to historical cost, suggested that "here is an admission that our financial statements based on historical cost are misleading and do not, in fact, fulfill the principal purpose for which they are designed." Similarly, Donald Gordon [1960, p. 42], President of the Canadian National Railway in 1960, suggested that "for twenty years you [professional accountants] have been arguing among yourselves about the most important accounting question of our generation and the shibboleth of generally accepted accounting principles has prevented your profession from coming up with forthright recommendations."[30] Submissions made to the Lawrence Committee in 1965, also recommended the use of current market values [W. Beaton and B. B. Shetker, 1965]. It was only in the late 1960s that the Canadian Institute commissioned a study, (unreleased as of 1970), on Changing Financial Values by Professor L. Rosen.

Balance Sheets and Income Statements

The prime emphasis on the income statement continued unabated during the 1940 - 1970 period. This continuing emphasis was not an unlikely happening during inflationary periods of time. An historical cost based income statement in inflationary times can be relatively easily modified, through the use of LIFO[31] and accelerated depreciation, to approximate the income statement that would be prepared had some current replacement cost basis been used. However the very modifications which make the income statement more current tend to make the balance sheet less current. Therefore without departing from historical cost, the challenge of price changes is largely met if the income statement is

---

[30]See also Byrd [1952, pp. 87-104] and Ross [1964, pp. 276-279].

[31]Admittedly, LIFO has not been generally used in Canada, however, "the Dominion Taxation Division accepted a basis that came very close to the LIFO theory in connection with the wartime excess profits tax, except that the result was achieved through the establishment of an inventory reserve" [Parkinson, 1950, p. 212].

regarded to be of prime importance and the balance sheet, a mere residual. It was against this residual concept of the balance sheet by the chairman of the Accounting and Auditing Research Committee of the Canadian Institute, G. K. Carr that Professor J. Smyth protested:

> . . . the balance sheet and the income statement are only two parts of the same process - they are each an integral part of the measurement of income. We can never measure income sensibly without reference to assets and liabilities. We would like to, but in the long run we are not going to be allowed to do so. To disparage the balance sheet is to disparage the income statement too. [Smyth, 1968, p. 157.]

Various Accounting and Auditing Research Bulletins, most notably No. 1 in 1946, No. 14 in 1957 and No. 20 in 1964, continued to both recommend and encourage increased financial statement disclosure. Bulletin No. 1 in 1946, indicated that in many cases it is desirable to disclose sales, but not until Bulletin No. 20 in 1964 was sales disclosure made a requirement. It was only in this same Bulletin in 1964, that statements of source and application of funds and disclosure of cost of sales and operating expenses were made "desirable." The list of the items to be covered in footnotes extended dramatically with each new disclosure bulletin. Many of these disclosure requirements relating especially to additional detail in financial statements lagged in time behind the recommendations of the academic and investment community [McEachern, 1949, p. 261]. That lag is both demonstrated and explained by reference to the comments of T. A. M. Hutchison, the Chairman of the Ontario Institute Committee that made representations to the Roberts Committee in 1952. Respecting disclosure of investment portfolios he states that:

> I think you are making such a great advance in disclosure of information to the shareholders, over anything that has been available so far in Canada, that it probably is a big enough step to take at this time without full disclosure of the investment . . . [Ontario, Legislature of the Province of Ontario, 1952, p. 2330.]

And again, respecting disclosure of sales:

> We considered that at length and we come to the conclusion that while it is <u>desirable</u>, it is not <u>necessary</u> to have the whole picture in order to obtain a fair presentation of the company's financial position and earnings. [Author's italics] [Ontario, Legislature of the Province of Ontario, 1952, p. 2331.]

In response to Professor Smail's request for the disclosure of source and application of funds statements, Mr. Hutchison said that the balance sheet, profit and loss and surplus statements should be adequate [Ontario, Legislature of the Province of Ontario, 1952, p. 2156].

The Institute Bulletins have, over time, been somewhat inconsistent in their recommendations relating to the treatment of extraordinary items. The 1957 Bulletin suggested that such items, if material, should be disclosed after the net profit or loss - but whether they are placed in the profit and loss or earned surplus statement is relatively unimportant. The Bulletin in 1964 suggested that such items, if non-routine and material, should be located in the earned surplus statement. In 1968 the CICA Handbook, following largely the recommendations of APB No. 9 of the American Institute,[32] permitted only rare items relating to litigation or settlement of taxes, as candidates for inclusion in the earned surplus statement.

Corporate Reporting Practices

Several generalizations can characterize the evolution of annual corporate reports during this period. The conventions of existing balance sheet classification and valuation were firmly accepted; the balance sheet came to be enormously simplified and aggregated, largely as a function of the increase in the notes to financial statements; the period of the 1940s occasioned a significant increase in the use of precautionary or anticipatory reserves that were later in the early '50s, rationalized by being taken back to the profit and loss statement or to retained earnings; and from the mid-1960s there was a significant increase in the provision of such data as sales, and source and application of funds statements.

Since 1953, the Canadian Institute has prepared and published a bi-annual edition of Financial Reporting in Canada which describes in great detail the corporate reporting practices of approximately three hundred Canadian companies.[33] A tabulation comparable to Table 1,

---

[32]Acknowledged by the Associate Director of Research of the Canadian Institute, G. Mulcahy [1968, p. 104].

[33]Its counterpart in America is Accounting Trends and Techniques issued by the American Institute of Certified Public Accountants.

relating to the years prior to 1940, is given in Table 2, for the 1940-1970 period. The results of this tabulation, together with a scrutiny of each of the annual reports from 1940 to 1970 of the ten companies listed in Appendix B, constitute the bases of the following remarks.[34]

For a few items, such as the presentation of comparative statements and consolidated statements, the provision of the source and applications of funds statement and the disclosure of sales, the increase in information has been very notable. The increase in the latter item of data occurred since the mid-1960s and is very likely a function of the federal legislation of 1964 - 1965. While the classification and segregation of similar balance sheet items improved notably over the period, the detailed breakdown of such items as inventories and fixed assets was relatively poor. Similarly, while the tabulation indicates that nearly all companies provided the basis of valuation for their inventory, the 1968 edition of Financial Reporting in Canada indicates that only 77 percent described the basis of "market" and a mere 17 percent described the basis of "cost". The latter anachronism may be ascribed to the 1957 Institute bulletin which permitted the term "cost" to be used when the method of determining cost did not "differ materially from recent cost" [Canadian Institute of Chartered Accountants, Bulletin #14, 1957, p. 31]. The only extensive evidence located of the "cost" methods used by Canadian firms was obtained from a Dominion Bureau of Statistics survey done in 1949. Of 414 firms, approximately 25 percent used specific identification, 20 percent used FIFO, 48 percent used average cost, and 4 percent used LIFO [Dominion Bureau . . . , 1949].

A very notable increase, which is not clearly evident from Table 2, took place in the amount of information being conveyed in financial statement footnotes. The increase in number of footnotes in each set of financial statements tended to rise in the early and mid-1950s. By the 1960s most firms had at least seven or eight footnotes. (The financial statements of Consolidated Paper Corporation Limited in 1966 occupy four pages, while the twenty-four notes appended to the statements occupy

---

[34]There is an abundance of available corporate annual reports for the years 1940 to 1970. Most university libraries have collections of them, and since 1960, one hundred annual reports are available on microfilm. Therefore Appendix D includes only one, not atypical, example of the 1940s.

TABLE 2

ANALYSIS OF FINANCIAL STATEMENT DISCLOSURE, 1950 - 1970

Year	1953	1962 (% of companies)	1968
All statements in comparative form	34	68	96
Classification and segregation of current assets, fixed assets and current liabilities	95	a	a
Separation of:			
- depreciable and non-depreciable fixed assets	41	44	57
- inventory components	10	14	31
Depreciation deducted from fixed assets	86	90	99
Companies presenting some footnotes	78[b]	86	98
Valuation bases indicated for:			
- accounts receivable	83	68	27
- inventories (cost or otherwise)	95	100	100
- fixed assets	93	99	98
Some indication of fixed asset appraisal	31	22	14
Profit and Loss:			
- separate statement	75	74	71
- combined with retained earnings statement	24	25	28
- disclosure of sales	7	37	91
- disclosure of cost of sales	5	25	32
- some type of segment reporting	N/A	N/A	15
Inappropriate using of the term "reserve"	44	3	N/A
Extraordinary and non-recurring items shown before profit or loss for period	29[c]	32	31
Source and Application of Fund Statement	14	31	95
Complete consolidated financial statements provided	39	72	84

[a]No longer presented. Can be assumed to be 100 percent.

[b]For 1957. 1953 data unavailable.

[c]For 1955. 1953 data unavailable.

Source: Relevant years of Financial Reporting in Canada (Toronto: The Canadian Institute of Chartered Accountants). The number of companies included in the survey for the years 1953, 1962 and 1968 are 275, 300 and 325 respectively.

seven and one-half pages!) The proliferation of footnotes is likely a function of the Ontario legislation of 1953, the federal legislation of 1964 - 1965 and the Canadian Institute disclosure bulletins of 1957 and 1964 - all of which specified in increasing numbers the items that should be disclosed in footnotes. A good number of the footnotes also included the details of what had heretofore been given in financial statements proper. This transference, particularly with regard to the details of long-term indebtedness, capital stock, inventories, investments and fixed assets, allowed the presentation of the balance sheet to be aggregated and therefore greatly simplified.[35]

Table 2 indicates that the majority of Canadian firms exclude extraordinary items from the calculation of the profit or loss for the period. This treatment, which diverges notably from that of the American, may be because of the inconsistency of the Canadian Institute bulletins in 1957 and 1964 - the former indicating that it was unimportant where such items were placed as long as they were disclosed, and the latter indicating a preference for the current operating concept. The effect of the recommendation in 1968 for the all-inclusive approach had not as of 1970, had an opportunity to be reflected in the evidence available. The difference in the Canadian and American treatment of extraordinary items may have also been influenced by the Securities and Exchange Commission's long-standing preference for the all-inclusive approach.

The scrutiny of each of the financial statements of ten companies for the years 1940 to 1970 confirmed many of the foregoing observations. In addition, that scrutiny revealed the great concern that existed in the 1940s for the uncertainty caused by the war and the strong increases in prices following the war. All ten companies charged to income, amounts (sometimes not disclosed!) labelled as "reserve for future possible decline in inventory value," or "reserve for contingencies" or "extra depreciation for increased cost of replacements."[36] The Excess Profits

---

[35]See, for details of the most common type of footnotes, <u>Financial Reporting in Canada</u> [The Canadian Institute of Chartered Accountants, 1969, p. 123].

[36]See additional commentary on anticipatory and precautionary reserves by J. H. Thompson [1948, pp. 239-243].

Tax Act which permitted companies to deduct a reserve from inventory beyond that which was needed to reduce the inventory to the lower of cost or market undoubtedly abetted such treatment. Generally, the reserves were rationalized in the early 1950s by being taken back into income or into retained earnings. The concern for inflation and the increased cost of replacements was reflected in the directors' reports:

> Because of the great advance in prices which has taken place during the past four years, your directors considered it advisable to establish reserves against a possible decline in the market value of supplies, for the greatly increased cost of replacement of worn out and obsolete equipment where such is necessary and for other needs. [Ontario Steel Products Co. Ltd. Annual Report, 1948.]

And again:

> The decreased purchasing power of the dollar has resulted in a substantial increase in the cost of replacement of plant and equipment. Normal depreciation is based on the original cost of fixed assets but is insufficient in an inflationary period to cover replacement of that portion of plant and equipment being consumed annually through production of the Company's products.
>
> Recognizing as an element of cost the annual additional loss in the value of fixed assets over and above allowable depreciation based on original cost, and having regard for cost of indispensable replacements at much higher levels, your Directors decided it was essential to set aside a reserve of $500,000 from current earnings. [Canada and Dominion Sugar Co. Ltd. Annual Report, 1948.]

More than a decade later, in 1961, the Imperial Tobacco Company of Canada Limited, recorded an appraisal of its fixed assets in the records because "a greatly improved measure of the depreciation requirements necessary to meet current replacement cost of assets concerned will be known and the erosion of real capital will be prevented," and secondly "a true concept of the value of the shareholders' investment in current dollars will be available, which is not the case where assets are shown at historic cost" [Imperial Tobacco Company of Canada Limited Annual Report, 1961]. In 1962, Canada and Dominion Sugar Company Limited also reflected an appraisal increase. As Table 2 indicates, it should be noted that Canada has had a limited tradition - as opposed to America where no divergence from historical cost occurs - of recording appraisals in the records. The reason for the differences between the two countries may be that there has been no Securities and Exchange Commission to prevent this treatment.[37]

It has sometimes been suggested that those Canadian companies that are listed on the New York Stock Exchange will increase the information content in their annual corporate reports. Though general evidence on this proposition is unavailable, it was noted that one such company, Distillers Corporation Seagram Limited, was included in the sample of ten companies examined. As early as 1944, this company provided ten explanatory footnotes to the financial statements; however, it was not until 1966 and 1967 that it introduced comparative statements and source and application of funds statements.[38]

In summary, the information presented in corporate annual reports during the period was vastly greater than that provided in the previous period. Much of the information increase related to the notes to the financial statements, the elaboration of the sales in the profit and loss statement and the provision of the source and application of funds statement. In turn, much of this arose in the mid-1950s and mid-1960s-a good portion of it coincidental in time with corporate legislation.

Summary of the Evolution of Financial Statements 1900 - 1970

Canadian corporate financial statements of 1970 differ markedly from those of the first decade of the century. The statements before 1910, while occasionally similar in form, provide nothing like the quantity of information now regarded as necessary. Classification and segregation of balance sheet data were beginning to be established about the time of World War I, as was the provision of consolidated statements. The 1934 - 1935 federal legislation enforced disclosure of valuation practices. Prior to the mid-1930s, the record of corporate operations for a period of time was generally disclosed in a statement called the "profit and loss account." This statement was little more than the present day retained earnings statement with the additional inclusion of interest revenue and expense, depreciation and taxes. The 1934 - 1935

[37]As happened to United States Steel Corporation in the late 1940s.

[38]No studies of the differences or similarities between Canadian Companies listed on American exchanges and those not listed were located.

legislation provided the impetus to separate this statement into its two components and to increase the detail being provided in that part pertaining to the current operations. The all-inclusive and current operating concepts of income were not really a point of dispute until that separation took place. When it did, Canadian practice has exhibited preference for the current operating concept together with significant inconsistencies in the handling of extraordinary items. Increasing use of footnotes began to arise in the mid-1950s and their proliferation was largely a function of the requirements of the Canadian Institute recommendations and the 1953 Ontario legislation together with a desire to simplify the body of the financial statements. Disclosure of greater operating detail such as sales and source and application of funds, while long advocated by certain academics, did not become something stronger than "desirable" by the Institute until the early 1960 period. Legislation in 1964 - 1965 again provided some of the immediate impetus for disclosure.

Most of the first federal legislation of 1917 had been anticipated by corporate practices of the time. This may have been partly due to the earlier Ontario legislation of 1907. As outlined in the preceding paragraph, the effect of the federal legislation of 1934 - 1935 and 1964 - 1965 was not insignificant. It should be noted that the latter legislation, as it relates to financial statement disclosure, was almost a direct copy of the Ontario legislation of 1953 (which in turn was based almost wholly upon Institute recommendations!). The changes in corporate practices that resulted from changes in the various companies acts illustrate that legislation can and does go beyond the standards of good average practice. This pattern may continue as the demands of the public are more promptly reflected in legislation and where those demands relate to areas of concern for which generally accepted accounting principles have not been resolved. It was noted that since mid-1960 there has been increasing concern for the restriction of acceptable accounting practices as opposed to their mere disclosure. Two particular financial scandals-one English, the Royal Mail Steam Packet case of 1930, and the other Canadian, the Atlantic Acceptance Corporation case of 1965 - served to dramatize the status of the law. The former together with the corporate and economic difficulties of the early 1930s influenced the content and timing of the 1934 - 1935 federal legislation; the latter, though having extremely broad ramifications, was not directly related to the post 1965 legislation that pertains to the financial statement changes which are considered here.

The Canadian Institute of Chartered Accountants has been the acknowledged leader in the Canadian accounting profession. Almost all of the existing legislation relating to financial statement disclosure is a direct copy of Institute recommendations. That national leadership mantle was, to a great extent, assumed in the 1930s when the Institute started its policy of commenting on the adequacy of corporate legislation and later in the 1940s when it initiated its concern for research and financial statement disclosure recommendations. Not unexpectedly, some groups - particularly that academic triumvirate, Professors Smails, Ashley and Smyth - have been ahead (earlier and more vocally) of the Institute's recommendations; however, in other instances in the late 1960s, the Institute has been embarrassed by either the inability to resolve generally accepted accounting principles or the inability to anticipate areas of legislative concern. This situation, of course, is not unlike that of America. The Institute in the latter country has provided since the 1930s, apart from certain aspects of the legislative tradition inherited from England, the prototype for much of the Canadian Institute's recommendations and organization. The relative proximity, articulateness, size and resources of the American Institute are so enormous that the appropriateness of some of the activities of the Canadian Institute is sometimes challenged. Similarly that country's Securities and Exchange Commission has been mirrored in the Ontario Securities Commission and just as the former has provided a spur for the American Institute, the latter together with other corporate legislation may well do the same for the Canadian Institute.

CHAPTER VI
THE EVOLUTION OF DEPRECIATION

Purpose

The purpose of this chapter is to describe the evolution of the depreciation concept in Canada from 1900 to the present. Sources of information include the academic, financial and professional literature, the depreciation conventions adopted by the Department of National Revenue (the tax department) and a review of the actual corporate practices of Canadian companies. The influence of the tax department on depreciation practices has been both profound and pervasive. The attempt here will be to comment on certain selected tax conventions that have had significant influence. No attempt is made to be encyclopedic in this regard.

Professional and Academic Commentary on Depreciation Theory

The Concepts of Depreciation

Early depreciation theory evolved out of a concern for the inter-related concepts of capital maintenance, asset replacement and dividend distribution [Yamey, 1961, p. 758]. It was only by 1920, when the cost basis of recording fixed assets had become firmly established, that there began to evolve a coherent cost (original) allocation concept of depreciation. In the 1930s this latter concept of depreciation had become established - even though this same period displayed as much variety in its depreciation practices as the very early 1900s.

Much of the early literature was devoted to whether depreciation related to asset replacement and also to dispelling such practices as considering depreciation an appropriation of profits and allowing expenditures on renewals and betterments as well as appreciation of property to take the place of depreciation. Fleming, in 1892 [p. 277], indicated that the purpose of plant depreciation "is to meet writing off a percentage from the value of the plant according to the time it will last, or provide for the investing of a sinking fund that will replace the plant when worn out." He goes on to ascribe the causes of depreciation to wear and tear and obsolescence. Eddis[1] and Tindall seem to suggest an appropriation concept:

> That every manufacturer should set a certain sum aside out of his profits every year to provide for depreciation or deterioration of buildings, machinery and plant, is universally admitted. [Eddis and Tindall, 1904, p. 153.]

They also suggest that "depreciation is supposed to build up a fund to replace the asset when it is worn out" [p. 154] and that with regard to machinery "probably the wisest course is to have all machinery revalued every five years, and readjust the reserves or the amount written off accordingly" [p. 156].[2] Eddis himself, at an earlier time, in Manual for Accountants, a compendium of questions and solutions for the examinations of the Institute of Chartered Accountants of Ontario, was careful to distinguish depreciation from changes in market values:

> Depreciation is the lessening in the value in assets through wear and tear, or change in fashion, or affluxion of time, and must not be confused with fluctuation in value which also affects the value of such assets as land, stocks, etc. [Eddis, 1899, p. 140.]

J. D. Warde elaborated the significant relationships that exist between depreciation, dividends and capital maintenance:

> Unless this depreciation fund is carefully thought out, and its deductions from profit rigidly insisted upon, the shareholders of the corporation and perhaps the bondholders, may in the course of years find that their securities cover a property of little or no business value. If certain sums are not set aside to meet this depreciation, and if because of this, dividends are paid larger than would otherwise be the case, to the extent to which this is carried, the returns received by the shareholders are not dividends but their capital returned to them piecemeal. [Warde, 1900, p. 112.]

David Hoskins [1901, p. 127], principal of the British American Business College, Toronto, and Vice-president of the Institute of Chartered Accountants of Ontario, admonished the auditor to make sure

---

[1]A sometime president of the Institute of Chartered Accountants of Ontario and a noted author.

[2]The suggestion is similar to that of R. T. Sprouse and M. Moonitz, A Tentative Set of Broad Accounting Principles for Business Enterprises [1962, p. 57]. The former suggestion represents a comment from the twilight of "valuation" accounting of the nineteenth century while the latter represents what may be the dawn of the return to "valuation."

that "in checking the profit and loss account . . . the usual and proper deductions are made for wear and tear and depreciation . . ."

By the end of the second decade of the century, both the tax department and a committee of the accounting profession recognized original cost as the basis for the calculation of depreciation [Breadner, 1918, p. 108]. However, within the cost concept, inconsistencies and differences abounded concerning the purpose of depreciation. One can feel a certain hesitancy in accepting the depreciation concept in the remarks of a correspondent to The Canadian Chartered Accountant who, while he felt that depreciation should be charged in loss years was nevertheless sympathetic with the "reluctance of making a charge to operations for which no liability to an outside party exists."[3] Parton a former president of the Canadian Institute suggested that:

> Charging depreciation does not necessarily provide for the replacement of the wasting article - it simply means that there has been a decline in the value of certain assets; consequently, if the capital is to be kept intact, there must be an increase in some of the others. [Parton, 1911, pp. 10-11.]

Apedaile however continued to emphasize the replacement aspect - a theme which was to invariably reappear in times of sizable increases in prices:

> If the whole of the profits are withdrawn without providing for this loss [depreciation], monies will not have accumulated out of revenue during the life of the asset for the purpose of replacing the same, and consequently when such replacement becomes necessary, new capital will have to be found in order to do so. [Apedaile, 1916, p. 306.]

Even in the 1920s it was necessary to admonish the auditor to "ascertain that a reasonable depreciation has been reserved for and should certainly not be put off with the time-worn excuse that the appreciation of the land is looking after the depreciation of the buildings" [Bennett, 1922, p. 336].

By 1933, however, the cost allocation concept was being well expressed by Smails:

> Depreciation is not designed to adjust an asset to value, but is merely the cost of that portion of the total serviceability of the asset which - according to the best estimates available - has been used up to date. The balance sheet figure of cost, less

---

[3]Correspondence of T. W. S. in The Canadian Chartered Accountant [Vol. 4, April 1915, p. 288].

> depreciation to date, therefore, represents the original cost of the serviceability remaining in the asset. [Smails, 1933, p. 110.]

The classic statement, <u>An Introduction to Corporate Accounting Standards</u> [Paton and Littleton, 1940] has since served to reinforce the cost-allocation concept.

Sporadically, throughout the period 1920 to 1970, and invariably in times of substantial general price increases, the replacement notion of depreciation clashed with the cost allocation concept. The editorial notes of <u>The Canadian Chartered Accountant</u> in 1924 indicated that:

> . . . there is, however, a rapidly growing tendency to set up a basis on which depreciation will replace buildings and equipment at prices higher than those paid for them. The corporations operating on this basis believe that depreciation reserves are intended to replace the outlay for the property. ["Depreciation," 1924, p. 387.]

Professor R. G. H. Smails himself a proponent of cost allocation, toyed with, but rejected a notion similar to replacement, on pragmatic grounds:

> . . . the depreciation charge each year should be based on the cost of installing in that year a plant with a life capacity identical with the life capacity of the plant actually in use. The resultant profit or loss would be the true operating profit or loss having regard to changes in the price level and improvements in the arts. If adjustment of the depreciation so charged against operations was considered desirable for financial reasons, such adjustment would be made through surplus account.
>
> Practically however, this conclusion is of no value because of the insuperable difficulty of determining from year to year the cost of installing a plant of similar capacity. It might, however, indicate to the accountant the desirability of making rough adjustment for changes in the price level and improvements in the arts . . . [Smails, February, 1936, p. 148.]

Dean Thompson in commenting upon the setting up of precautionary and anticipatory reserves indicated that:

> Such reserves are provided as a cushion against the shock of a sudden decline in the level of prices or for the replacement of plant at prices far in excess of the original cost of the asset to be replaced, or for other purposes generally designated as contingencies. [Thompson, 1948, p. 239.]

However, the revised tax regulations of 1949 which permitted much more generous depreciation deductions took much of the sting out of the replacement cost argument.[4] Concern for depreciation since that time, but especially in the 1960s, has been a part of a broader concern for a more complete revision of all accounting data to reflect changes in general and specific prices.

The Methods of Depreciation

Between the years 1932 and 1954, the depreciation methods of Canadian companies tended to follow those methods viewed as acceptable by the tax department. This practice was so because between those years the maximum depreciation allowable for tax purposes was restricted to the amount charged in the financial statements, providing that it did not exceed the amount allowable under the rates laid down by the Department. These rates were based on the straight line method between 1932 and 1949 and on the diminishing balance method between 1949 and 1954. Prior to 1932 and subsequent to 1954, no correspondence between depreciation for book and tax purposes was required.

The early textbook writers displayed no great preference for, nor particular theory to support, the straight line method (commonly assumed to be most in use) over the diminishing balance method. Fleming's [1892, p. 277] illustration uses straight line; however, those of Eddis [1899, p. 157] use diminishing balance. Somewhat later Eddis and Tindall [1904, p. 155] imply the straight line method. These commentators generally attempted to suggest that the rate of depreciation would depend on the extent to which the asset was kept in good repair, but they did not offer theoretical support for one method or another. It was only later in 1916 that Apedaile [1916, p. 304] discussed at greater length the merits not only of the straight line and diminishing balance methods, but also of the annuity and sinking fund methods. He notes that the diminishing balance method is commonly used for plant, furniture and fixtures and that it has the merit that the total charge of depreciation and repairs and maintenance is more level over the years.

Smails and Walker in 1926 [pp. 118-120] elaborated in greater detail the various depreciation methods. While they admitted that the diminishing balance method was in common use for factory plant and

[4]As will be detailed in the section on taxes, a certain correspondence between depreciation for book and tax purposes was required.

equipment and that this method tended to equalize the total annual charge for depreciation and repairs, they stated that in most cases the straight line method "reflects the true position of affairs."

General testimony supports the contention that the straight line method of depreciation was used by virtually all Canadian companies from 1932 to 1949. A. Gilmour [1950, p. 276] mentioned that he was aware of only a few instances where the diminishing balance method was in use. A. Hamilton [1954, p. 206], as did others, attributed this to the force of the income tax regulations which, while permitting any reasonable and consistent method,[5] set a pattern of depreciation rates based on the straight line method as a maximum for tax purposes. Moreover, this straight line method was generally regarded, both as to method and rates, as being in conformity with good accounting principles.[6]

The 1949 tax regulations altered corporate depreciation practices drastically. The most significant feature was that the maximum depreciation for tax purposes (referred to by the tax department since 1949 as "capital cost allowance"), could not exceed certain prescribed rates calculated on the basis of the diminishing balance method. The provision existing since 1932 that the amount claimed for tax purposes must not exceed the amount recorded in the books of the company, continued in force.

Mr. Douglas Abbott [1954, p. 23], the Minister of Finance, suggested that for tax purposes the accounting concept of depreciation was being "thrown overboard" and a system of capital cost allowances adopted. It was rather odd that at the same time that the tax department was breaking the nexus between the concepts of depreciation for tax and book purposes, it would insist that the tax method be used in corporate records if the company were to claim maximum capital cost allowance. When this requirement was rescinded in 1954, the problem relating to tax allocation arose. The Canadian Institute had issued no statements on the

---

[5]As indicated by the Department of National Revenue, Special Field Auditor, R. Swift [1938, p. 387].

[6]The only commentator who disagreed with this was R. G. H. Smails who pointed out that in some instances the rates are inadequate. [Smails, 1933, p. 111.]

appropriateness of the capital cost allowance methods of depreciation;[7] however, it did recognize directly the corporate reporting problems that arise when the depreciation for book purposes differs from that of the capital cost allowance. Bulletin No. 10 of the Institute, Depreciation, Capital Cost Allowances and Income Taxes, recommended the deferred credit method of allocation, but also permitted the taxes payable (flow-through) method if differences for the year and the years to date were footnoted.[8] Bulletin No. 26 Accounting for Corporate Income Taxes took this alternative away, as of 1968. It should be noted, on this occasion, that the Canadian Institute position has been independent of, at variance with, and ahead of that of the American Institute. The Latter organization has moved from an acknowledgement of the liability concept of tax allocation in rare instances in 1954, to recognition of the general propriety of tax allocation in 1958, and finally to the deferred credit method in 1968.[9] The latter position had been the recommended but not exclusive procedure, of the Canadian Institute from 1954 to 1968.[10]

---

[7]However, as previously mentioned, there had been some tradition for the theory and practice of the genus of the method prior to this time.

[8]Actually, the same problem had arisen for some companies during the depression when the tax department set up depreciation at 50 percent of maximum rates, even though the companies charged no depreciation in their financial statements. [Bennett, 1942, p. 390.]

[9]See the following publications of the American Institute of Certified Public Accountants: Chapter 9C of Accounting Research Bulletin No. 43, Restatement and Revision of Accounting Research Bulletins, 1953; Accounting Research Bulletin No. 44, Declining Balance Depreciation, 1954; Accounting Research Bulletin No. 44 (Revised), Declining Balance Depreciation, 1958; Accounting Principles Board Opinion No. 11, Accounting for Income Taxes, 1967.

[10]Apart from whatever theoretical merit attaches to tax allocation, it (and therefore the Institute's recommendations) can be viewed as being essentially a compromise position in which under usual circumstances, less income will be reported than companies using the flow-through method and more income will be reported than those companies using capital cost allowance for book purposes.

Depreciation for Tax Purposes

To 1940

The first income tax act, the Income War Tax Act of 1917 [Canada, Statutes, C. 28, Sec. 3(1)(a)], allowed depreciation to be deducted in arriving at the determination of taxable income. The deduction was permitted in reasonable amounts at the discretion of the Minister of National Revenue. As a consequence, no hard and fast rules were published but certain traditions and procedures developed over time. Some of the more notable aspects were: though any reasonable method could be used, maximum rates of depreciation were set in terms of the straight line method [Swift, 1938, p. 387]; the method and rates of depreciation were in conformity with what were generally regarded as good accounting principles [Gilmour, 1945, p. 147; and "Comment and Opinion," February, 1950, p. 47]; no allowances were made for obsolescence; and no provisions existed for carrying losses forward or backward nor for recapture or terminal loss on disposition of assets [Davis, 1966, p. 20].

In 1928, in order "to prevent a taxpayer from indirectly carrying forward a loss by not claiming depreciation," a minimum of 50 percent of the normal depreciation allowances was deemed by the department to be taken.[11] In 1933, Regulation I commenced a period lasting until 1954 in which a certain correspondence between depreciation for books and tax purposes was required:

> The maximum depreciation allowable in any period shall be the amount incorporated in the profit and loss, surplus, or similar account in the usual book of record of the taxpayer . . . , provided the said amount shall not exceed the amount allowable under the rates laid down by the Income Tax Division. [Frears, 1947, p. 207.]

In 1935 the department instituted the 80 percent rule, which required that unless fixed assets were recorded in such a manner that depreciation on fully depreciated assets would be avoided, the department would insist that once accumulated depreciation reserves amounted to 80

---

[11]Letter to the author from D. R. Pook, Director General Tax Policy, Legislation Branch, Department of National Revenue, July 14, 1970.

percent of the cost of the assets, that depreciation be calculated at the normal rates but only on the diminished net base of 20 percent.[12]

Given the foregoing operating rules of the department, companies would generally tend to charge in their records the maximum amounts allowable for tax purposes, since to charge less would not reduce the current liability for taxes to the allowable minimum and to charge more would mean that some of the depreciation would be lost for future tax deduction purposes.[13] The absence of loss carry-forward provisions would generally tend to motivate companies to smooth expenses (including depreciation) over time so that the tax deduction aspect of any expense incurrence would not be lost.

The manner in which Regulation I was applied however, may be subject to some debate since it has been suggested by Gilmour [1950, p. 277] that "even after the assets had been fully written off the books of account, the department continued to allow depreciation until the cost of the asset was fully written off at the rates recognized by them."[14] If indeed this was the case, then companies would not necessarily tend to charge in their records the maximum amounts allowable for tax purposes. While this latter amount would constitute the minimum - since charging less would not reduce the current liability for taxes - it would not constitute the maximum since any excess of depreciation for book purposes over depreciation for tax purposes would not be lost for future tax deductibility. A study by C. B. Wade [1943, p. 435] lends some support

---

[12]Letter to the author from D. R. Pook, Director General Tax Policy, Legislation Branch, Department of National Revenue, July 14, 1970.

[13]Similarly, in years where profits were not sufficient to carry full depreciation, companies would want to charge off not more than that amount that would reduce taxable profits to zero and in years where cash losses were incurred companies would not want to charge off more than the minimum 50 percent. This is so because of the absence of loss carry-forward and carry back provisions.

[14]Confirmed by the author with A. W. Gilmour in correspondence dated September 10, 1970. In correspondence with Mr. I. W. Linton, Director, Tax Research Division, the latter stated that exceptions to Regulation I might well have existed since the depreciation allowable was at the discretion of the Minister of National Revenue and that "Mr. Gilmour was a senior official of the Taxation Division and would have been aware of the Departmental practice at that time." Correspondence with author dated August 24, 1970.

to this interpretation in circumstances where companies had either cash loss years or profits insufficient to absorb full depreciation. Wade indicated that in 1938 of forty-three such companies, twenty-four continued to charge full depreciation. On the other hand, if as Gilmour admits the Department's depreciation rates "were generally considered to be reasonably generous,"[15] then the likelihood of book depreciation exceeding tax depreciation would be reduced and in the general case, companies would tend to record for book purposes the maximum amounts of depreciation allowable for tax purposes.

1940 to 1970

Commencing in 1940, special (increased) depreciation was permitted on war contracts equipment and in 1944, double depreciation was allowed for these industries planning post-war expansion, conversion or modernization [Perry, 1955, pp. 607-610]. In 1942, the carrying forward of losses (including depreciation) was permitted and in 1944 this provision was extended to three years forward and one year back. The latter provisions would have taken away any expense smoothing motivation. In 1949 the basis of calculating depreciation was revised significantly [Canada, Statutes, C. 25, Secs. 7 and 8]. Provisions for obsolescence, for recapture and terminal loss were introduced. No longer was there any requirement to justify that the depreciation for tax purposes was a necessary and proper charge [Richardson, 1953, p. 211]. In fact, the accounting concept of depreciation was replaced by the new concept (and even the wording!) of "capital cost allowances." Henceforth, the granting and withholding of capital cost allowance would be as much a function of general fiscal policy as it was of the need to amortize corporate fixed assets against corporate revenue. The method of determining the calculation was on the diminishing balance basis and by existing depreciation standards the maximum rates, to which all were entitled, were regarded as quite generous. Additionally, capital cost allowance was permitted on assets under construction and a full year's allowance permitted on assets purchased any time within the fiscal year.

---

[15]A. W. Gilmour, in testimony to the Newfoundland Board of Commissioners of Public Utilities concerning the Avalon Telephone Company Limited, August 25, 1967, p. 14. Copy obtained from Clarkson Gordon & Co., Montreal.

Consistent with previous regulations, the department insisted that the capital cost allowance could not exceed the depreciation taken on the company's books [Canada, "The Income Tax Regulations, P.C. 6471," 1949, p. 2209]. This requirement was rescinded only after a torrent of protest in 1954 ["Comment and Opinion," 1954, pp. 1-2]. In the 1960s, allowances for capital cost allowance became increasingly a function of government fiscal policy as write-offs over so short a period as two years were initiated under certain conditions.[16] Some of these conditions related to the manufacturing of new products, the modernization of old equipment, the investment in economically depressed areas and the degree of foreign ownership in the company [Davis, 1966, pp. 44-47]. The 1969 white paper on taxation indicated that the capital cost allowance rates may be too generous and that they should be reviewed [Benson, 1969, p. 62].

In retrospect, two things may be said of the revised depreciation regulations. Firstly, they have usually been regarded as the impetus for companies to change from straight line to the diminishing balance method of depreciating. Alternatively, the regulations, prior to 1949, could be viewed as the stumbling block that prevented companies from moving to the diminishing balance method before that date. Certainly the diminishing balance method had been used in a few instances and the uncertainty of the war years and the concern for inflation that followed the war years made management far more anxious to rationalize an increased charge for depreciation. Secondly, the requirement that the company's book and tax depreciation correspond was in the tradition of the tax department. This correspondence only became a problem when the revised regulations induced companies to charge more in their books than they otherwise would in order to reduce the current liability for taxes. This requirement for correspondence, together with the asset pool method of diminishing balance, also made the administration of the tax regulations easier for

---

[16]Instances also existed, for brief periods of time commencing in 1951 and again in 1966, in which capital cost allowances were either deferred or diminished on certain newly-acquired assets. The former instance gave rise to the Canadian Institute Bulletin No. 8, Deferred Depreciation in which accountants were reminded that depreciation for tax purposes was not to be confused with depreciation for book purposes. The fact that this kind of statement needed to be handed down is itself commentary on the influence of taxation on corporate depreciation practices.

the department. The 1949 correspondence requirement need not therefore be viewed as a commentary on the inability of the accounting profession to be influential in this matter.[17] On the other hand, the rescinding of the correspondence requirement in 1954 can be viewed as a measure of the influence of the accounting profession, since it meant that the department was breaking with a fairly long-established tradition.

Corporate Depreciation Practices

To 1940

Though the broad concept of depreciation was fairly generally accepted by 1917, the actual depreciation practices of Canadian companies, prior to 1920, were extremely varied. The review of the sample ten companies (see Appendix B) indicated that acceptance of a methodical fixed-asset amortization policy was somewhat slow and evolutionary. Only one of the ten companies examined did not record depreciation or what the author has interpreted as its equivalent (e.g. "amounts written off fixed assets or allowance for plant reserve") by 1910;[18] however, the amount of depreciation was often a function of the amounts of profits available.[19] Similarly, several companies confused the concept of depreciation with expenditures on renewals. According to the president of Dominion Iron and Steel Company Limited in 1909, wear and tear is made good by renewals and rebuilding "so that the property is always kept practically in as good condition as new."[20] The audit report of Ogilvie Flour Mills

---

[17]Briefs were presented by the Canadian Institute in 1946 and 1948. ["Brief to Senate Committee," 1946, pp. 194-218; and "Recommendations on Bill 454," 1948, pp. 265-312.] This latter brief recommended that tax regulations should be broad enough to permit various methods of depreciation when the circumstances so demanded. It went on to advocate that for purposes of government fiscal policy, the concept of tax credits be used rather than the adjusting of tax depreciation.

[18]The exception being Ogilvie Flour Mills Company Limited which commenced the practice in 1917, coincident with the Income War Tax Act.

[19]See, for example, Canadian General Electric Company Limited Annual Reports, 1905 to 1918; Canada Cycle and Motor Company Limited Annual Report, 1914; and Montreal Cottons Limited Annual Report, 1915.

[20]See also comments by A. K. Fisk. "It is further a well known fact that many manufacturers ignore the item of depreciation altogether and comfort themselves with the fact that all renewals, improvements and

Company Limited in 1904 indicated that "there is no provision for general depreciation as the properties stand on the books at figures considerably under those shown by recent expert valuation." In some instances the depreciation taken was credited directly to the asset account; in other instances, though depreciation was taken, the actual amount was not indicated. After a number of years of having "the inventory of the assets taken at a most conservative valuation before estimating profits, in addition to the precaution of writing off the usual percentage for depreciation" the Canadian General Electric Company Limited, in the low-profit year of 1914, indicated that "fortunately the conservative policy that has been pursued during prosperous years of accumulating large reserves and of writing down in our books of account of both capital and current assets to a minimum value, has placed the company in an exceptionally strong financial position." In no instances was there noted any comment in the financial statements concerning the method of depreciation being used.

The widespread revision of the depreciation provisions in the 1949 tax act gave rise to a number of depreciation and tax reviews in the literature. The comments by J. G. Glassco were not uncommon:

> It is fair to say that before income tax, the average businessman regarded the whole subject of depreciation as academic in the extreme and the fact is that many, probably the great majority of our larger corporations, refrained from adopting depreciation prior to the first great war. There is nothing reprehensible in their sudden change of policy but it is unfortunate that the influence of income tax upon depreciation did not cease at that point. [Glassco, 1948, p. 175.]

It has been noted that nine of the ten companies whose financial statements were examined recorded depreciation prior to 1910. Again, for the sixty-three "industrial" companies listed in The Annual Financial Review -Canadian of 1916,[21] thirty-two recorded depreciation in the profit and loss account in both 1915 and 1919, thirteen recorded depreciation in neither year, thirteen recorded depreciation in 1919 but not in 1915, and

---

replacements are paid for out of the manufacturing account." [Fisk, 1914, p. 173.]

[21]This edition would incorporate corporate annual reports ending in 1915.

the remaining five recorded depreciation in 1915 but not in 1919.[22] What the income tax act may well have done, however, is to make more methodical the depreciation when it was being charged. This indeed is likely to have taken place in years of profits after 1932 when the tax regulations required some correspondence between tax and book depreciation.

The practice of not charging depreciation in loss or less-profitable years was the most characteristic feature that was carried forward to the 1920 - 1940 period from the earlier two decades. At least six of the ten corporate financial statements examined failed to record depreciation under these circumstances.[23] However, less rationalizing of this lack of depreciation was noted in the sample companies relative to similar omissions in the earlier two decades. On the other hand, a study in 1935 by E. V. C. Smith [1935, pp. 75-86] of 187 companies for the years 1930 to 1934 revealed that in many instances much the same reasoning was being used. This study indicated that such practices as the augmenting of accumulated depreciation by transfers from surplus or other reserve accounts and the regarding of depreciation as an appropriation of profits to be made relative to the availability of profits, were not uncommon. The reasons given for the failure to record depreciation were that the charges to repairs were sufficient to allow for depreciation, that existing depreciation reserves were adequate or, more simply, that sufficient profits were unavailable.

The tax department requirement of 1933, which required some correspondence of book and tax depreciation likely served to regularize depreciation charges for companies having profits since that time. C. B. Wade [1943, p. 435], in a study of 199 public companies for the years 1934 to 1940 stated "with a few minor exceptions no corporation reduced its depreciation charges in any substantial amount so long as its earnings before depreciation were sufficient to absorb the usual amounts

---

[22]Glassco's comment is also supported by the Commissioner of Taxation, R. W. Breadner [1918, p. 107]. Possibly the allegation relates to non-large, non-public Canadian companies.

[23]Canadian Locomotive Company Limited, 1923 - 1925, 1935 - 1936; Brandram Henderson Limited, 1935 - 1936; Cockshutt Plow Company Limited, 1934; Dominion Rubber Company Limited, 1922; Penmans Limited, 1931-1932; Tooke Bros. Limited, 1933 - 1937.

of depreciation - this in spite of wide fluctuations in net income."[24] Moreover, for this period, Wade felt that the amounts being charged were such as to indicate that the straight line method of depreciation was being used. Though some writing-down of assets during the depression seemed to be related to the desire to distribute dividends, no instances were noted in either the ten sample companies or in the commentaries by Smith, Wade or Ashley wherein the concern for dividend distribution was related to foregoing the normal depreciation charge. The only commentary available on this point related to a very slight discussion of two English legal cases by Ashley [1931, p. 86] and the admonition of Smails [1933, pp. 211-212] to follow the prescription of Masten and Frazer [1929, pp. 551-552] to make sure that depreciation was being charged before dividends were declared.

1940 - 1970

The 1949 tax depreciation revision caused a notable change in the depreciation practices of Canadian companies. J. Kehler [1970, p. 23] reported that of seventy-eight companies, forty-seven altered their depreciation practices within three years to conform with the tax department, and thirty-one either gave no indication or inadequate indication of their depreciation policies. What this meant largely was that, by simple tax fiat, the depreciation policies of possibly the majority of Canadian companies changed dramatically from straight line to the diminishing balance method. Undoubtedly the path for higher depreciation charges had been well paved by the special and double depreciation allowances of the tax department between 1940 and 1948 and the general rise in post-war prices. The commentary in the Annual Report of Dominion Bridge Company Limited for 1948 indicated that "as the normal provision for depreciation is based on the original cost of fixed assets, your directors believe that it is prudent to give some recognition to this

[24] C. A. Ashley performed a much less comprehensive study for the years 1936 to 1940 noting that "some companies, particularly those with fairly steady profits, make almost constant annual changes for depreciation; many companies make changes which vary very considerably, and the variation often has a direct relation to the profits and, as far as can be determined, . . . this variation is not justified by changes in fixed assets." [Ashley, 1942, p. 293.]

increase in the cost of replacements . . . [by providing] an additional amount . . . out of current earnings."

Similarly, the enormous effect of the tax department was again felt in 1954 when the correspondence requirement was rescinded. Kehler [1970, p. 32] indicated that approximately twenty-seven of the forty-seven companies that changed depreciation policies because of the 1949 regulations, subsequently changed their policies again owing to the 1954 regulation. It would seem therefore that of this group of forty-seven companies, twenty wished to remain on the newly introduced capital cost allowance method while twenty-seven wanted to revert to straight line. No studies are available to indicate the impact on reported profits of the depreciation changes in 1949 or 1954. Possibly the single most significant change occurred with Aluminum Limited which reverted to straight line depreciation in 1954 and in the process put through its records a reduction of accumulated depreciation of seventy-six million, an increase of thirty-four million in deferred taxes arising from allocation and an increase in earned surplus of forty-two million. This latter figure reflected what the company felt to be an underestimation of profits for the four years 1950 to 1953 - representing approximately 40 percent of reported net profits for those years.

Various issues of Financial Reporting in Canada indicate the extent of the influence of the material differences between depreciation and capital cost allowance. In 1956, of three hundred companies, sixty-four indicated the use of the tax allocation or the taxes payable method [Canadian Institute . . . , 1957, p. 95]. In 1968, of three hundred and twenty-five companies, two hundred and sixty-four used the tax allocation or taxes payable method - with barely fifty using the latter [Canadian Institute . . . , 1969, p. 107]. Unfortunately, relatively few companies indicated their actual method of depreciation; though Financial Reporting in Canada indicates that 11 percent in 1959 and 21 percent in 1968 did so, the actual methods used are not reported by this publication.

Summary

Not surprisingly, the tax regulations have had an enormous effect on the depreciation practices of Canadian companies. Though the first income tax acts of World War I did not introduce the concept of depreciation to many large public companies, they may have served to make more methodical and regular its calculation. Between 1932 and 1954, tax requirements forced a certain correspondence between book and tax depreciation, which meant that between those years most companies used the straight line method of depreciation and between 1949 and 1954 most companies began to use the tax department version of the diminishing balance method. The rescinding of the correspondence requirement in 1954 again led many companies to change their depreciation methods.

Since 1950, as the capital cost allowance rules of the tax department have increasingly become a medium of government fiscal policy, the financial need to minimize the current tax liability together with the desire to reflect the depreciation of assets in an acceptable accounting fashion, have given rise to the tax allocation problem. The Canadian Institute, while recommending tax allocation, also permitted the taxes payable (i.e. flow-through) method between 1954 and 1967.[25] Beginning in 1968, the latter alternative was removed. Unfortunately no studies exist which attempt to measure the impact of tax allocation on profits[26] - other than an indication of the number of companies using the deferred credit or taxes payable methods as reported in Financial Reporting in Canada. With or without the correspondence of tax and book depreciation, the tax department by the very fact that it does not accept the company depreciation charge, but rather permits a greater or smaller deduction based upon its own rules, continues to influence corporate reporting practices - the expression of this influence being the large tax deferral charges and credits existing in most Canadian corporate financial statements.

---

[25]The Canadian Institute has always regarded the deferred credit method rather than the liability method of tax allocation as preferable. The former method emphasizes the deferral to subsequent periods of the tax effects of current timing differences in amounts based on existing tax rates; whereas, the latter emphasizes the accrual of the tax effects of current timing differences in amounts based upon anticipated tax rates.

[26]As does the American study Is Generally Accepted Accounting for Income Taxes Possibly Misleading Investors? by Price Waterhouse & Co. in 1967.

CHAPTER VII
SUMMARY

The purpose of this study has been to document the changes and to inquire into the background and processes that have influenced changes in selected annual corporate reporting practices in Canada from 1900 to 1970. The selected practices included: the evolution of the mandatory audit and the content of the auditor's standard report; the evolution of the balance sheet and the profit and loss statement including content, classification and general valuation base; the evolution of the earned surplus statement, footnotes to financial statements, secret reserves and extraordinary items - inasmuch as they bear upon the balance sheet and the profit and loss statement; and lastly, the evolution of corporate depreciation practices. These particular practices were chosen for observation because they involve important accounting concepts and because it was thought that they would reveal the various influences that have shaped corporate reporting practices in Canada over the years.

Various sources of evidence have been used. The study has continually anchored itself in actual reported corporate data. This has been done by reviewing a sample of annual financial statements for each year from 1900 to 1970. Test readings of corporate reporting practices were also made approximately every ten years throughout this period. In addition, whenever encountered, evidence in the literature from various studies and compilations have been included in the analysis. Other evidence includes various incorporating and regulating statutes, debates of the Senate and House of Commons, proceedings of governmental committee hearings, reports of government-appointed inquiries, briefs and submissions made by various parties to committees of inquiry, and lastly, the considerable professional, academic and financial literature. The path of change has been charted as a somewhat slow, evolutionary one-influenced in varying degrees by legislation, instances of corporate malfeasance, English and American institutions, and the accounting profession itself, and pressures from the public emanating in the financial press. In turn, these influences have taken place within an economic and social environment wherein there has come to be an increasing recognition of business as an acceptable and responsible social institution and wherein the ready means of communication exist such that the various publics of business can influence business and business practices.

Early Ontario and federal legislation in 1907 and 1917 was strongly influenced from England. That tradition involved a concern for the investor and a willingness to require the price of corporate disclosure and audit for the conferred benefit of limited liability. The expression of this tradition has been centered in the provision of minimum disclosure requirements in the various Canadian companies acts over time which like their English models - but unlike the later American Securities Acts - established no institutions to review corporate annual reports nor to set accounting principles. This tradition has persisted up to the present time, with only the activities of the Ontario Securities Commission, reflecting since 1966 something of a unique but possibly portentous exception.

The examination of actual financial statements has indicated that legislation has been on some occasions, and with regard to some matters, something more than a setting down of good existing corporate practices The federal act of 1917 may have been largely anticipated by corporate practices (possibly because of the earlier Ontario Act of 1907); however, the legislation of 1934 did alter valuation, earned surplus, and profit and loss presentation; and similarly the 1964 - 1965 legislation did alter the presentation of profit and loss information. Running parallel in time but largely unrelated, the various income tax acts since 1917 have had an enormous effect on the depreciation practices of Canadian companies. This influence was particularly strong during the 1933 to 1954 period in which a certain correspondence between tax and book depreciation was required. While the tax department no longer requires that correspondence, its concern for capital cost allowance as an instrument to effect government fiscal policy has given rise to the deferred tax allocation problem - the extent of which is reflected in the sizable deferred taxes accounts that now exist on a majority of Canadian corporate financial statements.

The extent to which financial scandals and corporate malfeasance in Canada have been prime movers in changes in the selected corporate practices that this study has examined is debatable. Certainly much of the concern for scandal has been of a vicarious nature. The financial and professional literature has dwelt at enormous length on such notable non-Canadian scandals as the English Royal Mail Steam Packet case and the American McKesson & Robbins case. Apart from the banking failures in the first two decades of the century and the financial failures of the mid-1960 period, Canada has been remarkably free of this order of grand notoriety. Uncertainty concerning the influence of Canadian financial scandals on annual corporate reporting practices also exists because the scandals that have existed related as much - or even more - to inappropriate corporate promotion and organization as it did to a lack of adequate financial statement reporting practices. Similarly, though the concern for scandals influenced the timing and content of the 1934 legislation, the mood for reform expressed in the 1964 - 1965 federal legislation and the 1966 Ontario Securities Act was already under way by the time the Atlantic Acceptance debacle broke across the Canadian financial scene. It should be noted here that the financial press, in particular The Financial Post, has been conspicuous in its attempts over the years to improve annual corporate reporting practices. A great deal of effort has also been spent by some leaders in the accounting profession, the accounting profession itself, and some of the accounting and financial academics to do likewise. It may be that the most important contribution of the Canadian academic has been in this regard.

Apart from the legal tradition previously mentioned, the English influence was felt in the ever-present Canadian awareness of the English profession's literature and practice. However these sources of influence waned as the relative size of the American investment in Canada increased - so that by the mid-1930 period the proximity and articulateness of the American Institute and of American academic contributions were having a relatively much greater effect on the Canadian scene. That influence has grown to such proportions that it poses an enormous problem for the Canadian accounting profession. If their research activities go beyond what are uniquely Canadian problems, their efforts can be considered to be redundant, or at least inefficient, in relation to the economies of scale achievable in these matters in America. On the other hand, dealing with only peculiarly Canadian problems is a constraint which both acknowledges and aggravates the dependence on America for the more general accounting theory.

Both the Ontario and Canadian Institutes of Chartered Accountants have been formative in their influence on Canadian accounting practices. From its early organization through the last two decades of the nineteenth century and the first two decades of the twentieth century, the Ontario Institute gave strong and prestigious leadership. The efforts of the Canadian Institute have been more notable since the 1930 period. It was largely at this time that that body began to accept the increasing and arduous burden of representing the profession nationally and of promoting the improvement in corporate reporting standards. That acceptance of professional responsibility expressed itself chiefly in the accounting bulletins which commenced in 1946. It has been noted that at two of the most fateful junctures in the evolution of accounting practices - 1907 and 1953 - the Ontario Institute has virtually written the Ontario legislation and the latter, on both occasions but with a ten year time lag, has been copied by the legislation at the federal level.

It is likely that the duties and tasks of the Canadian Institute will be even more time-consuming and burdensome in the future. Firstly, it has been noted that since mid-1960 much more attention has been paid by the financial community in narrowing the range of acceptable accounting alternatives as opposed to merely ensuring the disclosure of those alternatives that were being used. The increasing willingness of governments to respond to such demands will require much more research- a burden which will be transferred back on to the profession. This narrowing of the range of acceptable alternatives has never proved to be an easy task and its difficulty is compounded as the increasing rate of price changes aggravates the difference between historical and current cost recording. Secondly, as the legislation becomes increasingly identified with the professional recommendations, any inadequacies in such legislation will redound directly to the discredit of the profession. The willingness of such governmental agencies as the Ontario Securities Commission to provide guidelines where the profession has not already done so has also been noted.

The foregoing summary represents the most notable influences that have affected, since 1900, the annual corporate reporting practices selected for examination for this study. More particularized summaries are given at the end of Chapter II on auditing, Chapter V on financial statement practices and Chapter VI on depreciation and taxes.

BIBLIOGRAPHY

BIBLIOGRAPHY

Abbott, D. "Corporation Tax Policy." Canadian Tax Journal, Vol. 2 (February, 1954), pp. 20-25.

Accountants International Study Group. The Independent Auditor's Reporting Standards in Three Nations. Toronto: The Canadian Institute of Chartered Accountants, 1969.

"Accounting Terminology." Editorial, The Canadian Chartered Accountant, Vol. 25 (October, 1934), pp. 298-300.

"A Law for Amateurs." The Globe and Mail, May 18, 1968, p. 5.

American Accounting Association. "Report of the Committee on Accounting History." The Accounting Review, Supplement to Vol. 45, pp. 53-64. Evanston, Illinois: American Accounting Association, 1970, pp. 53-64.

American Institute of Accountants. Audits of Corporate Accounts. New York: American Institute of Accountants, 1934.

________. Extensions of Auditing Procedure. New York: American Institute of Accountants, 1939.

________. The Revised S.E.C. Rule on Accountants' Certificates. New York: American Institute of Accountants, 1941.

________. Revision in Short-Form Accountant's Report or Certificate. New York: American Institute of Accountants, 1948.

Annual Financial Review - Canadian, The. Toronto: Houston's Standard Publications, 1901 to 1941.

"Annual Meeting." The Canadian Chartered Accountant, Vol. 21 (September, 1931), pp. 119-121.

Annual Reports. Various companies for various years as indicated in body of text.

Appedaile, J. L. "The Management of a Manufacturing Concern or a Plea for the Manufacturer." The Canadian Chartered Accountant, Vol. 5 (October, 1915), pp. 132-147.

________. "Depreciation." The Canadian Chartered Accountant, Vol. 4 (April, 1916), pp. 297-308.

Ashley, C. A. An Introduction to Auditing for Canadians. Toronto: The MacMillan Company of Canada Limited, 1931.

________. "Audit Reports Fail in Too Many Cases." The Financial Post (May 27, 1933), p. 9.

_______. "The Use of Accounts." The Canadian Chartered Accountant, Vol. 38 (June 1941), pp. 389-400.

_______. "Precept and Practice in Accounting." The Canadian Chartered Accountant, Vol. 40 (May, 1942), pp. 290-296.

--------. "Uniform Accounting." The Commerce Journal (April, 1943), pp. 1-9.

Attorney General of Ontario, The. Report of the Attorney General's Committee on Securities Legislation in Ontario. (The Kimber Report.) Toronto: Queen's Printer, 1965.

"Auditing Balance Sheets." Commentary, The Canadian Chartered Accountant, Vol. 1 (April, 1912), p. 208.

"Auditor's Report." Canadian Institute of Chartered Accountants. Reprinted in The Canadian Chartered Accountant, Vol. 63 (July, 1953), p. 35.

"Auditor's Report to the Shareholders, The." Commentary, The Canadian Chartered Accountant, Vol. 33 (August, 1938), pp. 135-139.

_______. Memorandum Regarding Roundtable Discussion at Annual Meeting. The Canadian Chartered Accountant, Vol. 33 (July, 1938), pp. 63-65.

"Bank Auditing." Editorial, The Canadian Chartered Accountant, Vol. 12 (May, 1923), pp. 450-455.

"Bank Audit or Inspection Compulsory from Outside: Is It Justifiable and Expedient?" The Canadian Chartered Accountant, Vol. 1 (July, 1911), pp. 24-28.

"Bank Examinations in Canada." The Journal of Accountancy, Vol. 8 (May, 1909), pp. 40-42.

Beaton, W. and B. B. Shetker. Proceedings of the Select Committee Appointed by the Legislature of the Province of Ontario to Enquire into and Review the Companies Act of the Province of Ontario and Related Acts and Regulations Made Thereunder. Library, Province of Ontario, Queen's Park, Toronto, 1965.

Bell, W. H. Accountants Reports, 4th ed., New York: Ronald Press Co., 1949.

Bennett, E. J. "Some Points for Consideration in Connection with a Customer's Balance Sheet." The Canadian Chartered Accountant, Vol. 11 (March, 1922), pp. 325-340.

Bennett, H. L. "The Presentation of Fixed Assets." The Canadian Chartered Accountant, Vol. 41 (December, 1942), pp. 390-392.

Benson, E. J. Proposals for Tax Reform. Ottawa: Queen's Printer, 1969.

Benston, George. "The Value of the SEC's Accounting Disclosure Requirements." The Accounting Review. Vol. 44 (July, 1969), pp. 515-532.

Bentley, H. C. "Standardization of Accounting Forms and Methods." The Journal of Accountancy, Vol. 14 (August, 1912), pp. 99-106.

Boer, G. "Replacement Cost: A Historical Look." The Accounting Review, Vol. 61 (January, 1966), pp. 92-97.

Breadner, R. W. "The Business Profits and Income War Tax Acts." The Canadian Chartered Accountant, Vol. 8 (October, 1918), pp. 104-123.

"Brief to Senate Committee." The Canadian Chartered Accountant, Vol. 48 (April, 1946), pp. 194-218.

Brown, C. The Balance Sheet to the Income Statement: A Study in the History of Accounting Thought. Ph.D. dissertation. Ann Arbor: published on demand by University Microfilms, 1968.

Byrd, K. F. "Should Accounts be Corrected for Changing Money Values." The Canadian Chartered Accountant, Vol. 61 (September, 1952), pp. 87-104.

_______. Principles of Accounting - Intermediate. Canadian edition of H. A. Finney and H. E. Miller. Toronto: Prentice Hall of Canada Ltd., 1966.

"Call for Action." The Canadian Chartered Accountant, Vol. 42 (May, 1943), pp. 361-364

Canada. House of Commons Debates, Vol. 2, 1902.

_______. House of Commons Debates, Vol. 3, 1916.

_______. House of Commons Debates, Vol. 6, 1917.

_______. House of Commons Debates, Vol. 4, 1934.

_______. House of Commons. Bill C-4, 18 Eliz. II, 1969.

_______. House of Commons, Committee on Banking and Commerce, Vol. 84, 1944 - 1945, House of Commons Journals, Appendix #8.

_______. Senate Debates, 1934.

_______. Senate Debates, 1964.

_______. Senate. Proceedings of the Standing Committee on Banking and Commerce, 26 Parl., 1964.

Canada. Statutes, Canada Joint Stock Companies Act. 1877, 40 Vict., C. 43.

_______. Statutes, The Companies Act. 1902, 2 Edward VII, C. 15.

________. Statutes, The Bank Act. 1913, 3 and 4 George V, C. 9.

________. Statutes, The Loan Companies Act. 1914, 4 and 5 George V, C. 40.

________. Statutes, The Trust Companies Act. 1914, 4 and 5 Georve V, C. 55.

________. Statutes, Business Profits War Tax Act, 1916. 6 and 7 George V, C. 11.

________. Statutes, The Income War Tax Act, 1917. 6 and 7 George V, C. 28.

________. Statutes, The Companies Act Amendment Act, 1917. 8 George V, C. 25.

________. Statutes, The Income War Tax Act. 1917, 6, 7 and 8, George V, C. 28.

________. Statutes, Companies Act. 1934, 24 and 25, George V, C. 33.

________. Statutes, Companies Act. 1935, 25 and 26, George V, C. 33.

________. Statutes, An Act to Amend the Income Tax Act and the Income War Tax Act. 1949, 13 George VI, C. 25.

________. Statutes, Corporations and Labour Unions Returns Act. 1962, 10 and 11 Eliz. II, C. 26.

________. Statutes, Canada Corporations Act. 1964 - 1965, 13 and 14 Eliz. II, C. 52.

________. "The Income Tax Regulations, P.C.6471." Canada, Statutory Orders and Regulations, Consolidation 1949, II (1949), p. 2209.

"Canadian Bank Audits." The Canadian Chartered Accountant, Vol. 16 (October, 1913), pp. 309-312.

Canadian Institute of Chartered Accountants, The. "Report of the Committee on the Canadian Companies Act (1953)." Reprinted in The Canadian Chartered Accountant, Vol. 62 (April, 1953), pp. 151-176.

________. Accounting and Auditing Practices. Bulletins. Statements issued by the Committee on Accounting and Auditing Research. Toronto: The Canadian Institute of Chartered Accountants, 1946-1968.

________. Financial Reporting in Canada. Toronto: Bi-annual publication of The Canadian Institute of Chartered Accountants, 1954 - 1968.

________. "Report of the Special Committee on Shareholders' Audits." The Canadian Chartered Accountant, Vol. 93 (November, 1968), pp. 345-357.

CICA Handbook. Toronto: The Canadian Institute of Chartered Accountants (commenced in 1968 - successor to Bulletins on Accounting and Auditing Practices).

Capon, F. S. "Financial Statement Reform." The Canadian Chartered Accountant, Vol. 43 (December, 1943), pp. 380-385.

Carey, John L. The Rise of the Accounting Profession. New York: American Institute of Certified Public Accountants, 1969.

Carr, E. H. What is History. New York: Alfred A. Knopf, Inc. and Random House, Inc. 1967.

Carscallen, M. P. Ontario Securities and Companies Legislation. Toronto: The Institute of Chartered Accountants of Ontario, 1966.

Carter, K. LeM. "Statutory Duties of Auditors." The Canadian Chartered Accountant (July, 1943), pp. 7-8.

Chaston, J. G. "The Effect of a Fluctuating Monetary Unit on the Income Statement." The Canadian Chartered Accountant, Vol. 50 (February, 1947), pp. 70-73.

Clapperton, C. A. "The Balance Sheet." Cost and Management (July, 1927), pp. 2-13.

Clapperton, H. D. "What Are Profits?" The Canadian Chartered Accountant, Vol. 39 (July, 1941), pp. 75-83.

Cochrane, George. "The Auditor's Report, Its Evolution in the U.S.A." The Accountant, Vol. 123 (November 4, 1950), pp. 448-460.

"Comment and Opinion." The Canadian Chartered Accountant, Vol. 56 (February, 1950), p. 47.

_______. The Canadian Chartered Accountant, Vol. 63 (August, 1953), pp. 45-46.

_______. The Canadian Chartered Accountant, Vol. 64 (January, 1954), pp. 1-2.

"Companies Act, 1934, The." Editorial, The Canadian Chartered Accountant, Vol. 25 (July, 1934), pp. 73-81.

Coutts, W. B. "Accounting Research." The Canadian Chartered Accountant, Vol. 74 (February, 1959), pp. 134-140.

Dalglish, K. W. "Should the Statutory Form of the Auditor's Report to the Shareholders be Changed?" The Canadian Chartered Accountant, Vol. 33 (December, 1938), pp. 453-456.

Davis, R. W. Capital Cost Allowance - Studies of The Royal Commission on Taxation. Ottawa: Queen's Printer, 1966.

Davison, R. S. "Overhauling and Unifying Canadian Company Law." The Financial Post (September 30, 1933), p. 11.

"Depreciation." The Canadian Chartered Accountant, Vol. 13 (May, 1924), p. 387.

Dexter, Grant. "Commerce and the Canadian Constitution." Queen's Quarterly, Vol. 38 (May, 1932), pp. 250-260.

Dickerson, R. W. V. Accountants and the Law of Negligence. Toronto: The Canadian Institute of Chartered Accountants, 1966.

Dickinson, A. Lowes. "Accounting Practice and Procedure." The Journal of Accountancy, Vol. 9 (May, 1909), pp. 11-12.

Dominion Bureau of Statistics. Inventory of Accounting Methods of Canadian Manufacturers. DBS Reference Papers, 1949. Ottawa: Dominion Bureau of Statistics.

Dow, A. "CPR: Washington Gets the Facts." Toronto Daily Star (July 30, 1965), p. 8.

Eddis, W. C. Manual for Accountants. Toronto: Published by author, 1899.

________ and W. B. Tindall. Manufacturers' Accounts, 3rd ed. rev. Toronto: Published by the authors, 1904.

Edey, H. C. "Company Accounting in the Nineteenth and Twentieth Centuries." Certified Accountants Journal, Vol. 48 (April and May, 1956), pp. 95-96, 127-129.

________ and Prot Panitpakdi. "British Company Accounting and the Law 1844 - 1900." Studies in the History of Accounting, ed. by A. C. Littleton and B. S. Yamey. London: Sweet and Maxwell Limited, 1956, pp. 356-379.

Editorial. The Canadian Chartered Accountant, Vol. 30 (May, 1937), pp. 178-179.

________. The Canadian Chartered Accountant, Vol. 32 (May, 1938), p. 325.

Edwards, George. "The Educational Responsibilities of the Chartered Accountant Societies." The Canadian Chartered Accountant, Vol. 11 (September, 1921), pp. 150-159.

"Election of Auditors Versus Appointment by Governments Discussed." The Financial Post (February 25, 1933), p. 11.

Fanshaw, A. J. J. "Some Thoughts on the Balance Sheet." The Canadian Chartered Accountant, Vol. 29 (November, 1936), pp. 346-361.

Ferguson, W. S. and Crocombe, F. R. Elements of Accounting. Toronto: Sir Isaac Pitman & Sons, 1936.

"Finance Company Bill Arousing Business' Ire." Financial Times (December 2, 1968), p. 3.

Financial Post, The. Various issues indicated in body of text.

Financial Times, The. Various issues indicated in body of text.

Fisk, A. K. "Principles of Cost Accounting." The Canadian Chartered Accountant, Vol. 3 (January, 1914), pp. 167-177.

Fleming, C. A. Expert Book-keeping. Owen Sound: Northern Business College Steam Press, 1892.

"Form of Financial Statements." The Canadian Chartered Accountant, Vol. 47 (1945), pp. 345-348.

"Form of the Auditor's Report, The." Summary of Round Table Discussion at Annual Meeting. The Canadian Chartered Accountant, Vol. 39 (October, 1941), pp. 240-254.

Frears, R. I. Frears Annotated Income War Tax Act. Toronto: Canadian Law List Publishing Company, 1947, p. 207.

"General Notes." The Canadian Chartered Accountant, Vol. 34 (April, 1939), pp. 285-294.

Gilmour, A. W. "The Excess Profits Tax Act." The Canadian Chartered Accountant, Vol. 47 (July, 1945), pp. 141-160.

_______. "Diminishing Balance Depreciation Under the Income Tax Act." The Canadian Chartered Accountant, Vol. 56 (June, 1950), pp. 273-283.

Glassco, J. G. "Accounting in a Modern World." The Canadian Chartered Accountant, Vol. 66 (April, 1955), pp. 206-214.

_______. "Depreciation Accounting." The Canadian Chartered Accountant, Vol. 53 (October, 1948), pp. 172-180.

Goodman, M. "The Chartered Accountants of the Dominion - A Discussion and Suggestion." The Canadian Chartered Accountant, Vol. 7 (July, 1917), pp. 44-46.

_______. "The Income Tax." The Canadian Chartered Accountant, Vol. 7 (October, 1917), pp. 121-124.

Gordon, Donald. "Facing Facts in Financial Statements." The Canadian Chartered Accountant, Vol. 76 (January, 1960), pp. 37-42.

Gordon, H. D. Lockhart. "Fifty Years Ago." The Canadian Chartered Accountant, Vol. 79 (July, 1961), pp. 96-98.

Governor General in Council. Report of the Royal Commission on Banking and Finance. (The Porter Report.) Ottawa: Queen's Printer, 1964.

_______. Royal Commission on Canada's Economic Prospects - Final Report. (The Gordon Report.) Ottawa: Queen's Printer, 1957.

Grant, George W. "Auditing Balance Sheets." The Canadian Chartered Accountant, Vol. 2 (October, 1912), pp. 111-112.

Grant, R. R. "A Provincial Organization." The Canadian Chartered Accountant, Vol. 22 (February, 1933), p. 532.

Gray, J. C. "Standardization of Shareholders' Accounts and Auditors' Reports and Certificates." The Canadian Chartered Accountant, Vol. 8 (January, 1919), pp. 193-206.

Great Britain. Statutes, Joint Stock Companies Act. 1844, 7 and 8 Vict., C. 110.

_______. Statutes, Joint Stock Companies Act. 1856, 19 and 20 Vict., C. 47.

_______. Statutes, Companies Act. 1862, 25 and 26 Vict., C. 89.

_______. Statutes, Companies Act. 1900, 63 and 64 Vict., C. 48.

_______. Statutes, Companies (Consolidation) Act. 1908, 8 Edward VII, C. 69.

_______. Statutes, Companies Act. 1928, 18 and 19 George V, C. 45.

_______. Statutes, Companies Consolidation Act. 1929, 19 and 20 George V, C. 23.

_______. Statutes, Companies Act. 1947, 10 and 11 George VI, C. 47.

_______. Statutes, Companies Act. 1967, 15 and 16 Eliz. II, C. 81.

Hamilton, A. W. "Section 1100(4) The Effect of Its Removal." Canadian Tax Journal, Vol. 2 (May, June, 1954), p. 204-210.

Harris, E. C. "Access to Corporate Information." Studies in Canadian Company Law, ed. by J. S. Ziegel. Toronto: Butterworths, 1967, pp. 476-506.

Hatfield, H. R. Accounting. New York: D. Appleton and Company, 1927.

_______. "Variations in Accounting Practice." Journal of Accounting Research, Vol. 4 (Autumn, 1966), pp. 169-187.

Hawkins, D. F. "The Development of Modern Financial Reporting Practices Among American Manufacturing Corporations." Business History Review, Vol. XXXVII, No. 3 (1963), pp. 135-168.

Hein, Leonard W. "The Auditor and the British Companies Acts." The Accounting Review, Vol. 38 (July, 1963), pp. 508-520.

Hensel, P. H. "Corporate Reports." The Canadian Chartered Accountant, Vol. 27 (December, 1935), pp. 400-408.

"Here are Recommendations from the Atlantic Inquiry." The Financial Post (December 20, 1969), p. 22.

Hoskins, David. Bookkeeping for Joint Stock Companies. Toronto: Warwick Bros. and Rutter, 1901.

________. Joint Stock Company Accounts. Toronto: The Shaw Correspondence School, 1907.

Hyde, John. "The President's Address." The Canadian Chartered Accountant, Vol. 8 (October, 1918), pp. 93-103.

"Inventory Valuation." The Canadian Chartered Accountant, Vol. 32 (February, 1938), p. 80.

Jamieson, H. T. "Investigations." The Canadian Chartered Accountant, Vol. 9 (April, 1920), pp. 238-251.

Johnson, T. H. "The Form of the Balance Sheet." The Canadian Chartered Accountant, Vol. 22 (February, 1933), pp. 497-509.

Jones, R. H. "Do Those Financial Statements Really Inform the Shareholder?" The Financial Post (September 18, 1965), p. 13.

Joplin, J. Porter. "Secret Reserves." The Canadian Chartered Accountant, Vol. 4 (January, 1915), pp. 193-201.

Keen, T. "Business Accounts and How to Read Them." The Accountant, June 15, 1935. Reprinted in W. T. Baxter ed., Studies in Accounting, pp. 85-92. London: Sweet and Maxwell Limited, 1950.

Kehler, J. "A Historical Study to Determine the Effect of Taxation Regulations on Accounting Practice." Unpublished B.Comm. Honours Thesis, University of Saskatchewan, 1970.

Kerr, David S. "Consolidated Balance Sheets." The Canadian Chartered Accountant, Vol. 5 (October, 1915), pp. 107-114.

Kettle, Russell. "Qualifications in Auditor's Reports." The Canadian Chartered Accountant, Vol. 17 (May, 1928), pp. 325-365.

King, C. L. "Depreciation on Replacement Cost." The Canadian Chartered Accountant, Vol. 53 (August, 1948), pp. 77-84.

Leonard, W. G. "A Plea for Greater Frankness in Financial Representations." The Canadian Chartered Accountant, Vol. 41 (July, 1942), pp. 11-15

Littleton, A. C. and V. K. Zimmerman. Accounting Theory: Continuity and Change. Englewood Cliffs: Prentice-Hall, 1962.

"Low Audit Fees Lead to Inadequate Check." The Financial Post, March 25, 1933, p. 9.

"Lucidity and Success." The Canadian Chartered Accountant, Vol. 16 (November, 1926), pp. 185-187.

Lyons, P. H. "The Impact of Research Bulletins on the Chartered Accountant in Industry and Practice." Annual Conference Papers, 1965. Toronto: The Canadian Institute of Chartered Accountants, 1965, pp. 22-34.

Masten, C. A. and W. K. Frazer. Company Law of Canada, 3rd ed. Toronto: The Carswell Co. Limited, 1929.

Mautz, R. K. and H. A. Sharaf. The Philosophy of Auditing. American Accounting Association, 1961.

May, George O. "Wider Horizons." The Canadian Chartered Accountant, Vol. 30 (April, 1937), pp. 295-304.

_______. Financial Accounting, A Distillation of Experience. New York: The MacMillan Company, 1943.

_______. "Improvements in Financial Accounts," (1938). Dickenson Lectures in Accounting. Cambridge, Mass.: Harvard University Press, 1943.

Macintosh, W. A. "Economics and Accountancy." The Canadian Chartered Accountant, Vol. 23 (December, 1932), pp. 404-408.

Macpherson, L. G. "A Company's Annual Financial Statement to Shareholders." The Canadian Chartered Accountant, Vol. 24 (January, 1934), pp. 83-92.

McEachern, R. A. "The Role of the Accountant in a Changing Social Climate." The Canadian Chartered Accountant, Vol. 55 (December, 1955), pp. 261-265.

Members of the Department of Political and Economic Science at Queen's University. "Financial Manipulation: A Project of Reform." Queen's Quarterly, Vol. 40 (May, 1933), pp. 264-281.

Mitchell, V. E. Treatise on the Law Relating to Canadian Commercial Companies. Montreal: Southam Press Limited, 1916.

Moonitz, Maurice. Book Reviews. The Accounting Review, Vol. 39 (July, 1964), pp. 829-830.

Morgan, Henry. "The Auditor's Responsibility in Relation to Balance Sheets and Profit and Loss Accounts." The Fourth International Congress of Accounting, 1933. London: Gee & Co. Ltd., 1933, pp. 487-519.

Mulcahy, G. "The Auditor's Report on Consolidated Statements." The Canadian Chartered Accountant, Vol. 88 (April, 1966), pp. 288-289.

_______. "Accounting Research." The Canadian Chartered Accountant, Vol. 93 (August, 1968), pp. 104-106.

_______. "Financial Reporting by Diversified Companies - Part I." The Canadian Chartered Accountant, Vol. 4 (October, 1969), pp. 286-288.

Mulvey, Thomas. Canadian Company Law. Montreal: John Lovell and Sons Limited, 1913.

_______. "The Companies Act." The Canadian Chartered Accountant, Vol. 8 (October, 1918), pp. 124-141.

_______. Dominion Company Law. Toronto: The Ontario Publishing Co., 1920.

Nelson, L. M. "The Statutory Report." The Canadian Chartered Accountant, Vol. 91 (July, 1967), pp. 40-41.

"New OSC Recommendations Cover Broad Range of Business." Financial Times (March 23, 1970), p. 6.

Ontario, Legislative Assembly of Ontario. Interim Report of the Select Committee on Company Law. (The Lawrence Committee). Toronto: Queen's Printer, 1967.

Ontario, Legislature of the Province of Ontario. Proceedings of the Special Committee of the Legislature of the Province of Ontario Charged with the Revision of the Companies Act (Ontario) and Related Acts. (The Roberts Committee.) Vol. 15, October, 6, 1952. Library, Province of Ontario, Queen's Park, Toronto.

Ontario, Lieutenant Governor in Council. Report of the Royal Commission to Investigate Trading in the Shares of Windfall Oils and Mines Limited. Toronto: Queen's Printer, 1965.

_______. Report of the Royal Commission Appointed to Enquire into the Failure of Atlantic Acceptance Company Limited. Toronto: Queen's Printer, 1969. Four volumes.

"Ontario Moves with Deliberation in Company Law Reform." Financial Times (June 2, 1969), p. 10.

Ontario Securities Commission. Recognition of Profits in Real Estate Transactions. Toronto: Ontario Securities Commission, July, 1969.

Ontario. Statutes, The Ontario Companies Act. 1897, 60 Vict., C. 28.

_______. Statutes, The Ontario Companies Act. 1907, 7 Edward VII, C. 34.

_______. Statutes, The Corporation Act. 1953, 1 Eliz. II, C. 19.

_______. Statutes, An Act to Amend the Companies Act. 1964, 12 and 13 Eliz. II, C. 10.

_______. Statutes, An Act to Amend the Corporations Act. 1966, 14 and 15 Eliz. II, C. 28.

_______. Statutes, The Securities Act. 1966, 14 and 15 Eliz. II, C. 142, part XII.

"OSC Takes Hard Line on Private Placements, Disclosure." Financial Times (March 23, 1970), pp. 5-6.

Parker, R. H. "Accounting History: A Select Bibliography." Abacus, Vol. I, No. 1 (1965), pp. 62-84.

_______. "Lower of Cost and Market in Britain and the United States: An Historical Survey." Abacus, Vol. 1 (December, 1965), pp. 158-165.

Parkinson, R. M. "The LIFO Method of Inventory Valuation." The Canadian Chartered Accountant, Vol. 56 (May, 1950), pp. 206-214.

Parton, John C. "The Determination of Profits in a Joint Stock Company." The Canadian Chartered Accountant, Vol. 1 (July, 1911), pp. 7-15.

_______. "Merchandise Inventories and the Auditor's Responsibility Therefor." The Canadian Chartered Accountant, Vol. 7 (October, 1917), pp. 93-100.

_______. "Fifty Years Ago." The Canadian Chartered Accountant, Vol. 79 (July, 1961), pp. 94-96.

Paton, W. A. and A. C. Littleton. An Introduction to Corporate Accounting Standards. Ann Arbor, Michigan: American Accounting Association, 1940.

Perry, J. H. Taxes, Tariffs & Subsidies, Vol. 2. Toronto: University of Toronto Press, 1955.

"Pertinent Question." Financial Times, June 30, 1969, p. 3.

Pines, J. A. "The Securities and Exchange Commission and Accounting Principles." Law and Contemporary Problems, Vol. 30 (Autumn, 1965), pp. 727-751.

Privy Council Office. Foreign Ownership and the Structure of Canadian Industry. Ottawa: Queen's Printer, 1968.

Price Waterhouse & Co. Is Generally Accepted Accounting for Income Taxes Possibly Misleading Investors? New York: Price Waterhouse & Co., 1967.

"Provincial News." The Canadian Chartered Accountant, Vol. 20 (July, 1930), p. 60.

"Public Accountant and Publicity, The." Editorial, Journal of Accountancy, Vol. 1 (December, 1905), p. 137.

Ralston, J. L. "Discussions on Dominion Companies Act." The Canadian Chartered Accountant, Vol. 26 (February, 1935), pp. 87-94.

Raynauld, Andre. The Canadian Economic System. Toronto: The MacMillan Company of Canada Limited, 1967.

"Recognition of Profits in Real Estate Transactions." Ontario Securities Commission Bulletin. Toronto: Ontario Securities Commission, July, 1969.

"Recommendations on Bill 454." The Canadian Chartered Accountant, Vol. 52 (May, 1948), pp. 265-312.

Richardson, G. G. "The Impact of Income Taxes on Depreciation Accounting in Canada." The Canadian Chartered Accountant, Vol. 63 (November, 1953), pp. 211-216.

Rose, Harold. Disclosure in Company Accounts. "Eaton Paper." London: Institute of Economic Affairs, 1965.

Ross, Howard. "The Unsolved Problem of Fixed Asset Valuation." The Canadian Chartered Accountant, Vol. 84 (April, 1964), pp. 276-279.

_______. The Elusive Art of Accounting. New York: The Ronald Press Company, 1966.

_______. Financial Statements - A Crusade for Current Values. Toronto: Sir Isaac Pitman (Canada) Ltd., 1969.

Sands, J. E. Wealth, Income and Intangibles. Toronto: University of Toronto Press, 1963.

Schumpeter, J. A. History of Economic Analysis. New York: Oxford University Press, 1954.

Scully, V. W. "Problems Arising from the Decline in the Purchasing Power of the Dollar." The Canadian Chartered Accountant, Vol. 61 (November, 1952), pp. 179-184.

SEC Accounting Series Release No. 7. "Analysis of Deficiencies Commonly Cited by Commission in Connection with Financial Statements." May, 1938, reprinted in Federal Securities Law Reports. Washington: Commerce Clearing House Inc.

Shaw, W. H. and P. McIntosh. Bookkeeping. Toronto: The Central Business College, 1903.

Skelton, O. D. General Economic History of the Dominion 1867 - 1912. Toronto: The Publishers Association of Canada Limited, 1913.

Skeoch, L. A. Restrictive Trade Practices in Canada. Toronto: McClelland and Stewart Limited, 1966.

Skinner, R. M. "Generally Accepted Accounting Principles." The Canadian Chartered Accountant, Vol. 78 (May, 1961), pp. 463-468.

Smails, R. G. H. "Directors' Reports - A Criticism and Suggestion." The Canadian Chartered Accountant, Vol. 21 (September, 1931), pp. 100-106.

_______. Letter to the Editor. The Canadian Chartered Accountant, Vol. 19 (March, 1930), pp. 311-313.

_______. "Students' Department." The Canadian Chartered Accountant, Vol. 22 (November, 1932), pp. 361-362.

_______. Auditing. Toronto: The Commercial Text Book Co., 1933.

_______. "Students' Department." The Canadian Chartered Accountant, Vol. 25 (September, 1934), pp. 283-284.

_______. "Students' Department." The Canadian Chartered Accountant, Vol. 26 (May, 1935), pp. 367-368.

_______. "Students' Department." The Canadian Chartered Accountant, Vol. 28 (February, 1936), pp. 147-148.

_______. "The Balance Sheet and the Layman." The Canadian Chartered Accountant, Vol. 29 (November, 1936), pp. 362-367.

_______. "Students' Department." The Canadian Chartered Accountant, Vol. 30 (February, 1937), p. 165.

_______. "Students' Department." The Canadian Chartered Accountant, Vol. 42 (June 1943), pp. 454-455.

_______. "Students' Department." The Canadian Chartered Accountant, Vol. 43 (September, 1943), pp. 197-198.

_______ and C. E. Walker. Accounting Principles and Practice. Toronto: The Ryerson Press, 1926.

Smith, E. V. C. Depreciation Policies of Canadian Corporations During Depression. Unpublished Bachelor of Arts Thesis. London: University of Western Ontario, 1935.

Smyth, J. E. "Letter to the Editor." The Canadian Chartered Accountant, Vol. 93 (September, 1968), p. 157.

________. "Notes on the Development of the Accounting Profession." The Canadian Chartered Accountant, Vol. 63 (November, 1953), pp. 200-210.

________. "Notes on the Development of the Accountancy Profession." The Canadian Chartered Accountant, Vol. 63 (December, 1953), pp. 282-292.

Sprott, A. F. and F. G. Short. Canadian Modern Accounting. Toronto: The Commercial Text Book Company, 1921.

Sprouse, R. T. and M. Moonitz. A Tentative Set of Broad Accounting Principles for Business Enterprises. New York: American Institute of Certified Public Accountants, 1962.

Stacey, N. A. H. English Accounting: A Study in Social and Economic History 1800 to 1954. London: Gee and Company Limited, 1954.

Stans, M. H. "The Future of Accounting." Handbook of Modern Accounting Theory, ed. M. Backer. Englewood Cliffs: Prentice Hall Inc., 1953, pp. 583-601.

Staub, Walter A. Auditing Developments During the Present Century. Cambridge, Massachusetts: Harvard University Press, 1942.

Sterrett, J. E. "Legislation for the Control of Corporations." Journal of Accountancy, Vol. 9 (February, 1910), pp. 241-247.

Stettler, Howard F. Auditing Principles, 2nd Ed. Englewood Cliffs: Prentice Hall Inc., 1961.

"Stock Inventories." The Canadian Chartered Accountant, Vol. 8 (July, 1918), pp. 50-51.

"Stocks Disappearing." Financial Post, February 16, 1907, p. 1.

Storey, R. K. The Search for Accounting Principles. New York: American Institute of Certified Public Accountants, 1964.

Sutherland, J. B. "Reserves and Sinking Funds." The Canadian Chartered Accountant, Vol. 7 (October, 1917), pp. 101-109.

Swift, R. "Depreciation Allowance Under the Income War Tax Act." The Canadian Chartered Accountant, Vol. 32 (May, 1938), pp. 385-388.

Thompson, J. H. "The Income Statement." The Canadian Chartered Accountant, Vol. 53 (November, 1948), pp. 231-244.

Turgeon, W. F. A. Royal Commission on the Textile Industry. Ottawa: King's Printer, 1938.

"Uniform Accounting." The Canadian Chartered Accountant, Vol. 7 (May, 1917), pp. 5-33.

"Uniform Examinations." The Canadian Chartered Accountant, Vol. 6 (April, 1917), p. 311.

"Uniformity in Company Legislation." Editorial, The Canadian Chartered Accountant, Vol. 22 (October, 1932), pp. 287-288.

United States Federal Reserve Board. Uniform Accounting. Washington: Federal Reserve Board, 1917.

Urquhart, M. C. and K. A. H. Buckley, eds. Historical Statistics of Canada. Toronto: The Macmillan Company of Canada Ltd., 1965.

Wade, C. B. "Income and Cost Adjustments." The Canadian Chartered Accountant, Vol. 38 (February, 1941), pp. 98-108.

_______. "Depreciation Policies of Canadian Public Corporations." The Canadian Chartered Accountant, Vol. 42 (June, 1943), pp. 434-437.

Walsh, W. H. An Introduction to Philosophy of History, 3rd ed. rev. London: Hutchinson & Co. Publishers Ltd., 1967.

Warde, J. D. The Shareholders' and Directors' Manual. Toronto: The Canadian Railway News Co. Limited, 1900.

Wegenast, F. W. "Audit Clearing House Would Aid Investor." The Financial Post (January 24, 1934), p. 9.

Wilkinson, George. "The Auditor's Standing in England and America." The Canadian Chartered Accountant, Vol. 3 (April, 1914), pp. 237-243.

Williamson, J. Peter Securities Regulation in Canada. Toronto: University of Toronto Press, 1960.

Wilson, W. M. "Events Subsequent to Balance Sheet Date." The Canadian Chartered Accountant, Vol. 69 (July, 1956), pp. 35-38.

Yamey, B. S. "The Development of Company Accounting Conventions." Accountants' Magazine, Vol. 65 (October, 1961), pp. 753-763.

APPENDIX A

APPENDIX A

LIST OF AUDIT REPORTS EXAMINED

1904 to 1939

Firm Audited	Auditing Firm[1]	Period
Canadian Locomotive Company Limited	Geo. A. Touche & Co.	1912 - 1930
Cockshutt Plow Company Limited	Deloitte, Plender, Griffiths & Co.	1911 - 1939
Canadian Westinghouse Company Limited	C. S. Scott & Co.	1904 - 1920
Canadian Canners Limited	Price Waterhouse & Co.	1923 - 1939
Dominion Steel & Coal Corporation Limited	Price Waterhouse & Co.	1909 - 1920
Dominion Textile Company Limited	P. S. Ross & Sons	1906 - 1920
Howard Smith Paper Mills Limited	P. S. Ross & Sons	1926 - 1939
Massey-Harris Company Limited	Clarkson, Gordon, Dilworth & Co.	1923 - 1939
Ogilvie Flour Mills Company Limited	Creak, Cushing & Hodgson	1909 - 1920
Penmans Limited	C. S. Scott & Co.	1913 - 1939
Steel Company of Canada Limited	Riddell, Stead, Graham & Hutchison	1910 - 1939
Russell Industries Limited	Edwards, Morgan & Co.	1920 - 1939

1940 - 1970

Firm Audited	Auditing Firm[1]
British American Oil Company Limited	Clarkson, Gordon & Co.
Burns & Co. Limited	Peat, Marwick, Mitchell & Co.
Canada & Dominion Sugar Company Limited	Clarkson, Gordon & Co.
Consolidated Paper Corporation Limited	Touche, Ross & Co.
Distillers Corporation Seagrams Limited	Price Waterhouse & Co.
Dominion Bridge Company Limited	Riddell, Stead, Graham & Hutchison
Famous Players Canadian Corporation Limited	Price Waterhouse & Co.
George Weston Limited	Edwards, Morgan & Co.
Imperial Tobacco Company of Canada Limited	Deloitte, Plender, Haskins & Sells
Ontario Steel Products Company Limited	McDonald, Currie & Co.

---

[1] Indicates name of auditing firm for majority of time period.

APPENDIX B

APPENDIX B

LIST OF FINANCIAL STATEMENTS EXAMINED

1903 to 1919

Canada Cycle & Motor Company Limited
Canadian General Electric Company Limited
Canadian Salt Company Limited
Carter Crume Company Limited
Dominion Iron & Steel Company Limited
Lake of Woods Milling Company Limited
Montreal Cotton Company
Montreal Steel Works Limited
Ogilvie Flour Mills Company Limited
Victoria Rolling Stock Company Limited

1920 - 1939

Brandram Henderson Limited
Belding Corticelli Limited
Canadian Locomotive Company Limited
Cockshutt Plow Company Limited
Dominion Glass Company Limited
Dominion Rubber Company Limited
National Breweries Limited
Penmans Limited
Steel Company of Canada Limited
Tooke Bros. Limited

1940 - 1970

Same companies for this period as in Appendix A

APPENDIX C

APPENDIX C

TABLE 3

SELECTED HISTORICAL STATISTICS

Year	Estimated population (thousands)	Gross National Product (millions)	Gross Value of All Production Manufacturing (millions)
1880	4,255	581	303
1890	4,779	803	452
1900	5,301	1,057	575
1910	6,988	2,235	1,147
1915			1,330
1919			3,162
1920	8,556	5,529	
1926		5,152	3,108
1929			3,879
1930	10,208	5,728	
1932		3,827	
1933			1,953
1935		4,135	
1939			3,472
1940	11,381	6,743	
1946			8,033
1950	13,712	18,006	
1957			21,969
1960	17,870	36,287	
1965			33,389
1966	20,015	57,738	

Sources: M. C. Urquhart and K. A. H. Buckley, eds., Historical Statistics of Canada (Toronto: The Macmillan Company of Canada Ltd., 1965), pp. 14, 130 and 490 respectively for all figures up to 1960; Canada Year Book, for 1968 for all subsequent figures.

TABLE 4

SELECTED HISTORICAL STATISTICS

Estimates of Non Resident and Total Capital
Invested in Canada (in millions)

Year	Percentage of Non Resident Investment		Total of Non Resident Investment		Resident and Non Resident Total Investment[a] Increase During Year
	U.S.	U.K.	Accumulated Total	Increase during period	
1900	14	85	1,232		
1910	19	77	2,529	1,297	Statistics
1916	30	66	4,323	1,794	Unavailable
1920	44	53	4,870	547	
1926	53	44	6,003	1,137	
1930	61	36	7,614	1,611	4,465
1939	60	36	6,913	- 701	5,278
1945	70	25	7,092	179	5,612
1950	76	20	8,664	1,572	13,920
1955	76	18	13,473	4,809	25,587
1960	75	15	22,200	8,727	36,420
1966	80	11	32,012	9,812	56,804

Sources: M. C. Urquhart and K. A. H. Buckley, eds., Historial Statistics of Canada (Toronto: The Macmillan Company of Canada Ltd., 1965), pp. 136 and 169 for all figures up to 1960; National Income Accounts and Expenditures, 1967 and Quarterly Estimates of the Canadian Balance of International Payment, 1969 - both of the Dominion Bureau of Statistics for the subsequent years.

[a]Includes gross fixed capital investment and value of physical changes in inventories.

TABLE 5

SELECTED HISTORICAL STATISTICS

Number of Establishments and Gross Value of Production by Size of Establishment Measured by Gross Value of Production
(establishments in thousands and total value in millions)

	Up to $199,999		$200,000 to $999,999		$1,000,000 and over	
Year	Establishments	Total Value of Production	Establishments	Total Value of Production	Establishments	Total Value of Production
1900	14.2		.4		.04	
1910	18.1	431	.9	375	.1	359
1922	20.5	508	1.6	680	.4	1,250
1930	21.4	577	2.0	843	.6	2,046
1940	22.5	646	2.2	957	.8	2,924
1950	29.0	1,152	4.9	2,141	2.0	10,521
1959	26.1	1,268	6.8	3,069	3.4	18,972
1965	20.3	1,189	8.0	3,675	4.9	29,027

Sources: M. C. Urquhart and K. A. H. Buckley, eds., Historical Statistics of Canada (Toronto: The Macmillan Company of Canada Ltd., 1965), p. 489 for all figures up to 1959; Canada Year Book, 1968 for all subsequent figures.

TABLE 6

SELECTED HISTORICAL STATISTICS

Commercial Failures in Canada

Year	Number	Liailities (in thousands)
1890	1,847	18,000
1900	1,355	11,613
1905	1,347	9,855
1910	1,262	14,515
1913	1,719	16,979
1914	2,898	34,997
1915	2,661	41,130
1916	1,685	25,070
1919	755	16,256
1921	2,451	73,299
1922	3,695	78,069
1923	3,247	65,810
1926	1,773	32,291
1929	2,167	38,748
1933	2,044	32,954
1939	1,392	15,089
1946	278	5,966
1957	2,213	79,863
1962	3,185	147,452
1966	3,007	247,467

Sources: M. C. Urquhart and K. A. H. Buckley, eds. Historical Statistics of Canada (Toronto: The Macmillan Company of Canada Ltd., 1965), p. 659 for all figures up to 1957; Canada Year Book, 1968 for all subsequent figures.

TABLE 7

SELECTED HISTORICAL STATISTICS

Year	Price Index Numbers of a Family Budget (1913 = 100)	Consumer Price Index (1949 = 100)	Index of Common Stock Prices (1935-39 = 100)
1900	69.7		
1905	78.2		
1910	91.2		
1913	100.0		
1915	98.7	50.7	57.6
1917	129.4	65.0	
1920	184.7	93.6	55.3
1921	161.9		
1926	153.1	75.8	95.2
1929			142.6
1930	151.8	75.2	94.0
1932	118.4	61.6	47.6
1935	115.2	59.9	98.0
1940	122.6	65.7	70.3
1945		75.0	112.5
1950		102.9	146.3
1955		116.4	247.6
1960		128.0	261.5
1961			132.7*
1967		149.0*	174.3*

*(1956 = 100) for figures after 1960.

Sources: M. C. Urquhart and K. A. H. Buckley, eds., Historical Statistics of Canada (Toronto: The Macmillan Company of Canada Ltd., 1956), pp. 303, 304 and 277 respectively for all figures up to 1960; Canada Year Book, 1968 for Consumer Price Index and Bank of Canada Statistical Summary, 1967 Supplement, p. 84 for Common Stock Price Index for figures after 1960.

TABLE 8

SELECTED HISTORICAL STATISTICS

Year	Membership in the Canadian Institute of Chartered Accountants
1910	242
1921	724
1930	1,440
1942	2,489
1952	4,975
1959	8,552
1964	12,832
1969	17,155

Source: Relevant years of *The Canadian Chartered Accountant*.

APPENDIX D

THE CANADIAN SALT COMPANY, LIMITED

December 31, 1905

ASSETS

Real estate, buildings, plant, etc.	$553,544
Accounts receivable and cash on hand	57,608
Salt, coal and other stores, on hand	18,807
Unexpired insurance	526
	$630,487

Capital stock				$500,000
Authorized loan, account new construction work				55,000
Accounts payable				19,154
Dividend payable (since paid)				10,000
Surplus of assets over liabilities, being balance at credit of Profit and Loss Account, as follows:				
Balance at December 31, 1904			$33,228	
Net profit on operations for year 1905		$56,635		
Less: Dividends declared for year 1905	$40,000			
Interest on loan	3,531	43,531	13,104	46,333
				$630,487

Figure 6

THE CANADIAN GENERAL ELECTRIC COMPANY, LIMITED

December 31, 1905

ASSETS

Permanent investments--		
Patents and contracts	$ 263,067.08	
Factory plants	2,668,558.18	
Patterns and drawings	125,000.00	
Machinery and tools		
-Peterboro*	365,056.17	
-Davenport	649,652.12	$4,071,333.55
Cash and current assets--		
Cash	$ 8,544.76	
Accounts receivable	1,447,556.14	
Notes receivable	107,388.53	
Brantford Street Railway Co. bonds	125,000.00	
Bonds of other Companies	11,000.00	
	$1,699,489.43	
Merchandise inventory	2,239,481.96	
Expenditure on contracts, net	220,834.08	
Insurance unexpired	10,444.64	4,170,250.11
		$8,241,583.66

LIABILITIES

Capital stock, common	$3,579,705.00	
Capital stock, preferred	300,000.00	$3,879,705.00
+Accounts and bills payable		1,010,283.67
+Canadian Bank of Commerce, current		1,403,497.27
Canadian Bank of Commerce, special (Nassau power plant)		86,965.06
Northey Co., mortgage bonds		160,000.00
Mortgages payable		30,050.00
Reserve Fund	$1,480,320.00	
Contingent Account	100,000.00	
Profit and Loss Account	90,762.66	1,671,082.66
		$8,241,583.66

*Previously included in Canada Foundry Company's manufacturing plant.

+Since the expiration of the fiscal year the cash received from the sale of 11,000 shares has been applied to paying off the floating liability.

PROFIT AND LOSS ACCOUNT

To Dividends paid	$335,499.11	By Balance, January 1, 1905	$ 81,913.42
Interest paid and discounts allowed	125,988.61	Profit on operating	608,206.97
Amounts written off	137,870.01		
Balance at credit, Dec. 31, 1905	90,762.66		
	$690,120.39		$690,120.39

Figure 7

THE MONTREAL COTTON COMPANY

December 31, 1910

ASSETS

Cash	$ 12,982.86
Book debts, etc.	843,436.20
Real estate balances	3,631.50
Cloth and waste	525,837.70
Cotton in process	591,823.83
Raw cotton	345,521.01
Supplies	198,075.02
Unexpired insurance	6,137.20
Total working assets	$2,527,445.32
Bills receivable, discounted	106,019.87
Employees' cottages	154,349.51
Mills, land, power, &c	4,210,523.48
	$6,998,338.18

LIABILITIES

Open accounts		$ 347,970.00
Bills payable		None
Total current liabilities		347,970.00
Indirect		106,019.87
Bond issue	$1,000,000.00	
Redeemed	33,056.65	966,913.35
Capital account		3,000,000.00
Sales guarantee		291,392.66
Insurance reserve		283,457.92
Profit and loss (surplus)		1,982,040.67
Net profits, balance forward as per account No. 2		20,513.71
		$6,998,338.18

Figure 8

THE MONTREAL COTTON COMPANY

December 31, 1910

MANUFACTURING ACCOUNT

Raw cotton, wages, supplies, chemics, etc.	$2,276,732.78	Cloth sales	$3,194,220.42
Salaries, incidentals and general	143,057.17	Cloth in process	1,117,661.53
			4,311,881.95
Taxes, interest, insurance, repairs and fuel	304,978.01		
Depreciation	115,000.00		
Gross profits	295,024.42	Cloth stock, 31st December, 1909	1,177,089.54
	$3,134,792.41		$3,134,792.41

PROFIT AND LOSS ACCOUNT

Bond interest and bad debts	$ 48,472.92	Manufacturing profits	$295,024.42
Dividends	240,000.00	Farm rents, &c	13,962.21
Balance forward	20,513.71		
	$308,986.63		$308,986.63

Figure 8 (continued)

THE CARTER-CRUME COMPANY, LIMITED

December 31, 1910

ASSETS

Real Estate, Buildings, Plant, Patents, Good-will, Investments, etc.	$2,618,096.79	
Deduct Net Value Mortgage Loan	70,752.50	$2,547,344.29
Stock in Trade and Accounts and Bills Receivable	$ 515,468.85	
Cash at Bankers and in hand	43,266.72	
Expenditure on Account of Future Business	20,091.58	578,827.15
		$3,126,171.44

LIABILITIES

Capital Stock:		
Preference Shares	$ 927,700.00	
Common Shares	1,250,000.00	$2,177,700.00
Reserve Account	$ 325,000.00	
Real Estate and Plant Reserve Account	100,000.00	
Investment Reserve Account	199,686.11	624,686.11
Accounts and Bills Pay-able, Including Wages and all Accrued Charges	$ 140,376.11	
Dividend on Preferred Stock, Payable January 3, 1911	16,234.75	
Dividend on Common Stock, Payable January 3, 1911	12,500.00	169,110.86
Contingent Liability		26,875.00
Profit and Loss Account, Balance Forward		127,799.47
		$3,126,171.44

Figure 9

THE CARTER-CRUME COMPANY, LIMITED

December 31, 1910

PROFIT AND LOSS ACCOUNT

Dividends on Preferred Stock Nos. 41, 42 and 43, at the rate of 7% per annum	$ 48,704.25		The Balance at Credit of Profit and Loss Account December 31, 1909 was		$108,730.98
Dividend on Common Stock No. 21, at the rate of 2% per annum	12,500.00		The Net Earnings for the Year were	$111,614.62	
Reserved for Preferred Stock Dividend No. 44, Payable January 3, 1911	16,234.75		From Pacific-Burt Company Transaction	105,315.00	216,929.62
Reserved for Common Stock, Dividend No. 22, Payable January 3, 1911	12,500.00				
Auditors' and Directors' Fees	3,152.38				
In Extinction of New Patents, etc.	4,769.75				
Transferred to Investment Reserve	25,000.00				
Transferred to Real Estate and Plant Reserve Acct.	25,000.00				
Transferred to Reserve Account	50,000.00	$197,861.13			
Leaving a Balance at Credit of Profit and Loss Account of		127,799.47			
		$325,660.60			$325,660.60

Figure 9 (continued)

CANADIAN CONSOLIDATED RUBBER COMPANY, LIMITED

Combined Statement, Consolidated and
Constituent Companies

December 31, 1919

ASSETS

Cash	$ 163,854	
Investment in Dominion of Canada Victory Loan Bonds	557,100	
Accounts receivable	1,863,836	
Inventories of manufactured goods and materials	10,285,434	
Total Current Assets		$12,870,225
Investments in other companies	482,732	
Goodwill, patents and formulae	4,203,702	
Property and plants	10,047,734	
Prepaid and Deferred Assets	568,124	15,302,293
Total Assets		$28,172,519

INCOME

Net sales, footwear, tires, clothing, general rubber goods, reclaimed rubber and miscellaneous (in Canada and export.)		$22,162,977
Less: Cost of goods sold, selling and general expenses, provision for bad debts and Government taxes, including provision for depreciation of $562,300		19,765,399
		$ 2,397,577
Deduct:		
Interest on bonds	$ 501,000	
Other interest and bond discount	145,071	646,071
Net profit for year ending December 31st, 1919		$ 1,751,506
Add: Surplus December 31st, 1918		5,700,795
		$ 7,452,302
Deduct: Dividend on Preferred Shares		209,994
Surplus, December 31st, 1919		$ 7,242,307

Figure 10

CANADIAN CONSOLIDATED RUBBER COMPANY, LIMITED

December 31, 1919

LIABILITIES

Accounts payable, accrued wages, etc., and provision for Government taxes	$ 2,790,456	
Acceptances payable	522,392	
Accrued interest on bonds	38,997	
Total current liabilities		$ 3,351,846
First and Refunding 5% Gold Bonds due January 1st, 1917	6,900,000	
Bonds 6% due October 1st, 1946	2,600,000	9,500,000
Total Liabilities		$12,851,846
Contingent reserve	255,943	
Reserve for depreciation of plant and property	2,016,921	
Total Reserves	2,272,865	
Capital Stock Issued:		
Preferred	3,000,000	
Common	2,805,500	
Total Capital Stock	5,805,500	
Surplus, as per Consolidated Statement of Surplus and Profits	7,242,307	
Total Capital Stock and Surplus	13,047,807	
Total Reserves, Capital Stock and Surplus		15,320,673
Total Liabilities, Reserves and Capital		$28,172,519

Contingent Liabilities:

Guarantee of Bonds of Canadian Consolidated Felt Company, Limited	$364,500
Paper under discount	464,839

Figure 10 (continued)

THE STEEL COMPANY OF CANADA, LIMITED

Balance Sheet, December 31st, 1919

ASSETS

Cost of works owned and operated by the Company	$27,382,151	
Investments in Coal, Ore and other Companies and Company's own Bonds, including those acquired for Sinking Fund	3,734,545	$31,116,697
Sinking Fund Assets--		
In hand of Trustee		39
Advances to Subsidiary Companies		687,652
Current Assets--		
Inventories of raw materials and finished products less reserve	5,503,833	
Accounts receivable	4,310,211	
Bills receivable	21,736	
Cash on hand and in banks	2,076,403	
	$11,912,185	
Other securities	2,884,209	14,796,394
Securities set aside for Special Purposes--		
Stock of the Company held in trust for employees	281,902	
Victory Bonds deposited with Trustees for retirement of Western Coke Co. Bonds	450,000	
Victory Bonds appropriated for employees' pension fund	305,245	1,037,147
Deferred charges to operations--		
Insurance and other expenses paid in advance		22,457
		$47,660,389

Figure 11

THE STEEL COMPANY OF CANADA, LIMITED

December 31st, 1919

LIABILITIES

64,963 shares at $100 each, Preferred	$ 6,496,300	
115,000 shares at $100 each, Ordinary	11,500,000	$17,996,300
Bonds 6% First Mortgage and Collateral Trust Bonds--		
Issued	$ 8,850,000	
Less held in escrow for redemption of Montreal Rolling Mills Co. Bonds	500,000	
	$ 8,350,000	
Less redeemed through Sinking Fund	737,774	
	$ 7,612,225	
Bonds 6% of the Montreal Rolling Mills Co.	500,000	
Bonds 5% of the Western Coke Co.	450,000	8,562,225
Convertible Promissory Notes--		
Due July 1st, 1920		30,000
Current Liabilities--		
Accounts payable, including provision for War Tax, 1919	$ 3,185,270	
Bills payable	2,000	
Unclaimed dividends	10,344	
Preferred dividend payable Feb. 1st, 1920	113,685	
Ordinary dividend payable Feb. 1st, 1920	287,500	3,598,799
Employees' Pension Fund Appropriation		305,245
Reserves--		
Furnace relining and rebuilding reserves	$ 637,313	
Reserve for Accidents to Employees	68,573	
Contingent Reserve	509,853	
Betterment and Replacement Reserve	2,360,013	
Fire insurance reserve	150,000	
	$ 3,725,753	
Bond Sinking Fund Reserve	809,267	
Depreciation Account	4,437,495	8,972,516
Surplus--		
Balance as per Profit and Loss Account		8,195,302
		$47,660,389

Figure 11 (continued)

THE STEEL COMPANY OF CANADA, LIMITED

December 31st, 1919

PROFIT AND LOSS

Profits for the year ended December 31st, 1919 after deducting charges for repairs, maintenance and improvements, and providing for Inventory Reserve and War Tax, 1919, but before providing for Depreciation and Bond Interest		$ 4,000,940
Less Reserves--		
Bond Sinking Fund	$ 192,730	
Depreciation	911,133	1,103,864
		$ 2,897,075
Less Interest on Bonds		514,904
		$ 2,382,471
Less Dividends--		
Preferred at 7% per annum	454,741	
Ordinary at 7% per annum	805,000	1,259,741
		$ 1,122,430
Transferred to employees' pension reserve	200,000	
Transferred to fire insurance reserve	50,000	250,000
		$ 872,430
Balance brought forward December 31st, 1918		7,322,872
Balance, profit and loss, December 31st, 1919		$ 8,195,302

Figure 11 (continued)

CANADIAN LOCOMOTIVE COMPANY LIMITED

Balance Sheet at June 30, 1921

CAPITAL AND LIABILITIES

Capital Stock:—			
Authorized 35,000 shares of $100 each $3,500,000.00			
Issued in:			
15,000 7% Cumulative Preference Shares, fully paid	$1,500,000.00		
20,000 Ordinary Shares, fully paid	2,000,000.00		$3,500,000.00
First Mortgage 6% Forty-Year Gold Sinking Fund Bonds, due 1st July, 1951:—			
Authorized $2,000,000.00			
Whereof issued			1,500,000.00
Current Liabilities:—			
Trade Accounts payable, wages and other charges, including Income Tax		$ 99,716.18	
Bond Interest accrued Coupon No. 20 (paid 2nd July, 1921)		45,000.00	
Dividend No. 38 on Preference Shares for three months to date (paid 2nd July, 1921		26,250.00	
Dividend No. 16 on Common Shares for three months to date (paid 2nd July, 1921)		40,000.00	210,966.18
Reserves:—			
General Depreciation		$ 990,000.00	
Sinking Fund		105,518.01	1,095,518.01
Profit and Loss Account:—			
Balance at credit thereof, per Statement II.			1,536,275.34
			$7,842,759.53

ASSETS

Fixed Assets—		
Real Estate, Buildings, Plant and Equipment, including Goodwill ($2,722,006.24):		
Balance 1st July, 1920	$5,499,041.36	
Additions during year	43,565.23	
	$5,542,606.59	
Less: Sales	6,520.00	$5,536,086.59
Sinking Fund Investment Account:—		
93,400 Company's First Mortgage Gold Bonds purchased and held by Trustees, cost	$ 87,666.01	
Cash in hands of Trustees, including July, 1921, Coupons	2,852.00	
Cash payable to Trustees on or before 1st July, 1921	15,000.00	105,518.01
Investment in Dominion of Canada War & Victory Bonds, at market value	$1,057,400.00	
Add: Interest accrued thereon to date	9,199.64	
	$1,066,599.64	
Current Assets:—		
Work-in-Progress, at cost	$ 16,062.32	
Materials and Supplies, less Reserve, certified by officials of the Company	138,907.47	
Trade and Miscellaneous Accounts receivable, less Reserve for bad debts	90,010.05	
Cash in Banks and on hand	866,988.96	2,178,568.44
Deferred Charges to Operations		22,586.49
		$7,842,759.53

Figure 12

CANADIAN LOCOMOTIVE COMPANY, LIMITED

June 30, 1921

Net Profit for year ended 30th June, 1921, after charging Income Tax and all other charges as hereunder shown			$ 767,891.56
Add:			
Interest from Investments			59,200.06
			$ 827,091.62
Deduct:			
Interest on First Mortgage Bonds		$ 90,000.00	
Provision for General Depreciation ...		125,000.00	
Provision to reduce Investments to market value		6,800.00	221,800.00
			$ 605,291.62
Add: Balance at credit 1st July, 1920 brought forward			1,210,983.72
			$1,816,275.34
Balance appropriated as under:-			
Sinking Fund provision		$ 15,000.00	
Dividends for year:-			
On Preference Shares, Nos. 35 to 38 inclusive	$105,000.00		
On Common Shares, Nos. 13 to 16 inclusive	160,000.00	265,000.00	$ 280,000.00
Balance at credit 30th June, 1921, carried forward, per Balance Sheet Account No. 1			$1,536,275.34

Figure 12 (continued)

Penmans Limited

Balance Sheet

As at the 31st December, 1933

ASSETS

FIXED		
Comprising Real Estate, Buildings, Plant, Dwelling Houses, Water Powers, etc., - Less Depreciation		$4,813,245.17
Goodwill, Trade Marks, etc. - -		1.00
CURRENT		
Cash on hand and in Bank - -	$ 406,873.88	
Accounts Receivable - - - - -	643,542.83	
Bills Receivable - - - - -	12,128.80	
Deferred Charges - - - - -	6,731.80	
Inventory of Raw and Manufactured Stock, Less Reserve - - - -	1,230,103.83	
Investments - - - - - -	277,913.75	
TOTAL CURRENT ASSETS - - - -		$2,577,294.89
		$7,390,541.06

LIABILITIES

CAPITAL STOCK		
Authorized:		
15,000 shares Preferred Stock, of $100. each	$1,500,000.00	
75,000 " Common " of no par value	....	
Issued:		
10,750 shares Preferred Stock - - - -	1,075,000.00	
64,518 " Common " of no par value	2,150,600.00	$3,225,600.00
5½% FIRST MORTGAGE SINKING FUND BONDS DUE 1st NOVEMBER, 1951 -	2,000,000.00	
Less Redeemed and Cancelled -	167,500.00	1,832,500.00
Reserve Account - - - -		742,046.40
CURRENT LIABILITIES		
Accounts Payable, including Reserve for Income Tax - - - - -	147,199.63	
Bills Payable - - - - - - -	1,218.89	
Wages - - - - - - - -	29,269.89	
TOTAL CURRENT LIABILITIES - - - -		$ 177,688.41
Surplus — Balance Profit and Loss Account - - - - - -		1,412,706.25
		$7,390,541.06

Figure 13

Penmans Limited

Profit and Loss Account

For the Year ending 31st December, 1933.

Gross trading profits for year ending 31st December, 1933, after deduction of Operating and Administration Expenses and provision for Federal Income Tax . . .		$ 549,541.75
DEDUCT		
Interest on Bonds . . .	$ 110,000.00	
Depreciation	140,000.00	
Bad Debts written off . .	22,029.90	
		$ 272,029.90
Net Earnings		$ 277,511.85
DISBURSEMENTS		
Dividends Preferred Stock at the rate of 6% per annum . .	64,500.00	
Dividends Common Stock at the rate of $3.00 per share per annum	193,554.00	
		$ 258,054.00
Surplus for the year		$ 19,457.85
Brought forward from the 31st December, 1932 . .		1,393,248.40
Balance at Credit . . .		$1,412,706.25

Figure 13 (continued)

Penmans Limited

Balance Sheet

As at the 31st December, 1934

ASSETS

FIXED		
Comprising Real Estate, Buildings, Plant, Dwelling Houses, Water Powers, etc., at cost	$5,797,393.25	
Less Depreciation	977,023.94	
		$4,820,369.31
Goodwill, Trade Marks, etc.		1.00
Bonds purchased for Sinking Fund Requirements, at cost		29,831.25
CURRENT		
Cash on hand and in Banks	$ 383,929.36	
Accounts Receivable	555,624.26	
Inventory of Raw and Manufactured Stock at cost or market, whichever is lower, Less Reserve	1,513,400.82	
Marketable Securities, at cost	49,262.50	
Deferred Charges	5,670.94	
TOTAL CURRENT ASSETS		$2,507,887.88
		$7,358,089.44

LIABILITIES

CAPITAL STOCK		
Authorized:		
15,000 shares Preferred Stock, of $100. each	$1,500,000.00	
75,000 " Common " of no par value	....	
Issued:		
10,750 shares Preferred Stock	1,075,000.00	
64,518 " Common " of no par value	2,150,600.00	
		$3,225,600.00
5½% FIRST MORTGAGE SINKING FUND BONDS DUE 1st NOVEMBER, 1951	2,000,000.00	
Less Redeemed and Cancelled	195,000.00	
		1,805,000.00
Reserve Account		742,046.40
CURRENT LIABILITIES		
Accounts Payable, including provision for Taxes	$ 132,014.40	
Bills Payable	2,107.83	
Wages	22,077.18	
TOTAL CURRENT LIABILITIES		$ 156,199.41
SURPLUS—Balance Profit and Loss Account		1,429,243.63
		$7,358,089.44

Figure 14

Penmans Limited

Profit and Loss Account

For the Year ending 31st December, 1934.

Net Operating Profit . .		$ 629,984.14
Income from Investments .		7,422.60
		$ 637,406.74
DEDUCT		
Interest on Bonds . .	$ 110,000.00	
Depreciation on Plant . .	140,000.00	
Provision for Income Taxes .	50,000.00	
Bad Debts written off . .	49,765.36	
Directors' Remuneration . .	13,050.00	
		$ 362,815.36
		$ 274,591.38
Dividends paid on Preferred Stock at the rate of 6% per annum	64,500.00	
Dividends paid on Common Stock at the rate of $3.00 per share per annum . . .	193,554.00	
		$ 258,054.00
Surplus for the year		$ 16,537.38
Brought forward from the 31st December, 1933 . . .		1,412,706.25
Balance at Credit . . .		$1,429,243.63

Figure 14 (continued)

COCKSHUTT PLOW COMPANY LIMITED

Balance Sheet, December 31, 1925

ASSETS

Property, Fixed and Loose Plant and Business, after deducting Depreciation Provided to Date		$7,618,318.82
Shares in Capital Stocks of Affiliated Companies, Fully Paid Up—Value as per books		675,299.50
Stocks of Raw Materials and Supplies, Goods in Process and Finished Product, as per Inventories, on the basis of replacement values:		
Brantford	$ 839,334.58	
Western Branches	1,408,592.17	
		2,247,926.75
Accounts and Notes Receivable, less Provision for Doubtful Debts		3,486,700.21
Insurance and Other Items Paid in Advance		26,002.60
Cash in Bank and on Hand		21,859.51
		$14,076,107.39

Approved on behalf of the Board,

A. K. BUNNELL }
GEO. A. BAKER } Directors

LIABILITIES

Share Capital:		
Authorized:		
75,000 7% Cumulative Preference Shares of $100.00 each	$ 7,500,000.00	
75,000 Common Shares of $100.00 each	7,500,000.00	
	$15,000,000.00	
Issued:		
64,650 7% Cumulative Preference Shares of $100.00 each	$ 6,465,000.00	
50,000 Common Shares of $100.00 each	5,000,000.00	
		$11,465,000.00
Accounts Payable		135,856.62
Unclaimed Dividends		5,159.00
Reserves:		
Capital Reserve	$ 1,500,000.00	
Contingent Reserve	500,000.00	
Merchandise Reserve	400,000.00	
		2,400,000.00
Profit and Loss Account:		
Credit Balance at this date as per Account herewith		70,091.77
		$14,076,107.39

Note: The Dividends on the Cumulative Preference Shares have been declared and paid to 30th June, 1914 and further Dividends totalling 30½% have been declared during the eight and one half years ended 31st. Dec., 1925.

Figure 15

COCKSHUTT PLOW COMPANY

Profit and Loss Account

for the Year Ended December 31, 1925

To Uncollectable Accounts written off	$297,717.01	By Balance at Credit 1st January, 1925	$ 51,303.16
To Balance as per Balance Sheet	70,091.77	By Profit from Operations after Providing for Depreciation	313,505.62
	$367,808.78		$367,808.78

Figure 15 (continued)

COCKSHUTT PLOW COMPANY LIMITED AND ITS SUBSIDIARY
THE FROST AND WOOD COMPANY, LIMITED

CONSOLIDATED BALANCE SHEET (AND SUBSIDIARIES) **NOVEMBER 30, 1934**

ASSETS

PROPERTY, FIXED AND LOOSE PLANT AND BUSINESS:		
Parent Company—at the aggregate amount of the par value of securities issued therefor, plus subsequent additions at cost	9,589,731.54	
Subsidiary Company—at gross replacement values as appraised by the Canadian Appraisal Company Limited, at August 1, 1912, plus net additions to date at cost	1,102,660.53	
		$10,692,392.07
INVESTMENT IN CANADA CARRIAGE AND BODY COMPANY LIMITED—VALUE AS PER BOOKS:		
6% Redeemable Debenture Stock—par value	311,400.00	
2,475—6% Cumulative Preference Shares	247,500.00	
30,000—No Par Value Shares	1.00	
	558,901.00	
Less Reserve	87,687.54	
		471,213.46
INVENTORIES of raw materials and supplies, goods in process and finished product, as determined and certified by responsible officials of the Company, and valued at cost or under		2,296,142.47
ACCOUNTS AND NOTES RECEIVABLE: Less Reserve for Doubtful Debts		3,366,181.34
DEFERRED CHARGES TO FUTURE OPERATIONS		33,338.03
CASH IN BANKS AND ON HAND		75,091.72
		$16,934,359.09

LIABILITIES

SHARE CAPITAL:		
Authorized: 500,000 Common Shares without nominal or par value.		
Issued: 300,678 Shares		$11,585,780.00
BANK LOANS—Secured		1,449,000.00
ACCOUNTS PAYABLE:		
Trade	135,951.02	
Other	39,975.58	
		175,926.60
UNCLAIMED DIVIDENDS		14,415.19
RESERVE FOR DEPRECIATION		2,026,428.57
RESERVES:		
Contingent Reserve	250,000.00	
Merchandise Reserve	285,000.00	
		535,000.00
CAPITAL SURPLUS: (No change during year). Being excess of net worth of Subsidiary Company over book value of investment therein		971,247.09
CONSOLIDATED EARNED SURPLUS AS PER STATEMENT HEREWITH		176,561.64
		$16,934,359.09

Approved on behalf of the Board,

GEO. A. BAKER
G. K. WEDLAKE } *Directors*

Figure 16

COCKSHUTT PLOW COMPANY, LIMITED

AND ITS SUBSIDIARY

THE FROST & WOOD COMPANY, LIMITED

(AND SUBSIDIARIES)

CONSOLIDATED STATEMENT OF PROFIT AND LOSS FOR THE YEAR ENDED NOVEMBER 30, 1934

Operating Loss for year, before making any provision for depreciation	$182,931.63
Add: Interest on Bank Loans	110,559.36
Uncollectible Accounts Written Off	111,889.13
Depreciation Provided on Fixed Assets of Subsidiary Company	11,807.94
Loss on Property Demolished	7,149.60
Directors' Fees	1,600.00
	425,937.66
Adjustment of Inventory Values	100,000.00
Consolidated Loss for Year, Including Adjustment of Inventory Values	$525,937.66

COCKSHUTT PLOW COMPANY, LIMITED

AND ITS SUBSIDIARY

THE FROST & WOOD COMPANY, LIMITED

(AND SUBSIDIARIES)

CONSOLIDATED STATEMENT OF EARNED SURPLUS NOVEMBER 30, 1934

Balance at November 30, 1933		$ 2,499.30
Add: Transfer from General Reserve		600,000.00
		602,499.30
Deduct: Consolidated Loss for Year as stated	525,937.66	
Less Transfer from Merchandise Reserve	100,000.00	
		425,937.66
Consolidated Earned Surplus as per Balance Sheet		$176,561.64

Figure 16 (continued)

IMPERIAL TOBACCO COMPANY OF CANADA, LIMITED

BALANCE SHEET 31st DECEMBER, 1947

ASSETS

ASSETS			1946
Cash in Banks		$ 4,852,794.59	$ 5,224,457.17
Dominion Government Securities (Market Value $5,050,275.84)		5,045,000.00	2,886,325.00
Excess Profits Tax Currently Refundable		243,947.32	—
Sundry Debtors		556,449.03	498,753.47
Stocks of Leaf Tobacco, Manufacturing Materials and Supplies (at average cost or under)		29,574,833.69	22,653,040.55
		40,273,024.63	31,262,576.19
Investments in Subsidiary Companies (at cost or under)			
Shares	$ 5,930,118.69		
Advances (largely represented by Manufactured Goods—at cost and other net current Assets)	22,527,226.25	28,457,344.94	29,307,243.78
Shares in other Companies (at cost)		61,200.00	61,201.00
Excess Profits Tax Not Currently Refundable		787,786.93	1,031,734.25
Real Estate and Buildings (at cost)		3,171,476.50	2,324,420.64
Plant, Machinery, Furniture and Fittings (at cost)		5,347,795.91	4,201,579.40
Taxes, Insurance, etc. Paid in Advance		94,433.76	46,929.59
Discount on Funded Debt, less amounts written off		—	183,446.96
Goodwill, Trade Marks and Patents		28,816,800.96	28,816,800.96
		$107,009,863.63	$97,135,932.86

LIABILITIES

LIABILITIES			1946
Due to Subsidiary Companies		$ 1,255,450.98	$ 904,194.59
Sundry Creditors		2,177,585.19	2,045,807.72
Income and Excise Taxes		4,481,930.10	5,570,574.99
Provision for Dividends:			
Accrued on Preference Shares	$ 187,116.67		
Final for year on Common Shares	1,890,206.40	2,077,323.07	2,010,656.40
		9,992,289.34	10,531,233.70
Provision for Retirement Allowances to Employees		1,368,146.49	1,368,146.49
Reserve for Buildings, Machinery, etc.		6,989,688.41	6,348,880.52
Funded Debt:			
2¾% Debentures maturing $700,000.00 April 15th in each of the years 1954 to 1965 inclusive	$ 8,400,000.00		
2¾% Debentures maturing April 15th, 1966	6,600,000.00	15,000,000.00	15,000,000.00
Capital Authorized:			
6% Cumulative Preference Shares 1,650,000 shares of the par value of $4.86 2/3 each	$ 8,030,000.00		
Redeemable Sinking Fund Preference Shares 600,000 shares of the par value of $25.00 each	15,000,000.00		
Common Shares 10,800,000 shares of the par value of $5.00 each	54,000,000.00		
	$ 77,030,000.00		
Capital Issued:			
6% Cumulative Preference Shares 1,650,000 shares of the par value of $4.86 2/3 each	$ 8,030,000.00		
4% Cumulative Redeemable Sinking Fund Preference Shares 400,000 shares of the par value of $25.00 each	10,000,000.00		
Common Shares 9,451,032 shares of the par value of $5.00 each	47,255,160.00	65,285,160.00	55,285,160.00
General Reserve		5,000,000.00	5,000,000.00
Deferred Surplus—Excess Profits Tax Not Currently Refundable		787,786.93	1,031,734.25
Profit and Loss Account (Earned Surplus) Balance as per Statement herewith		2,586,792.46	(a) 2,570,777.90
		$107,009,863.63	$97,135,932.86

APPENDIX E

SELECTED SECTIONS OF THE CORPORATIONS ACT, 1953

OF ONTARIO

83.-(1) The directors shall lay before each annual meeting of shareholders,

(a) a financial statement for the period commencing on the date of incorporation and ending not more than six months before such annual meeting, or commencing immediately after the period covered by the previous financial statement and ending not more than six months before such annual meeting, as the case may be, made up of,

(i) a statement of profit and loss for such period,

(ii) a statement of surplus for such period,

(iii) a balance sheet made up to the end of such period;

(b) the report of the auditor to the shareholders;

(c) such further information respecting the financial position of the company as the letters patent, supplementary letters patent or by-laws of the company require. R.S.O. 1950, c. 59, s. 46 (2), amended.

(2) The statements referred to in subclauses i, ii and iii of clause a of subsection 1 shall comply with and be governed by sections 84 to 88, but it shall not be necessary to designate them the statement of profit and loss, statement of surplus and balance sheet. New.

(3) The report of the auditor to the shareholders shall be read at the annual meeting and shall be open to inspection by any shareholder. R.S.O. 1950, c. 59, s. 117 (3), amended.

84.-(1) Every statement of profit and loss to be laid before an annual meeting shall be drawn up so as to present fairly the results of the operations of the company for the period covered by the statement and so as to distinguish severally at least,

(a) the operating profit or loss before including or pfoviding for other items of income or expense that are required to be shown separately;

(b) income from investments in subsidiaries whose financial statements are not consolidated with those of the company;

(c) income from investments in affiliated companies other than subsidiaries;

(d) income from other investments;

(e) non-recurring profits and losses of significant amount including profits or losses on the disposal of capital assets and other items of a special nature to the extent that they are not shown separately in the statement of earned surplus;

(f) provision for depreciation or obsolescence or depletion;

(g) amounts written off for goodwill or amortization of any other intangible assets to the extent that they are not shown separately in the statement of earned surplus;

(h) interest on indebtedness initially incurred for a term of more than one year, including amortization of debt discount or premium and expense;

(i) total remuneration of directors as such from the company and subsidiaries whose financial statements are consolidated with those of the company, including all salaries, bonuses, fees, contributions to pension funds and other emoluments;

(j) taxes on income imposed by any taxing authority,

and shall show the net profit or loss for the financial period.

(2) Notwithstanding subsection 1, items of the natures described in clauses f, g, and i of subsection 1 may be shown by way of note to the statement of profit and loss. New.

85.-(1) Every statement of surplus shall be drawn up so as to present fairly the transactions reflected in such statement and shall show separately a statement of contributed surplus and a statement of earned surplus.

(2) Every statement of contributed surplus shall be drawn up so as to include and distinguish the following items:

1. The balance of such surplus at the end of the preceding financial period.

2. The additions to and deductions from such surplus during the financial period including,

(a) the amount of surplus arising from the issue of shares or the reorganization of the company's issued capital, including inter alia ,

(i) the amount of premiums received on the issue of shares at a premium,

(ii) the amount of surplus realized on the purchase for cancellation of shares; and

(b) donations of cash or other property by shareholders.

3. The balance of such surplus at the end of the financial period.

(3) Every statement of earned surplus shall be drawn up so as to distinguish at least the following items:

1. The balance of such surplus at the end of the preceding financial period.

2. The additions to and deductions from such surplus during the financial period and without restricting the generality of the foregoing at least the following:

   (i) The amount of the net profit or loss for the financial period.

   (ii) The amount of dividends declared on each class of shares.

   (iii) The amount transferred to or from reserves.

3. The balance of such surplus at the end of the financial period.

86.-(1) Every balance sheet to be laid before an annual meeting shall be drawn up so as to present fairly the financial position of the company as at the date to which it is made up and so as to distinguish severally at least the following:

1. Cash.

2. Debts owing to the company from its directors, officers of shareholders, except debts of reasonable amount arising in the ordinary course of the company's business that are not overdue having regard to the company's ordinary terms of credit.

3. Debts owing to the company, whether on account of a loan or otherwise, from subsidiaries whose financial statements are not consolidated with those of the company.

4. Debts owing to the company, whether on account of a loan or otherwise, from affiliated companies other than subsidiaries.

5. Other debts owing to the company, segregating those that arose otherwise than in the ordinary course of the company's business.

6. Shares or securities, except those referred to in items 8 and 9, stating their nature and the basis of valuation thereof and showing separately marketable securities with a notation of their market value.

7. Inventory, stating the basis of valuation.

8. Shares or securities of subsidiaries, stating the basis of valuation.

9. Shares or securities of affiliated companies other than subsidiaries, stating the basis of valuation.

10. Lands, buildings, and plant and equipment, stating the basis of valuation, whether cost or otherwise, and if valued on the basis of an appraisal, the date of appraisal, the name of the appraiser, the basis of the appraisal value and the disposition in the accounts of the company of any amounts added to or deducted from such assets on appraisal after the 30th day of April, 1954, and also the amount or amounts accumulated in respect of depreciation, obsolescence and depletion.

11. There shall be stated under separate headings, in so far as they are not written off, (i) expenditures on account of future business; (ii) any expense incurred in connection with any issue of shares; (iii) any expense incurred in connection with any issue of securities, including any discount thereon; and (iv) any one or more of the following: goodwill, franchises, patents, copyrights, trade marks and other intangible assets and the amount, if any, by which the value of any such assets has been written up after the 30th day of April, 1954.

12. The aggregate amount of any outstanding loans under clauses c, d and e of subsection 2 of section 23.

13. Bank loans and overdrafts.

14. Debts owing by the company on loans from its directors, officers or shareholders.

15. Debts owing by the company to subsidiaries whether on account of a loan or otherwise.

16. Debts owing by the company to affiliated companies other than subsidiaries whether on account of a loan or otherwise.

17. Other debts owing by the company, segregating those that arose otherwise than in the ordinary course of the company's business.

18. Liability for taxes, including the estimated liability for taxes in respect of the income of the period covered by the statement of profit and loss.

19. Dividends declared but not paid.

20. Deferred income.

21. Securities issued by the company, stating the interest rate, the maturity date, the amount outstanding and the existence of sinking fund, redemption requirements and conversion rights, if any.

22. The authorized capital, giving the number of each class of shares, and a brief description of each such class and indicating therein any class of shares which is redeemable and the redemption price thereof.

23. The issued capital, giving the number of shares of each class issued and outstanding and the amount received therefor that is attributable to capital, and showing,

(a) the number of shares of each class issued since the date of the last balance sheet and the value attributed thereto, distinguishing shares issued for cash, shares issued for services and shares issued for other consideration; and

(b) where any shares have not been fully paid,

(i) the number of shares in respect of which calls have not been made and the aggregate amount that has not been called, and

(ii) the number of shares in respect of which calls have been made and not paid and the aggregate amount that has been called and not paid.

24. Contributed surplus.

25. Earned surplus.

26. Reserves, showing the amounts added thereto and the amounts deducted therefrom during the financial period. R.S.O. 1950, c. 59, s. 46 (3), amended.

(2) Explanatory information or particulars of any item mentioned in subsection 1 may be shown by way of note to the balance sheet. New.

87.-(1) There shall be stated by way of note to the financial statement particulars of any change in accounting principle or practice or in the method of applying any accounting principle or practice made during the period covered that affects the comparability of any of the statements with any of those for the preceding period, and the effect, if material, of any such change upon the profit or loss for the period.

(2) Where applicable, the following matters shall be referred to in the financial statement or by way of note thereto:

1. The basis of conversion of amounts from currencies other than the currency in which the financial statement is expressed.

2. Foreign currency restrictions that affect the assets of the company.

3. Contractual obligations that will require abnormal expenditures in relation to the company's normal business requirements or financial position or that are likely to involve losses not provided for in the accounts.

4. Material contractual obligations in respect of long term leases, including, in the year in which the transaction was effected, the principal details of any sale and lease transaction.

5. Contingent liabilities, stating their nature and, where practicable, the approximate amounts involved.

6. Any liability secured otherwise than by operation of law on any asset of the company, stating the liability so secured, but it is not necessary to specify the asset on which the liability is secured.

7. Any default of the company in principal, interest, sinking fund or redemption provisions with respect to any issue of its securities or credit agreements.

8. The gross amount of arrears of dividends on any class of shares and the date to which such dividends were last paid.

9. Where a company has contracted to issue shares or has given an option to purchase shares, the class and number of shares affected, the price and the date for issue of the shares or exercise of the option.

10. The total remuneration of directors as such of a holding company from subsidiaries whose financial statements are not consolidated with those of the holding company, including all salaries, bonuses, fees, contributions to pension funds, and other emoluments.

11. In the case of a holding company, the aggregate of any shares in, and the aggregate of any securities of, the holding company held by subsidiary companies whose financial statements are not consolidated with that of the holding company.

12. The amount of any loans by the company, or by a subsidiary company, otherwise than in the ordinary course of business, during the company's financial period, to the directors or officers of the company.

13. Any restriction by the letters patent, supplementary letters patent or by-laws of the company or by contract on the payment of dividends that is significant in the light of the company's financial position.

(3) Every note to a financial statement is a part of it. New.

88. Notwithstanding sections 84 to 87, it is not necessary to state in a financial statement any matter that in all the circumstances is of relative insignificance. New.

89.-(1) Any company, in this section referred to as "the holding company", may include in the financial statement to be submitted at any annual meeting the assets and liabilities and income and expense of any one or more of its subsidiaries making due provision for minority interests, if any, and indicating in such financial statement that it is presented in consolidated form.

(2) Where the assets and liabilities and income and expense of any one or more subsidiaries of the holding company are not so included in the financial statement of the holding company,

(a) the financial statement of the holding company shall include a statement setting forth,

(i) the reason why the assets and liabilities and income and expense of such subsidiary or subsidiaries are not included in the financial statement of the holding company,

(ii) if there is only one such subsidiary, the amount of the holding company's proportion of the profit or loss of such subsidiary for the financial period of the holding company, or, if there is more than one such subsidiary, the amount of the holding company's proportion of the aggregate profits less losses, or losses less profits, of all such subsidiaries for the respective financial periods coinciding with or ending in the financial period of the holding company,

(iii) the amount included as income from such subsidiary or subsidiaries in the statement of profit and loss of the holding company and the amount included therein as a provision for the loss or losses of such subsidiary or subsidiaries,

(iv) if there is only one such subsidiary, the amount of the holding company's proportion of the undistributed profits of such subsidiary earned since the acquisition of the shares of such subsidiary by the holding company to the extent that such amount has not been taken into the accounts of the holding company, or, if there is more than one such subsidiary, the amount of the holding company's proportion of the aggregate undistributed profits of all such subsidiaries earned since the acquisition of their shares by the holding company less its proportion of the losses, if any, suffered by any such subsidiary since the acquisition of its shares to the extent that such amount has not been taken into the accounts of the holding company,

(v) any qualifications contained in the report of the auditor of any such subsidiary on its financial statement for the financial period ending as aforesaid, and any note or reference contained in that financial statement to call attention to a matter which, apart from the note or reference, would properly have been referred to in such a qualification, in so far as the matter that is the subject of the qualification or note is not provided for by the company's own financial statement and is material from the point of view of its shareholders;

(b) if for any reason the directors of the holding company are unable to obtain such information as is necessary for the preparation of the statement that is to be included in the financial statement of the holding company, the directors who sign the financial statement shall so report in writing and their report shall be included in the financial statement in lieu of the statement;

(c) true copies of the latest financial statement of such subsidiary or subsidiaries shall be kept on hand by the holding company at its head office and shall be open to inspection by the shareholders of the holding company on request during the normal business hours of the holding company but the directors of the holding company may by resolution refuse the right of such inspection if such inspection is not in the public interest or would prejudice the holding company or such subsidiary or subsidiaries, which resolution may, on the application of any such shareholder to the court, be set aside by the court;

(d) if, in the opinion of the auditor of the holding company, adequate provision has not been made in the financial statement of the holding company for the holding company's proportion,

(i) where there is only one such subsidiary, of the loss of such subsidiary suffered since acquisition of its shares by the holding company, or

(ii) where there is more than one such subsidiary, of the aggregate losses suffered by such subsidiaries since acquisition of their shares by the holding company in excess of its proportion of the undistributed profits, if any, earned by any of such subsidiaries since such acquisition,

the auditor shall state in his report the additional amount that in his opinion is necessary to make full provision therefor. New.

90.-(1) For the purposes of this Act, a company shall be deemed to be a subsidiary of another company if, but only if,

(a) it is controlled by,

(i) that other, or

(ii) that other and one or more companies each of which is controlled by that other, or

(iii) two or more companies each of which is controlled by that other; or

(b) it is a subsidiary of a company which is that other's subsidiary.

(2) For the purposes of this Act, a company shall be deemed to be another's holding company if, but only if, that other is its subsidiary.

(3) For the purposes of this Act, one company shall be deemed to be affiliated to another company if, but only if, one of them is the subsidiary of the other or both are subsidiaries of the same company or each of them is controlled by the same person.

(4) For the purposes of this section, a company shall be deemed to be controlled by another company or person or by two or more companies if, but only if,

(a) shares of the first-mentioned company carrying more than 50 per cent of the votes for the election of directors are held, otherwise than by way of security only, by or for the benefit of such other company or person or by or for the benefit of such other companies; and

(b) the votes carried by such shares are sufficient, if exercised, to elect a majority of the board of directors of the first-mentioned company. New.

91. In a financial statement, the term "reserve" shall be used to describe only,

(a) amounts appropriated from earned surplus at the discretion of management for some purpose other that to meet a liability or contingency known or admitted or a commitment made as at the statement date or a decline in value of an asset that has already occurred;

(b) amounts appropriated from earned surplus pursuant to the instrument of incorporation or by-laws of the company for some purpose other than to meet a liability or contingency known or admitted or a commitment made as at the statement date or a decline in value of an asset that has already occurred; and

(c) amounts appropriated from earned surplus in accordance with the terms of a contract and which can be restored to the earned surplus when the conditions of the contract are fulfilled. New.